D1245517

# Fulfilling the Promise of the
# COMMUNITY COLLEGE

## Increasing First-Year Student Engagement and Success

*Thomas Brown, Margaret C. King,*
*and Patricia Stanley, Editors*

**National Resource Center for**
**The First-Year Experience®**
**& Students in Transition**
UNIVERSITY OF SOUTH CAROLINA

**AACC**
AMERICAN ASSOCIATION
OF COMMUNITY COLLEGES

Cite as:

Brown, T., King, M. C., & Stanley, P. (Eds.). (2011). *Fulfilling the promise of the community college: Increasing first-year student engagement and success* (Monograph No. 56). Columbia, SC: University of South Carolina, National Resource Center for The First-Year Experience & Students in Transition.

Sample chapter citation:

Boggs, G. R. (2011). The American community college: From access to success. In T. Brown, M. C. King, & P. Stanley (Eds.), *Fulfilling the promise of the community college: Increasing first-year student engagement and success* (Monograph No. 56, pp. 3-14). Columbia, SC: University of South Carolina, National Resource Center for The First-Year Experience & Students in Transition.

ISBN 978-1-889-27174-3

The First-Year Experience® is a service mark of the University of South Carolina. A license may be granted upon written request to use the term "The First-Year Experience." This license is not transferable without written approval of the University of South Carolina.

Production Staff for the National Resource Center:
Project Manager           Tracy L. Skipper, Assistant Director for Publications
Project Editors           Dottie Weigel, Editor
                          Toni Vakos, Editor
Design and Production      Shana Bertetto, Graphic Artist

Additional copies of this monograph may be obtained from the National Resource Center for The First-Year Experience and Students in Transition, University of South Carolina, 1728 College Street, Columbia, SC 29208. Telephone (803) 777-6229. Fax (803) 777-4699.

---

Library of Congress Cataloging-in-Publication Data

Fulfilling the promise of the community college : increasing first-year student engagement and success / Thomas Brown, Margaret C. King, and Patricia Stanley, editors.
    p. cm. -- (The first-year experience monograph series ; no. 56)
  Published with the American Association of Community Colleges.
  Includes bibliographical references and index.
  ISBN 978-1-889271-74-3
1. College student orientation--United States. 2. Community colleges--United States. 3. College freshmen--United States. 4. College students--Conduct of life. I. Brown, Thomas. II. King, Margaret C. III. Stanley, Patricia. IV. National Resource Center for the First-Year Experience & Students in Transition (University of South Carolina) V. American Association of Community Colleges.
  LB2328.15.U6F85 2011
  378.1'98--dc22
                    2011000923

# Contents

## PART I: The American Community College and Its Students

## PART II:  Supporting Student Success in the Community College

## PART III: A Comprehensive First-Year Experience in the Community College

# Tables and Figures

## Tables

## Figures

# Foreword

Jennifer R. Keup

The community college is, at its core, an American invention and a foundational element of the social contract higher education has with its constituencies. Community colleges quickly gained prominence in the American higher education landscape when they first emerged in the early 20th century and are now more important than ever for a host of reasons. For example, two-year colleges are a key element in the national effort to increase college graduation and help the United States regain a position of prominence in a global economy. Additionally, due to issues of access, affordability, and academic preparation, greater numbers of college students are beginning their academic journey in the two-year sector of higher education with community college-to-university transfer becoming an increasingly common connection in the educational pipeline. Further, recent economic declines and the revitalization of the G.I. Bill have created a boon of adult learners entering community colleges for the purposes of retraining and career development. Whether to provide vocational training, a pathway to transfer, or continuing professional development, two-year colleges are about enhancing human capital, increasing access to college, and creating social equity through education in the 21st century.

Demands for accountability in higher education at large have also drawn greater attention to community colleges. In the past decade, advancements in national surveys, new methodologies, and more sophisticated and widespread assessment practices that focus on the community colleges and their students as units of observation have resulted in a growing body of research and scholarship on two-year institutions. With this increase in the availability of empirical evidence, there are also enhanced expectations for data-driven decision making at the campus level. Two of the important themes throughout this body of research and assessment on community colleges are: (a) The first year, as the springboard for student success, matters just as much in two-year institutions as it does in their four-year counterparts, and (b) even when considering specific institutional contexts and cultures, standards of best practice for institutional support and success of first-year students in community colleges are emerging.

When these social forces, state and federal policies, and scholarly findings are considered and combined, it is evident that time was ripe for a re-examination of the transition and success of new community college students. This volume addresses all of these influences as well as other challenges and opportunities that are important to first-year students in community colleges. The monograph provides a full description of the rich history of these institutions, the current social and political context in which they operate, and the wide range of students that they serve. The editors and authors draw from national data, current research, and institutional examples to identify best practices to support the transition and success of new students in two-year colleges and highlight the impact of various curricular and cocurricular interventions in a comprehensive first-year program. Finally, the expertise of the contributors to this volume is complemented by their diverse experiences and professional roles at community colleges, including faculty, institutional leaders, assessment staff, and nationally renowned researchers. Woven together, these contributions provide a rich tapestry of strategies and recommendations that is sure to inform any professional interested in and supportive of the success of first-year students in community colleges.

The National Resource Center for The First-Year Experience and Students in Transition is proud to provide this new resource in partnership with the American Association of Community Colleges (AACC). Both organizations share similar core values, such as lifelong learning, diversity and inclusiveness, leadership, and quality. Community colleges and the first-year experience each have a history that is embedded in activism and advocacy on behalf of student success and truly represent movements within higher education. Further, each organization serves as a national champion and international leader in their respective areas of concentration within higher education. This exploration of the first-year experience in community colleges represents the nexus of these bodies of work and the collective expertise drawn from both organizations. Given that both the first-year experience and community colleges are characterized by intentional and integrative connections between colleagues, programs, campus units, organizations, communities, higher education systems, and educational sectors, we are pleased to model such collaboration in the development and publication of this volume. We hope that it inspires similar partnerships in the scholarship and practice of serving and supporting first-year students in community colleges for those professionals who read this book.

I would like to thank the monograph editors, chapter authors, and the publication staff at the National Resource Center for lending their experience, expertise, and insight to this project. We are pleased to add this volume to the National Resource Center's monograph series as another resource and foundation for future research, professional development, publications, and policy work on the transition and success of students at community colleges. We hope that it will be the catalyst for thoughtful discussion, increased advocacy, and future work on behalf of community colleges and the students they serve.

Jennifer R. Keup
Director
National Resource Center for The First-Year Experience and Students in Transition
University of South Carolina

# Introduction

Thomas Brown, Margaret C. King, and Patricia Stanley

*Community colleges have gone from being the stepchild to the golden child.*—Frank Chong, Deputy Assistant Secretary for Community Colleges

Community colleges are being challenged to play a key role in the national effort to double the number of college graduates in the next 10 years. As such, there is no better time to examine the first-year student experience in community colleges. The first year, indeed the first few weeks of the beginning semester of college, is a pivotal point in students' academic careers. Students whose first experiences are positive are more likely to persist toward their goals, whether that is a certificate, an associate degree, or transferring to a four-year institution.

In examining the first-year experience, this volume is guided by several overarching principles. The first is shaped by the learning college movement, which called for an answer to the question, How do you know? regarding student learning and achievement. As such, this monograph endorses a culture of evidence and data-driven decision making concerning the first-year experience. The second is related to specific measures for documenting student success. While useful benchmarks have been established for four-year institutions, we argue that the measures for community colleges should differ due to greater diversity in student demographics, not only in terms of ethnicity, but also in terms of age, experience, socioeconomic status, and prior learning opportunities. Finally, the multiple missions of community colleges make them unique in the nation and world, and this monograph provides insights for developing thoughtful and purposeful first-year experience interventions in support of these missions.

Arranged in three parts, the monograph describes the distinctive character of first-year students' experiences and challenges in community colleges. Chapter authors share research and effective strategies (sometimes adapted from the four-year sector) that can help individual educators and institutions intervene effectively to assist these students in overcoming challenges and achieving their personal, educational, and career goals. Part I establishes the larger context for examining the first-year experience in community colleges. In chapter 1, George Boggs reviews the development of the American community college movement and its larger social value. He also describes the shift from a focus on access to student success and completion and points out several high-profile efforts to improve academic performance, persistence, and degree attainment among community college students. In chapter 2, Kay McClenney draws on data from the Survey of Entering Students Engagement (SENSE) and student focus groups to create a portrait of new community college students. The chapter highlights student voices as they report on what their earliest college experiences are like, what works, and what could be better. McClenney offers recommendations on institutional strategies for focusing on and improving student success. Part I concludes with a review of community college retention and persistence to degree data collected from 1983 to 2009 through ACT's Institutional Data Questionnaire. Here, Wes Habley summarizes the results of ACT's What Works in Student Retention Survey conducted in the spring of 2009 and offers recommendations on increasing the persistence of first-year community college students.

Part II examines broad strategies for supporting student success and opens with a discussion of the characteristics of underprepared first-year students and the challenges they confront in pursuing their goals. In chapter 4, Thomas Brown and Mario Rivas highlight individual and institutional strategies and interventions to increase the learning, engagement, and student success. In chapter 5, Brown is joined by Christine Johnson McPhail as they examine the relationship between professional development and first-year student success. Specifically, they describe what educators need to know, understand, and be able to do in order to support students to move into college successfully. They also suggest factors to consider in planning professional development programs, describe different formats and techniques, and recommend strategies and incentives to encourage and increase participation.

Because the community college serves as a gateway to a four-year degree for many students, Part II concludes by examining resources and strategies for creating transfer initiatives to support student learning and success. Thomas Grites and Susan Rondeau offer examples of effective models from both community colleges and four-year institutions and discuss strategies for funding and assessing those initiatives.

Many community colleges, be they small, medium, or large, urban, suburban, or rural, are engaged in first-year programs and many have achieved success in these endeavors. Part III addresses a number of specific interventions designed to foster first-year student learning, engagement, and persistence. These include comprehensive academic advising programs, career services, learning communities, and first-year programs and courses. Different approaches are to be expected, given each college's distinctive mission to serve its community's specific education and training needs.

In chapter 7, Betsy Barefoot is joined by Paul Arcario and Ana Guzman in examining the challenges and barriers to implementing effective first-year programs. They advocate for the importance of orientation programs and courses in both extended and preterm formats and offer successful case studies from Palo Alto College (San Antonio, Texas) and LaGuardia Community College (New York City).

Chapters 8 and 9 look at two critical services for student success—academic advising and career development. In chapter 8, Margaret King and Rusty Fox describe the importance of academic advising and make the case for establishing program goals and learning outcomes to support first-year student success. The authors provide an overview of seven organizational models and delivery systems for academic advising and discuss the importance of effective evaluation, assessment, recognition and reward in maximizing program outcomes. Patricia Stanley, in chapter 9, discusses how the career development process assists students in understanding the essential connection between education and their academic, career, and life goals. She reviews the career development process, describes how understanding this process is an essential aspect of responding to the needs of diverse students, and provides descriptions of effective community college programs, offering insights and recommendations for educators involved in this work.

Learning communities can help first-year students persist and achieve academic success in a variety of settings. In chapter 10, Randy Jedele with Vincent Tinto explores the adoption of learning community models in the community college. The chapter opens with a brief discussion of the history of learning communities, a rationale for developing them, and an overview of the effectiveness of learning communities for students and faculty. The authors provide examples of successful community college learning community programs and offer implications for practice.

Community colleges play a critical role in educating students in science, technology, engineering, and math (STEM) fields. Part III concludes with a chapter focused on creating access to and success in STEM fields for community college students, whether a student's ultimate goal is a certificate, an associate degree, a bachelor's degree, or beyond. Kim Armstrong reviews barriers to success for students enrolled in STEM disciplines and highlights successful individual and programmatic efforts to support and retain first-year students in these fields.

The editors close the monograph in chapter 12, offering recommendations for practice drawn from preceding chapters. They also look to high-ranking community college administrators, presidents, and trustees to provide insights into the continuing importance of first-year programs for both student and institutional success.

The United States needs citizens who are educated to meet the many challenges of the 21st century world, and community colleges will play a central role in improving educational access for increasing numbers of U.S. college students. Yet in order for increased access to be meaningful, students must persist in college, complete their programs, and where applicable, transfer to four-year institutions. Effective first-year programs turn access into success by keeping students in college and helping them overcome barriers that might otherwise prevent them from reaching their goals. To that end, we have endeavored to provide ideas and models that will help educators create more accessible, unified, and effective first-year programs. We have encouraged the development of cross-discipline and cross-service interactions that will enhance efforts to promote and document student success. We hope that educators will find the information presented here useful as they design programs and strategies to fulfill the promise of community colleges for this and future generations of college students.

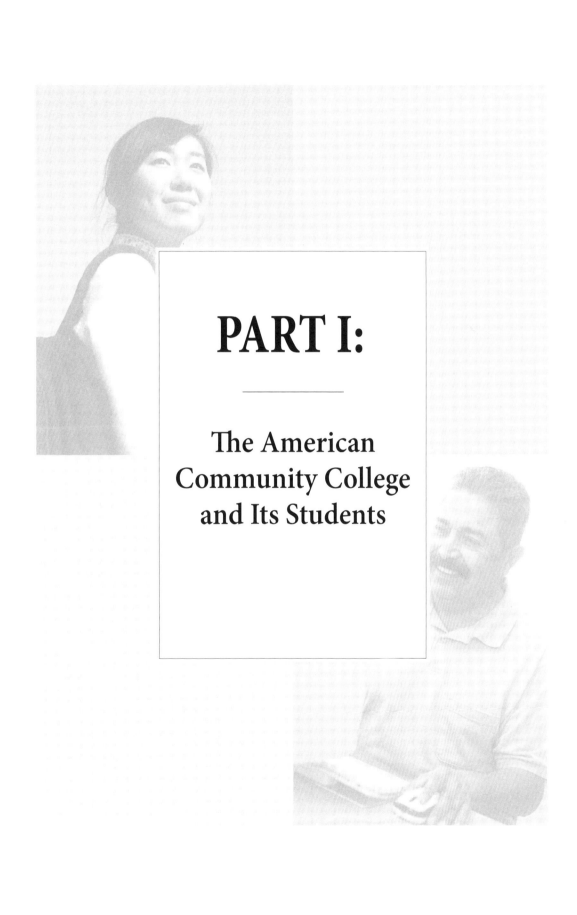

# PART I:

## The American Community College and Its Students

 # Chapter 1

## The American Community College:
## From Access to Success

George R. Boggs

T he focus on educational attainment has taken on a renewed sense of national urgency. It is now commonly accepted that educational achievement is correlated with higher individual lifetime earnings and a better quality of life. Increasing the general level of education is also seen as important for the well-being of society and the economic competitiveness of a country. The more education any one of us gets, the better off we all are. Because they are the largest, most accessible, and fastest-growing sector of higher education, community colleges have a substantial role to play in increasing the national level of educational attainment. Educators and policy makers need to know about the important contributions of community colleges and how they are different from any other sector of education anywhere in the world. Community colleges are a uniquely American contribution to higher education. From their early beginnings as junior colleges, two-year institutions have been shaped from within by visionary leaders and policy makers and also by external forces, such as the Great Depression, World War II, the baby boomer generation, and the demands of industry for skilled workers. This chapter will provide a review of the development of the American community college movement and its unique values. In particular, the origins of the recent values of student success and completion are presented, and the efforts to improve rates of success and completion are discussed.

### The Evolution of Colleges of Opportunity

*Origins: 1835 to the 1970s*

Around 1835, private academies began to appear in the United States (Palinchak, 1973). Combining secondary and postsecondary curricula, these academies offered vocational classes and courses that could transfer to a university. These academies included what were called two-year normal schools or teachers' colleges, as well as institutions meant specifically to serve female and Black students.

By the latter part of the 19th century, some higher education leaders, influenced by the German system, argued that the first two years of collegiate education should be left to the secondary schools. This model would allow universities to concentrate on upper-division, graduate, and professional curricula. In the view of these educators, some students from junior colleges, as they were beginning to be called, would transfer to the university for additional study, while others would end their education at grade 14 (Boggs & Cater, 1994). This model helped stimulate the creation of the first community colleges.

In 1901, Joliet Junior College was established near Chicago. Joliet was founded on a rather elitist concept—that it would accept Joliet High School graduates who wanted to begin college, but only the very best could transfer to the University of Chicago. Despite that elitist beginning, most community college historians point to the founding of Joliet, the oldest community college still in existence, as the true beginning of the community college movement—a social movement that opened access to higher education and training to students who would not otherwise have considered it an option due to economic, mobility, and social barriers. This model soon began to be replicated elsewhere. For example, in 1907, California legislation allowed local school districts to offer the first two years of college work.

In 1917, the North Central Association of Schools and Colleges established standards for accrediting junior colleges, based on factors such as admissions policies, faculty qualifications, and funding levels. These standards helped ensure uniformity across these colleges and enabled them to be included in the nation's unique education system of self-regulation and quality assurance (Vaughan, 2006). Today, all community colleges are accredited by one of the same six regional agencies that accredit four-year colleges and universities.

The Great Depression in the 1930s brought an unexpected boost to the community college movement (Brint & Karabel, 1989). The pressures of economic hard times, high unemployment rates, and a substantial increase in the number of college-age youth led states to establish 65 public junior colleges between 1933 and 1939. These colleges opened the doors for thousands of students at a cost they could afford and offered them future employment opportunities.

The conclusion of World War II signaled a second significant growth period for community colleges. Millions of returning veterans who were eager to move back into the workforce needed affordable education and training opportunities. The Servicemen's Readjustment Act of 1944, commonly called the GI Bill of Rights, provided financial aid that allowed veterans to consider the possibility of higher education, and many of them chose community colleges.

To further accommodate the enrollment demand caused by the GI Bill, President Harry S. Truman established the Commission on Higher Education in 1946. The commission's 1947 report recommended that higher education transform itself from "merely being an instrument for producing an intellectual elite" to becoming "the means by which every citizen, youth, and adult, is enabled and encouraged" to pursue higher learning. The report marked the first official use of the term *community college* and encouraged national expansion of community colleges to provide universal access to postsecondary education (President's Commission, 1947).

The greatest expansion of community colleges in the United States took place between 1960 and 1970. During that decade, more than 450 new community colleges opened their doors to accommodate the education and training needs of the baby boomer generation (i.e., children of returning World War II soldiers). As a result, about 45% of all 18-year-olds who attended college enrolled in a community college (Phillippe & González-Sullivan, 2005).

With the approval of the Higher Education Facilities Act of 1963 and the Higher Education Act of 1965, the federal government dramatically expanded its direct aid to community colleges and their students. The Facilities Act gave communities the means to construct new campuses and enlarge existing facilities. Through this act and its subsequent reauthorizations, the government provided to students a range of direct grants and loans based on financial need as a means of lessening the barrier of cost to higher education access (Vaughan, 2006).

Beginning with the Navajo Community College in 1971, the government began to support the development of tribally controlled community colleges. These efforts culminated in 1978 with the adoption of the Tribally Controlled Community College Assistance Act of 1978 (Pub. Law 95-471) and expansion of community colleges to serve previously underserved communities throughout the western United States (Vaughan, 2006).

*1970 to the Present: Continued Evolution of a Unique and Comprehensive Mission*

The early junior colleges focused on providing students with the first two years of a baccalaureate education before transferring to a university; transfer is still integral to the community college mission today. However, as community colleges evolved, this mission expanded in two significant ways. One was to provide alternatives for students whose primary goal was not to transfer to a university but rather to enter the workforce immediately after graduating. Another was to develop noncredit courses to provide yet more educational avenues for those with specific needs. Technical colleges began to emerge, developing certificate, degree, and noncredit programs to meet the more specialized needs of students and employers.

Certificate and degree programs provide students with a combination of liberal arts and a more focused set of courses that give them technical or occupational skills. Many of these programs were developed to prepare students for in-demand careers in allied health, public service, and computer fields. In fact, more than half of new nurses and the majority of other health-care workers (e.g., emergency medical technicians) and first responders (e.g., firefighters, police officers) are educated at community colleges (National Commission on Community Colleges, 2008). Although these degrees are not designed to lead to transfer to four-year institutions, often students are able to transfer credits from these programs.

At the heart of the evolving community college mission is a sense of responsibility for the economic development of the communities surrounding the colleges. Responding to local employers' needs for workers with specific types and levels of skills, community colleges offer a wide variety of noncredit programs and courses. Noncredit courses do not typically lead to a formal college degree, but they provide targeted, high-quality education and training for specialized careers, typically in demand by employers, such as industry-specific IT certifications. Noncredit courses also provide students with opportunities for academic and personal growth (e.g., remedial, ESL, community service, and professional development courses). According to the most recent data collected in fall 2007, an estimated 5 million noncredit students were enrolled in community colleges (AACC, 2010).

Gradually, the missions of the junior colleges and technical colleges started to overlap and merge into today's comprehensive mission, which remains unique in higher education. Technical colleges began to offer transfer courses while junior colleges offered vocational courses. The colleges also introduced developmental education to prepare students for college-level work, community service courses to meet the needs of community members, and contract education classes to serve local industry. Depending on their location, these institutions go by several different names: community colleges, technical colleges, technical community colleges, state colleges, or even junior colleges. As an integral part of the higher education system, they are most commonly referred to as community colleges and are generally affected by the same laws and regulations that apply to four-year colleges and universities.

## The Distinctive Characteristics of Community Colleges

Clearly, as the preceding history shows, one of the primary characteristics that distinguish community colleges from four-year institutions is their comprehensive service mission—offering a broad array of postsecondary alternatives to a bachelor's degree. But other unique values and characteristics also set community colleges apart within higher education.

## Access and Inclusion

Often referred to as open-door institutions, community colleges provide access to higher education not only to those who intend to continue their education beyond two years of post-secondary work, but also for people who, for academic, lifestyle, or economic reasons choose not to or are unable attend a four-year institution. The wide array of course and program options, the significantly lower cost of tuition, and the proximity of the colleges to home or work make them a more convenient and affordable option for close to 12 million students—and nearly half of all undergraduates earning college credit. In fall 2009, the average cost of tuition at a community college was $2,544 a year, compared with $7,020 at a four-year institution (College Board, 2009). Moreover, 90% of the U.S. population lives within 25 miles of a community college (National Commission on Community Colleges, 2008). Further enhancing access and convenience, students at 45% of public community colleges can earn a degree entirely online, and 97% of all institutions offer at least one Internet-based course (Parsad & Lewis, 2008).

Largely because of their accessibility, community colleges enroll the most diverse student body in higher education, along every major demographic dimension. The average age of community college students is 28; 46% are under 21, and 40% are between 22 and 39 years of age. An additional 16% are over 40. More than half (56%) of community college students are females, and 36% are non-White. The largest representations of students of color are Hispanic (15%) and Black (14%). A large percentage (42%) of community college students are first-generation, and nearly two thirds (60%) attend part time. Community college students are also likely to have multiple family obligations, and 16% of them are single parents (NCES, 2009).

## Community Responsiveness and Innovation

As noted earlier, community responsiveness is an integral part of the service mission of community colleges. Community colleges develop in-demand career programs, partner with local institutions and agencies, provide contract education to businesses, and offer both credit and noncredit community service programs. Some colleges provide facilities and support services to incubate new entrepreneurial businesses; others are seen as cultural centers for their communities. When new immigrants enter a community, it is the community college that provides courses in English language and citizenship. When a factory closes down in a community, it is the community college that retrains the workers who are displaced, sometimes through rapid-response programs that help workers gain reemployment more quickly.

Community colleges are especially innovative in partnering with local businesses and industry to design unique training programs to meet specific local workforce needs. For example, the Community College of Southern Alabama has a paper technology program to meet the needs of the pulp industry in that region. Napa Valley College in California has a viticulture program to support the local wine industry. The Maricopa County Community Colleges in Phoenix, Arizona, have computer chip manufacturing programs to support the needs of the technology industry in that area. And the community colleges along the Gulf Coast offer petrochemical technician training programs for the oil and natural gas industries.

Far beyond the specific program offerings reflecting the needs of local industries, community colleges often encourage entrepreneurship, hosting Small Business Development Centers or business incubators that nurture fledgling entrepreneurs. Two-year institutions may also develop or participate in consortia that collaborate in economic development ventures or with clusters of like businesses to focus on strengths of a specific economic region. The local community college may be part of a team focused on economic development that works to attract new industry to a community or region, with the incentive of training or retraining that the college might help provide.

### Small Class Sizes and Focus on Instruction

Class sizes are generally much smaller than those found in the lower-division classes in four-year colleges and universities, leading to more one-on-one relationships between students and instructors. Community college faculty are not required to conduct discipline-focused research or publish, as are their colleagues in other segments of higher education, to gain tenure or advancement; as a result, instructors can concentrate on teaching and typically expend a greater percentage of their work time in or preparing for the classroom. Faculty members most commonly have at least a master's degree in the field in which they teach, although an increasing number have a doctorate. They are typically involved in setting up the courses and the standards for academic achievement, often within the framework of specific academic disciplines. In many cases, community college instruction is made more current and relevant by adjunct faculty valued for their knowledge and expertise in a specific or highly specialized field. For example, the Gulf Coast colleges with petrochemical technician training programs mentioned earlier are likely to employ adjunct instructors who have long-time professional experience in the oil and gas industry. Or local professionals, such as accountants or financial planners, may lend real-world immediacy to business curricula. In the case of nursing professionals, hospital personnel may be recruited or, occasionally, provided on loan to help college nursing programs meet enrollment demand.

## The Learning College Model

In the foregoing section, several values and characteristics that define the uniqueness of community colleges are outlined: access, inclusion, community responsiveness, innovation, small class sizes, and focus on instruction. But what may best distinguish community colleges from their four-year counterparts is the unique learning-centered model on which the colleges are based. More than 25 years ago, under the direction of former President Ronald Reagan, the U.S. Department of Education formed the National Commission on Excellence in Education to undertake a study of the U.S. education system. The Commission published its final report, *A Nation at Risk*, in 1983, triggering an education reform movement that many consider still underway today. In this report, higher education came under fire for failing to give adequate attention to teaching and learning outcomes. The Commission's recommendations were as follows:

◇ Graduation requirements should be strengthened so that all students establish a foundation in five new basics: English, mathematics, science, social studies, and computer science.
◇ Schools and colleges should adopt higher and measurable standards for academic performance.
◇ The amount of time students spend engaged in learning should be significantly increased.
◇ The teaching profession should be strengthened through higher standards for preparation and professional growth. (National Commission on Excellence, 1983)

America's community colleges had long been committed to quality teaching, but in the wake of *A Nation at Risk*, they responded with a renewed focus on learning. The American Association of Community Colleges (AACC) Commission on the Future of Community Colleges report,

*Building Communities: A Vision for a New Century* (1988), called on community colleges to be the nation's premier teaching institutions and stated that quality instruction should be the hallmark of the movement. Later in a related analysis, the 2000 New Expeditions report, *The Knowledge Net* (AACC, 2000), challenged community colleges to shift the focus from producer-driven delivery of teaching to consumer-driven acquisition of learning. Focus began to shift beyond that of ensuring access to ensuring success once students gained access. This focus underscored the importance of the learning paradigm and the learning college movement that was already underway and that many community colleges are modeled on today.

Palomar College in southern California was an early adopter of the new learning paradigm. College leaders worked to transform the college into a more effective institution by establishing a new paradigm that defined community colleges as learning, not teaching, institutions. In an early article, what came to be referred to as a new learning paradigm was described as follows: "The mission is student learning. The most important people in the institution are the learners. Everyone else is there to facilitate and support student learning" (Boggs, 1993, p. 2). Many community college colleagues then and since have supported and advanced this paradigm. (For more on the history and development of the learning paradigm, see, e.g., Barr & Tagg, 1995; Boggs, 1993, 1993–1994, 1995, 1995–1996, 1999; Boggs & Michael, 1997; O'Banion, 1997.)

The learning paradigm called on colleges to accept responsibility for more than just providing students with an opportunity to learn. It encouraged colleges and all of their employees to accept responsibility for the learning and talent development of their students and to base their success as institutions on the success of their students. In principle, the learning paradigm served as a foundation to promote practices such as collaborative learning, learning communities, focus on learning outcomes, and better use of technology. In practice, the paradigm was implemented at Palomar College at every level, including the following:

⬦ A new mission statement defined student learning as the college's purpose.
⬦ Catalogs, publications, and job descriptions were changed to include language that articulated and supported the idea that everyone at the college was equally responsible for promoting, supporting, and facilitating student learning.
⬦ Orientation programs for faculty, staff, and board members emphasized the principles of the learning paradigm.

The Learning College Project, initiated in 2000 by The League for Innovation in the Community College, established a framework that would assist other colleges in putting this model into practice. Twelve Vanguard Colleges and 61 Champion Colleges were chosen to serve as incubators and catalysts for the learning college model by building on values that placed learning first throughout their institutions. These colleges developed and strengthened policies, programs, and practices across their institutions with a focus on five areas: (a) organizational culture, (b) staff recruitment and development, (c) technology, (d) learning outcomes, and (e) underprepared students. As this model took root in community colleges across the country, institutional structures were redesigned to support it. Planning and decision making are now based on consequences to student learning and success. Programs are evaluated based on the impact they have on student learning.

## The Success and Completion Agenda

As was stated earlier in this chapter, community colleges provide access to higher education to the most diverse student body along every demographic dimension. Despite their success at providing open access, however, the fact remains that the children of minorities and low-income families still do not have the same opportunities for access as do children from more advantaged families. Nor do they have the same success in college if they are admitted. The need to improve access and success rates for students, especially those who are first-generation college students, minorities, or students from low-income families, is a compelling issue for all institutions of higher education but one that is of special concern to community colleges, which have traditionally provided greater access for these students.

The open door of the community college has been criticized many times as being a revolving door. Students who are enrolled all too often drop out or stop out before meeting their learning goals. Bailey and Leinbach (2005) reported that of all first-time college students who entered a community college in 1995, only 36% earned a certificate, associate, or a bachelor's degree within six years. Although many students who did not complete degrees may have met other personal or professional goals, policy makers and educators judged these rates to be too low (Bailey & Leinbach). Moreover, Berkner, He, and Cataldi (2002) reported that completion rates for Black, Hispanic, Native American, and low-income students were lower than those for other groups, suggesting racial, educational, and income gaps. More recently, the Organisation for Economic Co-Operation and Development (OECD, 2009) has estimated the overall higher education graduation rate to be as low as 40%.

The traditional standard for measuring postsecondary completion rates is that established by OECD, which makes international comparisons that are based on attainment of associate or bachelor's degrees. As community colleges and others have become increasingly aware, however, OECD's standards are ineffective at capturing accurate completion and success rates at community colleges. Why? Because they do not take into consideration the array of reasons for community college attendance, and metrics are not calibrated to reflect the majority of community college students who are of limited economic means and attend part time while working.

A significant number of community college students, including many students who could be referred to as disadvantaged, do not enroll for the purpose of attaining an associate degree or transferring to a university to earn a bachelor's degree. Among this highly diverse student body are three groups in particular who attend for different reasons:

◇ High school students, who earn college credits while still in high school or who attend community colleges to receive remedial education or prepare for GEDs.
◇ Swirlers—Students who attend four-year institutions but concurrently take courses at community colleges.
◇ Retoolers—Students, most of whom are working adults, who enroll for one course or a complete program for the purpose of attaining the skills needed to gain or retain sustainable employment. (Mullin, 2010)

For these kinds of students, success and completion clearly need to be defined differently and more meaningfully. Fortunately, community colleges have received support from federal policy makers and major foundations to advance the success and completion agenda.

### Achieving the Dream

A significant effort to improve success in community colleges was set in motion by Lumina Foundation for Education in 2004. The Foundation seeks to identify and promote practices leading to improvement in the rates of entry and success in education beyond high school, particularly for low-income or other underrepresented students. Lumina's (2010) Big Goal is to increase the percentage of students receiving high-quality degrees and credentials to 60% by the year 2025 (today, 40% of adults in the United States hold a two- or four-year degree; OECD, 2009). Lumina asserts that this goal is achievable if the nation directs attention to three critical outcomes:

◇ Students are prepared academically, financially, and socially for success beyond high school.
◇ Higher education completion rates are improved significantly.
◇ Higher education productivity is increased to expand capacity and serve more students.

To advance its goal, Lumina was the initial funder in 2004 of Achieving the Dream: Community Colleges Count (ATD), a national initiative to help more community college students succeed, especially students of color, working adults, and students from low-income families. Eight national partner organizations have worked with Lumina to guide the initiative and provide technical and other support to the colleges and states: the American Association of Community Colleges; the Community College Leadership Program at the University of Texas-Austin; the Community College Research Center, Teachers College, Columbia University; Institute for Higher Education at the University of Florida; Jobs for the Future; MDC (formerly the North Carolina Manpower Development Corporation); MDRC (formerly Manpower Demonstration Research Corporation); and Public Agenda. Begun with a cohort of 26 colleges, ATD has now expanded to 128 colleges in 24 states, including the District of Columbia. Plans are being developed to expand ATD throughout the country.

The ATD initiative emphasizes the use of data and the creation of a culture of evidence at the colleges to inform decision making and to measure progress against a specific set of student success metrics. In particular, ATD colleges will maintain a high degree of access for historically underrepresented groups while working to increase the percentage of students who

◇ Successfully complete the courses they take
◇ Advance from remedial to credit-bearing courses
◇ Enroll in and successfully complete gatekeeper courses
◇ Enroll from one semester to the next
◇ Earn degrees or certificates (ATD, 2010)

ATD colleges begin by examining student outcomes data in an open, straightforward, and rigorous way. They involve faculty, students, staff, and the larger community in developing and implementing strategies to improve student achievement. They closely monitor their progress and share findings broadly. The initiative is intended to generate new knowledge about practices and policies that enhance student success. College teams share strategies across institutions and assess progress by noting the trends in the percentage of students who successfully complete the courses they take, advance from remedial to credit-bearing courses, enroll from one term to the next, and earn a degree or a certificate. ATD efforts have focused on improving or expanding developmental education, gatekeeper courses, first-year experience, learning communities, academic and personal advising, student support services, and tutoring. The colleges are also working to strengthen linkages to K-12 and to engage the community. In addition, the initiative is focused on improving state and federal policies that create barriers for students.

### Gates Foundation Postsecondary Success Initiative

The Bill and Melinda Gates Foundation (2009) announced a major success initiative, intended to ensure that postsecondary education results in a degree or a certificate with genuine economic value. It has set an ambitious goal to double the number of young people who reach that milestone by the time they reach age 26. The Foundation notes that the types of jobs fueling our economy continue to change rapidly and that success in the workplace demands advanced skills in critical thinking and problem solving as well as the ability to shift readily from one task or project to another. Workers with strong language, math, and technology skills and an ability to work well in teams are most likely to succeed. Carnevale, Smith, and Strohl (2010) project that, through 2018, nearly two thirds (63%) of all new jobs will require more than a high school diploma; nearly half of those will require some college but less than a bachelor's degree. The Bureau of Labor Statistics projects that, 21 of the 30 fastest-growing occupations require postsecondary education (Lacey & Wright, 2009).

The Gates Foundation postsecondary success initiative will begin with an emphasis on public community colleges rather than four-year institutions as the best complement to access and success efforts currently happening in U.S. higher education. A particular focus of the initiative is to generate innovation in remedial education, which is seen as a significant barrier to college completion.

### The Obama Administration Higher Education Agenda

In an address to a joint session of Congress, President Obama (2009) asked every American to commit to at least one year of higher education or career training so that America would once again have the highest proportion of college graduates in the world. The president made the point that in an increasingly competitive world economy, the economic strength of the United States depends on the education and skills of its workers and that, in the coming years, jobs requiring at least an associate degree are projected to grow twice as fast as those requiring no college experience.

The administration has had notable successes in enacting elements of its broader college affordability agenda. The American Recovery and Reinvestment Act (ARRA), passed in February 2009, increased the Pell Grant maximum award by $500 and created the American Opportunity Tax Credit, which temporarily replaces the Hope Scholarship tax credit and better serves community college students. ARRA also contained significant resources for job training programs.

In July 2009, President Obama unveiled the American Graduation Initiative: Stronger Skills Through Community Colleges (AGI) at Macomb Community College in Michigan. The president's plan was an ambitious one, calling on community colleges to prepare an additional 5 million graduates and program completers by 2020, nearly a 50% increase over current levels. The initiative components would modernize community college facilities, create new online learning opportunities, and fund strategies to promote access and completion.

The U.S. House of Representatives acted in September 2009, to approve its version of AGI in a bill that was called the Student Aid and Fiscal Responsibility Act (SAFRA). However, because SAFRA was considered budget reconciliation legislation, the bill became intertwined with the health-care reform legislation, part of which was also passed using the reconciliation process. This legislation, the Health Care and Education Reconciliation Act, did not become law until March 2010, when it was signed by President Obama at Northern Virginia Community College. The long delay in enacting SAFRA greatly diminished the amount of savings it produced for the federal government—money that would, in turn, be used to pay for new programs. As a result, most of SAFRA's new programs, including AGI, were not included in the final legislation, which devoted most of its resources to Pell Grants.

However, the bill did provide $2 billion over four years for the Community College and Career Training Program. This program, which is part of the Trade Adjustment Assistance (TAA) Act, was originally created in ARRA but never funded. It will provide funds to community colleges and other higher education institutions to create and expand programs that serve TAA-certified and other dislocated workers. While it will not have the same breadth as AGI, the U.S. Department of Labor is expected to focus on reforms at community colleges that will help more workers obtain postsecondary credentials. At the reconciliation bill signing in March, President Obama announced a White House summit on community colleges to be hosted by Jill Biden in fall 2010. The administration's completion agenda was a central focus of the event, at which U.S. Secretary of Education Arne Duncan also called for a future virtual summit to directly engage more community colleges.

### Voluntary Framework of Accountability

As was alluded to earlier, because of the complex and comprehensive missions of community colleges, measuring completion or student success is not as simple as examining graduation rates. In partnership with the Association of Community College Trustees and the College Board, and with the financial support of the Lumina Foundation for Education and the Bill and Melinda Gates Foundation, AACC is leading the development of the voluntary framework of accountability (VFA) for U.S. community colleges. VFA will provide metrics developed by community colleges, which will allow colleges to consistently report student progress and success measures to their stakeholders, as well as providing benchmarks for internal use.

## Conclusion

Since the founding of Joliet Junior College more than a century ago, community colleges have evolved to become the most egalitarian of all higher education institutions—what some describe as democracy's colleges. They have expanded their mission to include workforce, community, and developmental education and lifelong learning. The colleges adopted values that distinguished them as unique institutions of higher education: access, inclusion, community responsiveness, innovation, small class sizes, and a focus on instruction. In the 1980s, community colleges further distinguished themselves by adopting another value, that of student learning and success.

Today, however, improving the success rates of students is an ambitious goal for institutions that are the least well funded in American higher education and that attract the most at-risk students. Since community colleges now enroll 43% (NCES, 2007) of all of the undergraduate credit students in the United States (and, since the colleges attract most of the nation's minority and disadvantaged students), major foundations and policy makers have begun to pay increasing attention to them and have supported key initiatives to help the colleges improve the success rates of students. Most notably, the colleges have been identified as critical to the success of the nation, and President Obama has called for more investment in them while challenging them to significantly improve completion rates. These least well-funded institutions are being counted on to play a pivotal role in ensuring the future competitiveness and well-being of the country.

Improving student persistence and success rates, although a worthy goal, is not easy work, especially in times of economic recession and retrenchment. However, dedicated college faculty, researchers, and leaders are discovering together what structures, practices, and methods can help students persist, learn, and be successful in accomplishing their educational goals. What is being learned or verified by the initiatives now underway to increase student success and to improve student learning is not only impressive, it is also essential to the success of the learning enterprise of the future. College faculty, staff, and administrators are working to create a culture of evidence on campuses and to develop strategies to increase student retention and completion while maintaining high quality—a daunting goal requiring an unprecedented level of operational effort and transparency.

This difficult balancing act—preserving the access and inclusion that are cornerstones of the community college mission while implementing informed practices that ensure greater success for students— will test the strength and resolve of these institutions. But the growing commitment of organizations, college leaders, and faculty, buttressed by essential support from policy makers and major foundations, makes the focus on completion a pivotal turning point in the long and successful evolution of America's community colleges.

## References

Achieving the Dream (ATD). (2010). *Goals*. Retrieved from http://www.achievingthedream.org/ABOUTATD/GOALS/default.tp

American Association of Community Colleges (AACC). (1988). *Building communities: A vision for a new century*. (Report of the Commission on the Future of Community Colleges). Washington, DC: Community College Press.

American Association of Community Colleges (AACC). (2000). *The knowledge net*. (Report of the New Expeditions Initiative). Washington, DC: Community College Press.

American Association of Community Colleges (AACC). (2010). *2010 fact sheet*. Retrieved from AACC website: http://www.aacc.nche.edu/AboutCC/Pages/fastfacts.aspx

Bailey, T. R., & Leinbach, D. T. (2005). *Is student success considered institutional failure? The accountability debate at community colleges*. New York, NY: Community College Research Center.

Barr, R. B., & Tagg, J. (1995, November/December). From teaching to learning: A new paradigm for undergraduate education. *Change Magazine*, 12-25.

Berkner, L., He, S., & Cataldi, E. F. (2002). *Descriptive summary of 1995-96 beginning postsecondary students: Six years later* (NCES 2003-151). Washington, DC: U.S. Department of Education, National Center for Education Statistics.

Bill & Melinda Gates Foundation. (2009). *Postsecondary success*. Redmond, WA: Author. Retrieved from http://www.gatesfoundation.org/postsecondaryeducation

Boggs, G. R. (1993). Community colleges and the new paradigm. *Celebrations* (An occasional publication of the National Institute for Staff and Organizational Development [NISOD]). Austin, TX: The University of Texas at Austin, NISOD. (ERIC Document Reproduction Services No. ED366363)

Boggs, G. R. (1993-1994). Reinventing community colleges. *Community College Journal, 64*(3), 4-5.

Boggs, G. R. (1995). Focus on student learning. *Crosstalk, 3*(2), 6, 10-11.

Boggs, G. R. (1995-1996). The learning paradigm. *Community College Journal, 66*(3), 24-27.

Boggs, G. R. (1999). What the learning paradigm means for faculty. *AAHE Bulletin, 51*(5), 3-5.

Boggs, G. R., & Cater, J. J. (1994.). The historical development of academic programs in community colleges. In G. A. Baker, III (Ed.), *A handbook on the community college in America: Its history, mission, and management* (pp. 218-226). Westport, CT: Greenwood Press.

Boggs, G. R., & Michael, D. G. (1997). The Palomar College experience. In T. O'Banion (Ed.), *A learning college for the 21st century* (pp. 189-210). Washington, DC: Community College Press and Oryx Press.

Brint, S., & Karabel, J. (1989). *The diverted dream: Community colleges and the promise of educational opportunity in America, 1900-1985*. New York, NY: Oxford University Press.

Carnevale, A. P., Smith, N., & Strohl, J. (2010, June). *Help wanted: Projections of jobs and education requirements through 2018*. Washington, DC: Georgetown University, Center on Education and the Workforce.

College Board. (2009). *Trends in college pricing: 2009*. Washington, DC: Author. Retrieved from http://www.trends-collegeboard.com/college_pricing/pdf/2009_Trends_College_Pricing.pdf

Lacey, T. A., & Wright, B. (2009, November). Occupational employment projections to 2018. *Monthly Labor Review, 132*(11), 82-123.

League for Innovation in the Community College. *The Learning College Project (2000)*. Phoenix, AZ: Retrieved from http://www.league.org/league/projects/lcp/index.htm

Lumina Foundation for Education. (2010). *Goal 2025*. Retrieved from http://www.luminafoundation.org/goal_2025/

Mullin, C. M. (2010, June). *Rebalancing the mission: The community college completion challenge* (Policy Brief 2010-02PBL). Washington, DC: American Association of Community Colleges.

National Center for Education Statistics (NCES). (2007). *Integrated postsecondary education data system (IPEDS) fall enrollment survey* [Data file]. Washington, DC: U.S. Department of Education.

National Center for Education Statistics (NCES). (2009, April). *National postsecondary student aid study: 2007-08*. Washington, DC: U.S. Department of Education.

National Commission on Excellence in Education. (1983). *A nation at risk: The imperative for educational reform. A report to the nation and the Secretary of Education, United States Department of Education*. Ann Arbor, MI: University of Michigan Library.

National Commission on Community Colleges. (2008, January). *Winning the skills race and strengthening America's middle class: An action agenda for community colleges*. New York, NY: The College Board. Retrieved from http://professionals.collegeboard.com/profdownload/winning_the_skills_race.pdf

Obama, B. (2009, July 14). *Remarks by the president on the American Graduation Initiative*. Washington, DC: The White House, Office of the Press Secretary. Retrieved from http://www.whitehouse.gov/the_press_office/Remarks-by-the-President-on-the-American-Graduation-Initiative-in-Warren-MI/

O'Banion, T. (1997). *A learning college for the 21st century*. Washington, DC: Community College Press and Oryx Press.

Organisation for Economic Co-Operation and Development (OECD). (2009). *Education at a glance 2009: OECD indicators*. Retrieved from www.oecd.org/edu/eag2009

Palinchak, R. (1973). *The evolution of the community college*. Metuchen, NJ: Scarecrow Press.

Parsad, B., & Lewis, L. (2008). Distance education at degree-granting postsecondary institutions: 2006-07 (NCES 2009-044). Washington, DC: U.S. Department of Education, National Center for Education Statistics, Institute of Education Sciences. Retrieved from http://nces.ed.gov/pubs2009/2009044.pdf

Phillippe, K., & González-Sullivan, L. (2005). *National profile of community colleges: Trends and statistics*. Washington, DC: Community College Press.

President's Commission on Higher Education. (1947). *Higher education for democracy: A report of the President's Commission on Higher Education* (vols. 1-2). New York, NY: Harper.

Vaughan, G. B. (2006). *The community college story* (3rd ed.). Washington, DC: Community College Press.

# Chapter 2

## Understanding Entering Community College Students: Learning From Student Voices

Kay McClenney

E ngagement matters. That is the beginning and the end of this chapter. The more engaged students are—with faculty, staff, other students, and the subject matter they are studying— the more likely they are to persist and succeed in college. For community college students, who are typically juggling multiple challenges and obligations outside the classroom, engagement is critical. Effective student engagement also may even the playing field, heightening chances of success for students who bring an assortment of risk factors to college with them.

Community colleges are increasingly recognizing the importance of focusing attention and effort on the front door of the college. Though data are hard to find, many leaders believe that far too many students are lost in the intake process, before they ever get to class. Beginning with the official census date (typically the 10th or 12th day of class), more information about student matriculation is available. Achieving the Dream college data show that 14% of students who begin community college credit classes in the fall term earn no credits in their first term (Clery & Topper, 2008). Further, the same study shows that only 15% of students who earn no credits in their first term will persist to the second term, compared to 74% persistence for students who do earn first-term credits. Nationally, we know that of the students who begin in the fall, about 25% will not return for the spring term; and close to 50% will be gone by the subsequent fall term.

This picture illustrates the importance of understanding what is happening and, therefore, where improvements can be made in the ways colleges design and manage the entering student experience. Focal concerns include students' first contacts with the college; entry or intake processes, including assessment and course placement, academic planning and advising, financial aid, registration, and the like; college orientation and student success courses or first-year seminars; early classroom experiences; and academic support.

The purpose of this chapter is to focus attention on the characteristics and earliest experiences of community college students, as revealed through national data, student surveys, and focus groups. Specifically, the chapter will highlight the key characteristics of entering students, potential challenges, the quality of their earliest educational experiences in the community college, and their perceptions of what is important to them as they enter college and navigate their first few weeks on campus. The chapter concludes with a brief set of recommendations about how community colleges can understand and serve their first-year students more effectively.

## Understanding the Entering Student Cohort

National data indicate that community college students comprise 40% of all first-time, first-year students in U.S. colleges and universities (AACC, 2010). A critically important task for any community college committed to its students' success is to understand the characteristics of entering community college students as a distinctive cohort with particular needs. Newly available information about the characteristics and experiences of students entering community colleges—data provided by the students themselves—shed light on opportunities and issues for community colleges as they seek to improve student success. The Survey of Entering Student Engagement (SENSE), conducted by the Center for Community College Student Engagement at The University of Texas at Austin, was developed to ensure that community colleges can obtain timely and actionable information about new students' characteristics—and importantly, their experiences from the time of their first contacts with a college through the end of their first three weeks of class (Appendix A).[1] To learn more about the human experiences behind the survey numbers, the Center also conducts, through its Initiative on Student Success, a series of student focus groups that explore students' experiences as they enter college. Employing both the quantitative survey results and the qualitative focus groups, it becomes possible to lift up student voices to inform work aimed at improving student success.

Data from the first national administration of SENSE (Center for Community College Student Engagement [CCCSE], 2010a) provide a picture of the differences between entering community college students and their classmates who have previously been enrolled in at least one academic term in college. The distinctions between these two subpopulations (i.e., entering vs. returning students) provide preliminary insights, while raising additional questions and also some concerns regarding the apparent attrition among certain groups of students (Table 2.1). For example, males comprised 44% of entering students completing the survey, but only 39% of returning students. In addition, the returning group included significantly more students who were working 20 or more hours per week; and part-time enrollees comprised a larger portion of the returning student group than of the entering cohort. Comparisons of entering and returning student respondents in terms of race and ethnicity revealed few differences (Table 2.2).

Typically, the data initially raise more questions than they answer. Thus begins the important campus process of building a culture of evidence and inquiry. Guiding questions for discussions prompted by a general review of data might include the following:

◇ In demographic or descriptive terms, how do our entering students differ from returning students at the college?
◇ In terms of educational experiences, how do our entering students differ significantly from returning students?
◇ How might we reasonably understand these differences?
◇ What findings from these comparisons capture the attention of college faculty, staff, and administrators?
◇ What specific findings are pertinent to the college's current student success initiatives, particularly including programs that focus on the first-year experience?

Table 2.1

*Student Characteristics by Status*

| Characteristic | Percentage of entering students | Percentage of returning students | Percentage of all respondents |
|---|---|---|---|
| Male | 44 | 39 | 42 |
| Female | 56 | 62 | 58 |
| Enrolled part time | 26 | 36 | 30 |
| Enrolled full time | 74 | 64 | 70 |
| Traditional age (18-24) | 80 | 64 | 73 |
| Nontraditional age (25 and older) | 20 | 37 | 27 |
| Work more than 20 hours per week | 32 | 46 | 38 |
| English is their first language | 87 | 83 | 85 |
| Married | 11 | 19 | 15 |
| Have children living with them | 20 | 30 | 24 |

*Note.* Adapted from *Data Set for 2009 Survey of Entering Student Engagement* (CCCSE, 2010a).

Table 2.2

*Students' Race and Ethnicity by Status*

| Characteristic | Percentage of entering students | Percentage of returning students | Percentage of all respondents |
|---|---|---|---|
| White | 53 | 50 | 52 |
| Latino/Hispanic | 20 | 21 | 21 |
| African American | 17 | 17 | 17 |
| Asian | 4 | 5 | 5 |
| Other | 4 | 5 | 4 |
| Native American | 2 | 2 | 2 |
| Native Hawaiian | < 1 | < 1 | < 1 |

*Note.* Adapted from *Data Set for 2009 Survey of Entering Student Engagement* (CCCSE, 2010a).

Progressing to greater detail, those involved in data analysis might ask, for example, questions such as these:

◇ Why are we enrolling fewer men than women?
◇ Why is the proportion of part-time enrollees increasing for returning students? Are students finding that they can not handle full-time enrollment financially or because of competing commitments?
◇ Are we losing some younger students because they are not connecting with the college?
◇ To what extent are these data affected by students completing developmental education and/or first-year English and math in their first term?
◇ In our college, are high levels of engagement in the first term associated with improved persistence rates for students of color?

Addressing these questions often requires that colleges conduct further quantitative analysis or systematic focus groups with their students, probing to understand the human experience behind the survey numbers.

## Benchmarks of Effective Practice With Entering Students

Based on data analysis during a pilot year, an expanded field test, and the fall 2009 national survey administration, SENSE has produced a set of six benchmarks of effective practice with entering students in community colleges. Item development for the survey was strongly informed by the extant literature on effective practice with students during the first year of college. For each participating college, therefore, student responses to particular items, as well as institutional performance on each of the six benchmarks, provide useful insights regarding the quality of students' earliest collegiate experiences.

This section introduces the benchmarks, lists the SENSE items comprising each benchmark, and offers illustrative findings from the survey (CCCSE 2010a; 2010b), as well as selected observations from student focus groups.

### Benchmark #1 – Early Connections

In focus groups, community college students frequently described occasions when they considered dropping out of college. Asked why they persisted, they typically referred to a strong, early connection to someone at the college. Very often, they even offered that person's name. Thus, SENSE includes several items indicating the extent to which entering students feel welcome at their colleges and develop early connections with people on campus.

◇ *The very first time I came to this college I felt welcome*—73% agreed or strongly agreed; 3% disagreed or strongly disagreed
◇ *The college provided me with adequate information about financial assistance (scholarships, grants, loans, etc.)*—50% agreed or strongly agreed; 24% disagreed or strongly disagreed
◇ *A college staff member helped me determine whether I qualified for financial assistance*—35% agreed or strongly agreed; 39% disagreed or strongly disagreed

◇ *At least one college staff member (other than an instructor) learned my name*—46% agreed or strongly agreed; 36% disagreed or strongly disagreed
◇ *A specific person was assigned to me so I could see him/her each time I needed information or assistance*—23% responded Yes; 77% responded No

In focus groups, students used the word personal with notable frequency. They sought personalized orientation and advising, for example, and they commonly spoke of the value of structured opportunities, early in their college experience, to interact with faculty and with other students.

## Benchmark #2 – High Expectations and Aspirations

With striking consistency, new students at community colleges described their belief that they have the motivation and commitment necessary to succeed in college. What becomes clear is that when students perceive that college faculty and staff hold high expectations for their success, they often will rise to meet those expectations. Further, their early college experiences may contribute to a heightening of their own aspirations about what they are capable of achieving, even as they come to a better understanding of what it takes to be a successful college student. Accordingly, this benchmark includes items that explore respondents' motivation, as well as both college and student expectations and, again, the result are revealing:

◇ *The instructors at this college want me to succeed*—87% agreed or strongly agreed
◇ *I have the motivation to do what it takes to succeed in college*—91% agreed or strongly agreed
◇ *I am prepared academically to succeed in college*—86% agreed or strongly agreed

The response to the academic preparedness item is particularly noteworthy since other data indicate that more than 60% of students arrive at U.S. community colleges needing at least one course in developmental education (Bailey, 2009). This discrepancy raises the question of whether students are fully aware of the skill levels needed to meet expectations for success in college-level work.

Other survey items ask students to provide information on their frequency of turning in an assignment late, not turning in an assignment, coming to class without completing readings or assignments, or skipping class. Large numbers of entering students report behaving in ways—even as early as the first three weeks of class—that most college instructors would regard as not conducive to academic success. For example, reflecting on their first three weeks in college, 32% of entering students indicated that they were late in turning in at least one assignment while 26% failed altogether to turn in at least one assignment. In addition, 46% reported coming to class unprepared at least once, and 26% had skipped at least one class. Asked about these behaviors in focus groups, some students observed that one of the reasons they behaved in these ways was that there were no consequences. Thus, they underscored the importance of institutions and faculty members setting clear expectations and holding students accountable for meeting them. Further, students often acknowledged that they initially underestimated—because they had no experience with college—the amount of time and the kinds of effort that success in their courses would require of them.

## Benchmark #3 – Clear Academic Plan and Pathway

One of the most critical tools for helping students stay on track toward college success is an academic plan that identifies goals and charts the path toward their achievement. Effective academic advising addresses not only course selection but also the critical planning process. The items in this benchmark, therefore, assess the extent to which students are experiencing various key components of the advising process:

◇ *I was able to meet with an academic advisor at times convenient for me*—62% agreed or strongly agreed; 11% disagreed or strongly disagreed
◇ *An advisor helped me to select a course of study, program, or major*—60% agreed or strongly agreed
◇ *An advisor helped me to set academic goals and to create a plan for achieving them*—38% agreed or strongly agreed
◇ *An advisor helped me to identify the courses I needed to take during my first semester/ quarter*—72% agreed or strongly agreed
◇ *A college staff member talked with me about my commitments outside of school (work, children, dependents, etc.) to help me figure out how many courses to take*—48% disagreed or strongly disagreed

Student focus group participants strongly expressed the importance of academic goal setting accompanied by advising and planning for attainment of those goals. They often worried that advisors concentrated mostly on the class schedule and less on longer-term plans and the challenges of time management.

These data, both quantitative and qualitative, reflect the challenges that community colleges face as large numbers of students enter the institution, many at the last minute; but they may also point to the advantages of group advising, which promotes student-to-student interaction while addressing time and workload issues, and of first-term courses that integrate important elements of academic planning into inescapable classroom experiences.

## Benchmark #4 – An Effective Track to College Readiness

One of the greatest challenges to student success in community colleges is the significant proportion of entering students—more than 6 in 10—who arrive at the institution's doors underprepared for college-level work (Bailey, 2009). Thus, critical components of the entering student experience will include actionable assessment of academic skills, appropriate course placements, and instructional and support strategies that ensure students build the skills requisite to success. Accordingly, this benchmark includes a collection of items capturing students' experiences with academic skills assessment, course placement, study skills development, and the like. Addressing the crucial need to improve developmental education policy and practice and to monitor the effectiveness of those strategies is the cornerstone of a community college student success agenda.

◇ *Before I could register for classes I was required to take a placement test (COMPASS, ASSET ACCUPLACER, SAT, ACT, etc.) to assess my skills in reading, writing, and/or math*—88% indicated a placement test was required for registration
◇ *I took a placement test (COMPASS, ASSET ACCUPLACER, SAT, ACT, etc.)*—91% responded Yes
◇ *This college REQUIRED me to enroll in classes indicated by my placement test scores during my first semester/quarter*—For students who took placement tests, 74% reported they were required to enroll in prescribed classes.
◇ *Within a class or through another experience at this college, I learned to improve my study skills (listening, note taking, highlighting readings, working with others, etc.)*—73% agreed or strongly agreed

◇ *Within a class or through another experience at this college, I learned to understand my academic strengths and weaknesses*—69% agreed or strongly agreed
◇ *Within a class or through another experience at this college, I learned skills and strategies to improve my test-taking ability*—54% agreed or strongly agreed

Student focus group participants often admitted to surprise and/or initial discouragement when they learned upon entering college that they needed to take one or more remedial courses. On the other hand, the same students frequently acknowledged that taking those college-prep courses helped them become better prepared for success in the more advanced academics that are requisite to meeting their goals. Overall, though, student comments on the quality of developmental courses are decidedly mixed. They criticized teaching approaches that have failed them in the past and material that seemed to bear little relationship to the directions they hoped to take with their college studies.

## *Benchmark #5 – Engaged Learning*

Student engagement in the classroom is key to student success. Furthermore, given the multiple obligations (i.e., jobs, family, community) of most community college students, effective engagement is unlikely to happen by accident. Rather, "the most effective learning experiences will be those the college intentionally designs" (CCCSE, 2010b, p. 13). Items comprising this benchmark are based on research indicating that engaged learning is associated with a variety of desired academic outcomes in the community college environment (McClenney & Marti, 2006). Students were asked to report on the frequency with which they engaged in the following behaviors during the first three weeks of class:

◇ Asking questions in class or contributing to class discussions
◇ Preparing at least two drafts of a paper or assignment before turning it in
◇ Participating in Supplemental Instruction (i.e., extra class sessions with an instructor, tutor, or experienced student)
◇ Working with other students on projects during class
◇ Working with classmates outside of class on projects or assignments
◇ Participating in a required study group outside of class
◇ Participating in a student-initiated (not required) study group outside of class
◇ Using an electronic tool (e.g., e-mail, text messaging, Facebook, MySpace, class website) to communicate with another student about coursework
◇ Using an electronic tool (e.g., e-mail, text messaging, Facebook, MySpace, class website) to communicate with an instructor about coursework
◇ Discussing an assignment or grade with an instructor
◇ Asking for help from an instructor regarding questions or problems related to a class assignment
◇ Discussing ideas from readings or classes with instructors outside of class
◇ Using face-to-face tutoring
◇ Using writing, math, or other skills lab
◇ Using computer lab

In the earliest weeks of the semester, students tended to work with each other on projects during class time with greater frequency than outside of class (81% vs. 37%, respectively). Furthermore, when asked about their participation in certain high-impact experiences related to their coursework, students offered these observations: (a) 32% took part in a Supplemental Instruction session at least once (68% did not) and (b) only 17% participated in at least one required, out-of-class study group compared to 83% who never had that experience.

Regarding their early interactions with faculty members, 66% reported discussing an assignment or grade with an instructor at least once compared to 34% who never did so. Even more students approached instructors for course assistance, with 76% asking for help often or very often compared to 24% who did not seek help. However, out-of-class contact with instructors to discuss ideas or readings was limited, with only 34% making an outside connection. Although 40% of students claimed they never used technology to communicate with an instructor, many of those who requested course assistance could have done so online, since 60% of students indicated that during the first three weeks of class they communicated with an instructor about course work at least once via technology. In assessing feedback given by an instructor, 75% of entering students indicated they had received feedback in the first three weeks of class compared to 25% who reported it had never happened.

When asked in focus groups to describe a good class—a learning experience that is working well for them—students were, perhaps unsurprisingly, quite consistent in their responses. They typically described highly active learning environments (i.e., classroom discussions, small group work) as well as instructors who are passionate both about their subject matter and about their students' success.

### Benchmark #6 – Academic and Social Support Network

Community college students benefit significantly from having a network of support that ensures they receive timely information about college services and that makes it easy—even inescapable—for them to take advantage of academic and student support services. An important note: "Because entering students often don't know what they don't know, colleges must purposefully create those networks" (CCCSE, 2010b, p.16). The SENSE survey items comprising this benchmark ask respondents to indicate the extent to which they received various kinds of information and other support during their first three weeks at the college. Items included

◇ *All instructors clearly explained academic and student support services available at this college*—67% agreed or strongly agreed
◇ *All instructors clearly explained course grading policies*—88% agreed or strongly agreed
◇ *All instructors clearly explained course syllabi (syllabuses)*—91% agreed or strongly agreed
◇ *I knew how to get in touch with my instructors outside of class*—88% agreed or strongly agreed
◇ *At least one other student whom I didn't previously know learned my name*—84% agreed or strongly agreed ; 7% disagreed or strongly disagreed
◇ *At least one instructor learned my name*—87% agreed or strongly agreed; 5% disagreed or strongly disagreed
◇ *I learned the name of at least one other student in most of my classes*—81% agreed or strongly agreed; 8% disagreed or strongly disagreed

Apart from these benchmark items, a matter of some concern is the number of students who report, during the fourth or fifth week of class when the SENSE survey is conducted, that they are unaware of certain key support services (CCCSE 2010a). For example, more than one quarter

(27%) of entering students indicated that they did not know about academic advising and planning services. A similar number of students (24%) reported being unaware of financial assistance advising and face-to-face tutoring services.

## Implications and Recommendations

The emerging data on first-year students and their earliest experiences in the community college point to a number of implications for institutions interested in improving student persistence and success. In summary, the early lessons from the work include the following:

◇ Community college students arrive at their institutions with the conviction that they are motivated and prepared to succeed in college—a potential asset.

◇ On the other hand, large numbers of students, even during the first three weeks of class, behave in ways not conducive to their own academic success. Often, it appears that is the case because they have not yet learned the skills and habits for college success, and there are no immediately evident consequences of skipping class, failing to turn in assignments, and the like. Strategies such as student success courses that provide college know-how are showing promising results in many colleges. Serious discussion about the collective expectations of the faculty, followed by clear communication of those expectations to students, is also important.

◇ Too many students are unaware of key support services when surveyed or interviewed several weeks into their first term of enrollment. Other students know about services or experiences available to them but do not take advantage of them when they are optional rather than required. While it is obvious that effective communication about support services is needed, it also becomes increasingly evident that integrating key services and experiences into courses helps to make them an inescapable part of students' experiences.

◇ Developing an academic plan, including milestones marking the path toward goal achievement, is a critically important process for new students, but the academic planning and advising process appears to be underdeveloped in many colleges.

◇ Students are remarkably clear in describing the kinds of learning strategies that work for them: active learning; collaborative work; and frequent, helpful interactions with their instructors. While some colleges excel in promoting these aspects of student engagement, there is ample room for improvement at most institutions.

Data that assist in better understanding students and their earliest collegiate experiences are enormously valuable. But substantial change and lasting improvement in community college programs and services depend on the commitment to create new organizational cultures, processes, and habits of mind. Accordingly, this chapter concludes with a set of broader recommendations for creating and sustaining a powerful agenda focused on strengthening success rates for entering students.

### Build a Culture of Evidence

For any community college, finding the right answers for the entering student experience rests on an institution-wide commitment to engage the college community with data about their own students. Systematically collected data are indispensable, first in creating a heightened understanding of entering students and then in designing more effective entering-student experiences. Furthermore, a culture of evidence also involves a willingness to rigorously evaluate institutional strategies for improving student success.

### Treat Each Entering Group of Students as a Distinct Cohort

Entering students are different from continuing students. Understanding the unique characteristics and needs of a new-student cohort is fundamental to an effective student success agenda.

### Commit to the Discipline of Routine Student Cohort Tracking

Many community colleges across the country—particularly those affiliated with the national initiative on Achieving the Dream or the California Leadership Alliance for Student Success (CLASS)—are finding that routine longitudinal cohort tracking is a powerful tool for understanding student academic progress and outcomes; generating productive discussions on campus; and prompting appropriate, constructive, and targeted initiatives for change. Without the advantage of an accurate and honest picture of what happens to all students as they move into and through community colleges (or do not), the institutions essentially are operating in the dark. Tracking cohorts of students helps to heighten understanding, inform strategies, and focus efforts. Continuing the cohort tracking with each entering group makes it possible to gauge the effectiveness of these strategies over time.

### Purposefully Design the Entering Student Experience

In community colleges, where multitasking students abound, effective student engagement is critical; but it happens only when faculty and staff intentionally design educational experiences, rather than relying on serendipity or good intentions. Making student engagement inescapable is a worthy goal, and the SENSE benchmarks of effective practice provide a set of design principles for the entering-student experience.

### Overcome the Reluctance to Require

Emerging evidence suggests that certain educational experiences may contribute significantly to the likelihood of student success. Examples include college orientation, first-year seminars, student success courses, learning communities, and other experiences that help campus newcomers connect to classmates, faculty, and the college while learning to be effective college students. At some point, it behooves community college educators to overcome their reluctance to institute requirements for students and to make mandatory the experiences shown to enhance college learning, persistence, and attainment.

### Take Key Experiences Where the Students Are

One way to ensure that students receive the services and experiences they need to be successful is to abandon the traditional referral model and take the services where the students are. Colleges are demonstrating this principle, for example, when they incorporate academic advising into a learning community or require tutoring or Supplemental Instruction as part of a course.

*Bring Programs to Scale*

Given resource constraints, the central task for community colleges is not to create boutique experiences for a few fortunate students but to define evidence-based experiences that will produce the biggest positive effects for the largest possible number of students. Innovative approaches to the first college semester or year should be designed from the beginning to be scaled up, becoming the norm rather than the exception.

## Conclusion

Understanding data—whether quantitative or qualitative—about their students is only the first step for community colleges committed to strengthening entering student success. Moving the needle on success indicators for first-year students requires more than data collection and isolated programmatic interventions. Ultimately, it requires a sustained institution-wide commitment and a willingness to engage in continuous inquiry about the way the institution organizes itself to meet each cohort of entering students, purposefully designing first-year experiences to heighten their chances of success.

## Notes

[1]SENSE is administered in class at participating colleges during the fourth and fifth weeks of the fall academic term. Random samples are drawn from each college's population of courses that analysts have identified as enrolling the highest proportions of first-time students: developmental education courses in reading, writing, and math and first-college-level courses in English and mathematics. The fall 2009 national administration produced responses from more than 50,000 entering students and more than 36,000 returning students from 122 colleges in 30 states and one U.S. territory.

## References

American Association of Community Colleges (AACC). (2010). *Community college facts at a glance.* Retrieved from AACC website: http://www.aacc.nche.edu/AboutCC/Documents/factsheet2010.pdf

Bailey, T. (2009). *Rethinking developmental education in community college* (CCRC Brief No. 40). New York, NY: Community College Research Center.

Center for Community College Student Engagement (CCCSE). (2010a). *Data set for 2009 Survey of Entering Student Engagement (SENSE).* Austin, Texas: The University of Texas at Austin, Community College Leadership Program.

Center for Community College Student Engagement (CCCSE). (2010b). *Benchmarking and benchmarks: Effective practice with entering students.* Austin, TX: The University of Texas at Austin, Community College Leadership Program.

Clery, S., & Topper, A. (2008, October/November). Students earning zero credits. *Data Notes, 3*(5), 1-3.

McClenney, K. M., & Marti, C. N. (2006). *Exploring relationships between student engagement and student outcomes in community colleges: Report on validation research* (CCSSE Working Paper). Retrieved from CCSSE website: http://www.ccsse.org/publications/CCSSE%20Working%20Paper%20on%20Validation%20Research%20December%202006.pdf

## Appendix A

**Instructions: It is essential that you use a No. 2 pencil to complete this survey. Mark your answer as shown in the following example:**

CORRECT MARK  ●
INCORRECT MARKS  ⊘ ⊗ ⊖ ⊙

1. **Have you taken this survey in another class THIS SEMESTER/QUARTER?**
   ○ Yes                    ○ No

2. **Thinking about THIS SEMESTER/QUARTER, how would you describe your enrollment _at this college_?**
   ○ Full-time              ○ Less than full-time

3. **Did you begin college at this college or elsewhere?**
   ○ Started here           ○ Started elsewhere

4. **While in high school, did you earn college credit for one or more courses?** (Mark all that apply)
   ○ No
   ○ Yes, at this college
   ○ Yes, at a different college
   ○ Yes, at my high school

5. **In addition to taking courses at this college, were/are you also enrolled at a 4-year college or university during YOUR FIRST SEMESTER/QUARTER?**
   ○ Yes                    ○ No

6. **How many semesters/quarters have you been enrolled _at this college_?**
   ○ This is my first semester/quarter
   ○ This is my second semester/quarter
   ○ This is my third semester/quarter
   ○ This is my fourth semester/quarter
   ○ I have been enrolled more than four semesters/quarters

7. **How many courses did you enroll in for YOUR FIRST SEMESTER/QUARTER _at this college_?**
   ○ One                    ○ Three
   ○ Two                    ○ Four or more

8. **Did you add or drop any classes within the FIRST THREE WEEKS OF YOUR FIRST SEMESTER/QUARTER _at this college_?**
   ○ Yes, without discussing my decision with a college staff member or instructor
   ○ Yes, after discussing my decision with a college staff member or instructor
   ○ No, I did not add or drop any courses

9. **Of the courses you enrolled in during YOUR FIRST SEMESTER/QUARTER _at this college_, how many did you drop after the first day of class?**
   ○ None            ○ Two            ○ Four or more
   ○ One             ○ Three

10. **When did you register for your courses for YOUR FIRST SEMESTER/QUARTER _at this college_?** (Mark only ONE)
    ○ More than one week before classes began
    ○ During the week before classes began
    ○ During the first week of classes
    ○ After the first week of classes

PLEASE DO NOT MARK IN THIS AREA

SERIAL #

3/8" spine perf

11. **The following statements are about this college's orientation for new students.** (Mark all that apply)
- ○ I took part in an online orientation prior to the beginning of classes
- ○ I attended an on-campus orientation prior to the beginning of classes
- ○ I enrolled in an orientation course as part of my course schedule during my first semester/quarter at this college
- ○ I was not aware of a college orientation
- ○ I was unable to participate in orientation due to scheduling or other issues

12. **This set of items asks you about your earliest experiences _at this college_. To respond, please think about your experiences FROM THE TIME OF YOUR DECISION TO ATTEND THIS COLLEGE THROUGH THE END OF THE FIRST THREE WEEKS OF YOUR FIRST SEMESTER/QUARTER.**

| | Yes | No |
|---|---|---|
| a. Before I could register for classes I was _required_ to take a placement test (COMPASS, ASSET, ACCUPLACER, SAT, ACT, etc.) to assess my skills in reading, writing, and/or math | ○ | ○ |
| b. I took a placement test (COMPASS, ASSET, ACCUPLACER, SAT, ACT, etc.) | ○ | ○ |
| c. I was exempt from taking a placement test at this college | ○ | ○ |

13. **My placement test scores indicated that I needed to take a Developmental course (also referred to as Basic Skills, College Prep, etc.) in the following areas.** (Mark all that apply)
- ○ Didn't take a placement test
- ○ Developmental Reading
- ○ Developmental Writing
- ○ Developmental Math
- ○ Didn't place into any Developmental courses

14. **This college _required_ me to enroll in classes indicated by my placement test scores during my FIRST SEMESTER/QUARTER.**
- ○ Yes          ○ No

15. **With regard to financial assistance (scholarships, grants, or loans, etc.) to help with your college costs, mark a response for each of the following items.**

| | Yes | No |
|---|---|---|
| a. I applied for financial assistance (scholarships, grants, or loans, etc.) | ○ | ○ |
| b. I was notified I was eligible to receive financial assistance (scholarships, grants, or loans, etc.) | ○ | ○ |
| c. I received financial assistance funds (scholarships, grants, or loans, etc.) before classes began | ○ | ○ |

16. **When did you first apply for financial assistance.** (Mark only ONE)
- ○ 3 or more months before classes began
- ○ 1 to 2 months before classes began
- ○ Less than 1 month before classes began
- ○ After classes began
- ○ I did not apply for financial assistance

17. **In which of the following types of courses were you enrolled during your FIRST SEMESTER/QUARTER _at this college_?** (Respond to each item)

| | Enrolled | Not enrolled |
|---|---|---|
| a. Developmental Reading (also referred to as Basic Skills, College Prep, etc.) | ○ | ○ |
| b. Developmental Writing (also referred to as Basic Skills, College Prep, etc.) | ○ | ○ |
| c. Developmental Math (also referred to as Basic Skills, College Prep, etc.) | ○ | ○ |
| d. An English course taught specifically for students whose first language is not English (ESL, ESOL) | ○ | ○ |
| e. A course specifically designed to teach skills and strategies to help students succeed in college (e.g., a college success or student success course) | ○ | ○ |
| f. An organized "learning community" (two or more courses that a group of students take together) | ○ | ○ |

3/8" spine perf

18. This set of items asks you about your earliest experiences _at this college_. To respond, please think about your experiences FROM THE TIME OF YOUR DECISION TO ATTEND THIS COLLEGE THROUGH THE END OF THE FIRST THREE WEEKS OF YOUR FIRST SEMESTER/QUARTER. (Respond to each item)

| | Strongly agree | Agree | Neutral | Disagree | Strongly disagree |
|---|---|---|---|---|---|
| a. The very first time I came to this college I felt welcome | ○ | ○ | ○ | ○ | ○ |
| b. The instructors at this college want me to succeed | ○ | ○ | ○ | ○ | ○ |
| c. All the courses I needed to take during my first semester/quarter were available at times convenient for me | ○ | ○ | ○ | ○ | ○ |
| d. I was able to meet with an academic advisor at times convenient for me | ○ | ○ | ○ | ○ | ○ |
| e. An advisor helped me to select a course of study, program, or major | ○ | ○ | ○ | ○ | ○ |
| f. An advisor helped me to set academic goals and to create a plan for achieving them | ○ | ○ | ○ | ○ | ○ |
| g. An advisor helped me to identify the courses I needed to take during my first semester/quarter | ○ | ○ | ○ | ○ | ○ |
| h. A college staff member talked with me about my commitments outside of school (work, children, dependents, etc.) to help me figure out how many courses to take | ○ | ○ | ○ | ○ | ○ |
| i. The college provided me with adequate information about financial assistance (scholarships, grants, loans, etc.) | ○ | ○ | ○ | ○ | ○ |
| j. A college staff member helped me determine whether I qualified for financial assistance | ○ | ○ | ○ | ○ | ○ |
| k. All instructors had activities to introduce students to one another | ○ | ○ | ○ | ○ | ○ |
| l. All instructors clearly explained academic and student support services available at this college | ○ | ○ | ○ | ○ | ○ |
| m. All instructors clearly explained course grading policies | ○ | ○ | ○ | ○ | ○ |
| n. All instructors clearly explained course syllabi (syllabuses) | ○ | ○ | ○ | ○ | ○ |
| o. I knew how to get in touch with my instructors outside of class | ○ | ○ | ○ | ○ | ○ |
| p. At least one college staff member (other than an instructor) learned my name | ○ | ○ | ○ | ○ | ○ |
| q. At least one other student whom I didn't previously know learned my name | ○ | ○ | ○ | ○ | ○ |
| r. At least one instructor learned my name | ○ | ○ | ○ | ○ | ○ |
| s. I learned the name of at least one other student in most of my classes | ○ | ○ | ○ | ○ | ○ |
| t. I have the motivation to do what it takes to succeed in college | ○ | ○ | ○ | ○ | ○ |
| u. I am prepared academically to succeed in college | ○ | ○ | ○ | ○ | ○ |

3/8" spine perf

**SERIAL #**

19. **During the FIRST THREE WEEKS OF YOUR FIRST SEMESTER/QUARTER _at this college_, about how often did you do the following?** (Respond to each item)

| | Never | Once | Two or three times | Four or more times |
|---|---|---|---|---|
| a. Ask questions in class or contribute to class discussions | ○ | ○ | ○ | ○ |
| b. Prepare at least two drafts of a paper or assignment before turning it in | ○ | ○ | ○ | ○ |
| c. Turn in an assignment late | ○ | ○ | ○ | ○ |
| d. Not turn in an assignment | ○ | ○ | ○ | ○ |
| e. Participate in supplemental instruction (extra class sessions with an instructor, tutor, or experienced student) | ○ | ○ | ○ | ○ |
| f. Come to class without completing readings or assignments | ○ | ○ | ○ | ○ |
| g. Work with other students on a project or assignment during class | ○ | ○ | ○ | ○ |
| h. Work with classmates outside of class on class projects or assignments | ○ | ○ | ○ | ○ |
| i. Participate in a required study group outside of class | ○ | ○ | ○ | ○ |
| j. Participate in a student-initiated (not required) study group outside of class | ○ | ○ | ○ | ○ |
| k. Use an electronic tool (e-mail, text messaging, Facebook, MySpace, class Web site, etc.) to communicate with another student about coursework | ○ | ○ | ○ | ○ |
| l. Use an electronic tool (e-mail, text messaging, Facebook, MySpace, class Web site, etc.) to communicate with an instructor about coursework | ○ | ○ | ○ | ○ |
| m. Discuss an assignment or grade with an instructor | ○ | ○ | ○ | ○ |
| n. Ask for help from an instructor regarding questions or problems related to a class | ○ | ○ | ○ | ○ |
| o. Receive prompt written or oral feedback from instructors on your performance | ○ | ○ | ○ | ○ |
| p. Receive grades or points on assignments, quizzes, tests, or papers, etc. | ○ | ○ | ○ | ○ |
| q. Discuss ideas from your readings or classes with instructors outside of class | ○ | ○ | ○ | ○ |
| r. Discuss ideas from your readings or classes with others outside of class (students, family, co-workers, etc.) | ○ | ○ | ○ | ○ |
| s. Skip class | ○ | ○ | ○ | ○ |

3/8" spine perf

## SERIAL #

○○○○○○○○○○○○○○○○○○○○○○○○○ ▢

20. **This section asks three questions about a variety of college services.** Answer ALL THREE QUESTIONS for each service indicating (1) whether you knew about it, (2) how often you used it, and (3) how satisfied you were. To respond, please think about your experiences FROM THE TIME OF YOUR DECISION TO ATTEND THIS COLLEGE THROUGH THE END OF THE FIRST THREE WEEKS OF YOUR FIRST SEMESTER/QUARTER.

| | (1) Did you KNOW ABOUT it? | | (2) How often did you USE it? | | | | (3) How SATISFIED were you with it? | | | |
|---|---|---|---|---|---|---|---|---|---|---|
| | Yes | No | Never | Once | Two or three times | Four or more times | Very | Some-what | Not at all | N/A |
| a. Academic advising/planning | ○ | ○ | ○ | ○ | ○ | ○ | ○ | ○ | ○ | ○ |
| b. Career counseling | ○ | ○ | ○ | ○ | ○ | ○ | ○ | ○ | ○ | ○ |
| c. Job placement assistance | ○ | ○ | ○ | ○ | ○ | ○ | ○ | ○ | ○ | ○ |
| d. Face-to-face tutoring | ○ | ○ | ○ | ○ | ○ | ○ | ○ | ○ | ○ | ○ |
| e. Online tutoring | ○ | ○ | ○ | ○ | ○ | ○ | ○ | ○ | ○ | ○ |
| f. Writing, math, or other skill lab | ○ | ○ | ○ | ○ | ○ | ○ | ○ | ○ | ○ | ○ |
| g. Financial assistance advising | ○ | ○ | ○ | ○ | ○ | ○ | ○ | ○ | ○ | ○ |
| h. Computer lab | ○ | ○ | ○ | ○ | ○ | ○ | ○ | ○ | ○ | ○ |
| i. Student organizations | ○ | ○ | ○ | ○ | ○ | ○ | ○ | ○ | ○ | ○ |
| j. Transfer credit assistance | ○ | ○ | ○ | ○ | ○ | ○ | ○ | ○ | ○ | ○ |
| k. Services to students with disabilities | ○ | ○ | ○ | ○ | ○ | ○ | ○ | ○ | ○ | ○ |

21. **This set of items asks you about your earliest experiences _at this college_.** To respond, please think about your experiences FROM THE TIME OF YOUR DECISION TO ATTEND THIS COLLEGE THROUGH THE END OF THE FIRST THREE WEEKS OF YOUR FIRST SEMESTER/QUARTER. (Respond to each item)

| Within a class, or through another experience at this college: | Strongly agree | Agree | Neutral | Disagree | Strongly disagree |
|---|---|---|---|---|---|
| a. I learned to improve my study skills (listening, note taking, highlighting readings, working with others, etc.) | ○ | ○ | ○ | ○ | ○ |
| b. I learned to understand my academic strengths and weaknesses | ○ | ○ | ○ | ○ | ○ |
| c. I learned skills and strategies to improve my test-taking ability | ○ | ○ | ○ | ○ | ○ |

22. Thinking about your experiences FROM THE TIME OF YOUR DECISION TO ATTEND THIS COLLEGE THROUGH THE END OF THE FIRST THREE WEEKS OF YOUR FIRST SEMESTER/QUARTER, what has been your MAIN source of academic advising (help with academic goal-setting, planning, course recommendations, graduation requirements, etc.)? (Mark only ONE)

- ○ Instructors
- ○ College staff (not instructors)
- ○ Friends, family, or other students
- ○ Computerized degree advisor system
- ○ College Web site
- ○ Other college materials

3/8" spine perf

23. **Was a specific person assigned to you so you could see him/her each time you needed information or assistance?**
○ Yes    ○ No

24. **During the FIRST THREE WEEKS OF YOUR FIRST SEMESTER/QUARTER _at this college_, about how many hours did you spend in a typical 7-day week doing each of the following?**

| | None | 1–5 | 6–10 | 11–20 | 21–30 | More than 30 |
|---|---|---|---|---|---|---|
| a. Preparing for class (in a typical 7-day week) | ○ | ○ | ○ | ○ | ○ | ○ |
| b. Working for pay (in a typical 7-day week) | ○ | ○ | ○ | ○ | ○ | ○ |

25. **When do you plan to take classes _at this college_ again?**
○ I will accomplish my goal(s) during this semester/quarter and will not be returning
○ I have no current plans to return
○ Within the next 12 months
○ Uncertain

26. **While in high school, did you**

| | Yes | No | N/A |
|---|---|---|---|
| a. Take math every school year? | ○ | ○ | ○ |
| b. Take math during your senior year? | ○ | ○ | ○ |

27. **Would you recommend this college to a friend or family member?**
○ Yes    ○ No

28. **In what range was your overall high school grade average?**
○ A   ○ A- to B+   ○ B   ○ B- to C+   ○ C   ○ C- or lower

29. **Your sex:**
○ Male   ○ Female

30. **Mark your age group.**
○ Under 18   ○ 20 to 21   ○ 25 to 29   ○ 40 to 49   ○ 65+
○ 18 to 19   ○ 22 to 24   ○ 30 to 39   ○ 50 to 64

| | Yes | No |
|---|---|---|
| 31. Are you married? | ○ | ○ |
| 32. Do you have children who live with you and depend on you for their care? | ○ | ○ |
| 33. Is English your native (first) language? | ○ | ○ |
| 34. Are you an international student or nonresident alien? | ○ | ○ |

35. **What is your racial/ethnic identification?** (Mark only ONE)
○ American Indian or Native American
○ Asian, Asian American, or Pacific Islander
○ Native Hawaiian
○ Black or African American, Non-Hispanic
○ White, Non-Hispanic
○ Hispanic, Latino, Spanish
○ Other

36. **What is the highest academic certificate or degree you have earned?** (Mark only ONE)
○ None              ○ Vocational/technical certificate   ○ Bachelor's degree
○ GED               ○ Associate degree                   ○ Master's/Doctoral/Professional degree
○ High school diploma

**37. Please indicate whether your goal(s) for attending _this college_ include the following:** (Respond to all three)

|  | Yes | No |
|---|---|---|
| a. To complete a certificate | ○ | ○ |
| b. To obtain an Associate degree | ○ | ○ |
| c. To transfer to a 4–year college or university | ○ | ○ |

**38. Who in your family has attended at least some college?** (Mark all that apply)

- ○ Mother
- ○ Father
- ○ Brother/Sister
- ○ Child
- ○ Spouse/Partner
- ○ Legal Guardian
- ○ None of the above

**39. Please provide your student identification number by filling in the corresponding ovals. For example, in the first column, indicate the first number or letter in your student ID number, and so forth.** (OPTIONAL)

(Please begin here)

3/8" spine perf

## Additional Items
(Please respond to these items if requested)

| | A | B | C | D | E | | | A | B | C | D | E |
|---|---|---|---|---|---|---|---|---|---|---|---|---|
| 1 | Ⓐ | Ⓑ | Ⓒ | Ⓓ | Ⓔ | | 13 | Ⓐ | Ⓑ | Ⓒ | Ⓓ | Ⓔ |
| 2 | Ⓐ | Ⓑ | Ⓒ | Ⓓ | Ⓔ | | 14 | Ⓐ | Ⓑ | Ⓒ | Ⓓ | Ⓔ |
| 3 | Ⓐ | Ⓑ | Ⓒ | Ⓓ | Ⓔ | | 15 | Ⓐ | Ⓑ | Ⓒ | Ⓓ | Ⓔ |
| 4 | Ⓐ | Ⓑ | Ⓒ | Ⓓ | Ⓔ | | 16 | Ⓐ | Ⓑ | Ⓒ | Ⓓ | Ⓔ |
| 5 | Ⓐ | Ⓑ | Ⓒ | Ⓓ | Ⓔ | | 17 | Ⓐ | Ⓑ | Ⓒ | Ⓓ | Ⓔ |
| 6 | Ⓐ | Ⓑ | Ⓒ | Ⓓ | Ⓔ | | 18 | Ⓐ | Ⓑ | Ⓒ | Ⓓ | Ⓔ |
| 7 | Ⓐ | Ⓑ | Ⓒ | Ⓓ | Ⓔ | | 19 | Ⓐ | Ⓑ | Ⓒ | Ⓓ | Ⓔ |
| 8 | Ⓐ | Ⓑ | Ⓒ | Ⓓ | Ⓔ | | 20 | Ⓐ | Ⓑ | Ⓒ | Ⓓ | Ⓔ |
| 9 | Ⓐ | Ⓑ | Ⓒ | Ⓓ | Ⓔ | | 21 | Ⓐ | Ⓑ | Ⓒ | Ⓓ | Ⓔ |
| 10 | Ⓐ | Ⓑ | Ⓒ | Ⓓ | Ⓔ | | 22 | Ⓐ | Ⓑ | Ⓒ | Ⓓ | Ⓔ |
| 11 | Ⓐ | Ⓑ | Ⓒ | Ⓓ | Ⓔ | | 23 | Ⓐ | Ⓑ | Ⓒ | Ⓓ | Ⓔ |
| 12 | Ⓐ | Ⓑ | Ⓒ | Ⓓ | Ⓔ | | 24 | Ⓐ | Ⓑ | Ⓒ | Ⓓ | Ⓔ |

*Your responses will remain confidential.*
*No individual responses will be reported.*

Thank you for sharing your views.

PLEASE DO NOT MARK IN THIS AREA

SERIAL #

SCANTRON  Mark Reflex® EM-276910-2:654321

# Chapter 3

## Enhancing First-Year Success in the Community College: What Works in Student Retention

Wesley R. Habley

With more and more students pursuing postsecondary education in community colleges, it is essential that community college educators understand both the student and the institutional characteristics that have an impact on student attrition. In addition, scarce resources dictate that retention efforts target program interventions most likely to contribute to student success. This chapter will provide a review of community college retention and persistence-to-degree data collected from 1983 to 2009 through ACT's Institutional Data Questionnaire (IDQ). In addition, the chapter will summarize the results for the 305 community colleges that responded to ACT's What Works in Student Retention (WWISR) survey conducted in the spring of 2009. The WWISR study was designed to identify institutional retention interventions and explore the perceived impact of those interventions on student success rates. Finally, the chapter will close with three sets of recommendations for increasing the success of first-year community college students.

### Community College Retention and Persistence to Degree Rates

Since 1983, ACT has been collecting data on first-to-second-year retention and degree completion rates through its IDQ. Institutional respondents are asked to report the percentage of first-time, full-time entering students who returned for a second year on campus. In addition, community college respondents were asked to report on the percentage of first-time, full-time entering students who had completed an associate degree within three years. Between 900 and 950 colleges report these data annually. The highest retention rate for community colleges was 53.7%, reported in both 2008 and 2009. The lowest retention rate (51.3%) was recorded in 2004. Three observations can be drawn from these data. First, the rate is hauntingly stable. Over a 26-year period, the range from high to low (1.6%) is very narrow. In addition, the highest rates have taken place in the last two reporting cycles. While there are many plausible explanations for this, it is difficult to deny that the current economic conditions in the United States are causing community college students to delay transfer to more expensive four-year colleges or to remain in the community college due to an inability to find meaningful work. A final observation is that these data represent only first-time, full-time students—about one third of all community college students. As a result, what we know about persistence at the community college level is limited.

Another measure of persistence is the percentage of students who complete an associate degree (ACT, 2010a). The highest three-year degree completion rate for first-time, full-time community college students (38.8%) was recorded in 1989, the lowest rate (27.1%) recorded in 2007. The current rate (28.3%) is up only slightly from the 2007 low. Clearly, there are many factors that have an impact on community college degree completion rates. These include student transfer rates, those who take longer than three years to earn a degree, and students who achieve educational goals that do not include a degree, to name a few. As a result, the current degree-completion rate of 28.3% should be viewed as neutral. Institutional goals for retention and persistence to degree should not be based on a national average. Rather, current institutional retention and persistence to degree rates should be used as baselines from which to improve.

## What Works in Student Retention

ACT conducted its fourth national WWISR survey in the late spring and early summer of 2009. This chapter focuses only on selected highlights of the retention survey reported by respondents from 305 community colleges (ACT, 2010b). The 2009 survey was in many ways parallel to the 2004 survey (ACT, 2010b). Revisions of the earlier instrument were based on low response to particular items, new issues, new interventions, and rewording of the item stems. Although the 2009 survey included seven sections, only selected data elements are reported here and include:

◇ Background items, including coordination of retention programs and institutional cooperation on transfer-enhancement programs
◇ Institutional goals for retention and timelines for goal achievement
◇ Ratings of the contribution to attrition of 42 student and institutional characteristics or factors
◇ The incidence of and ratings of the contribution to retention of 94 retention interventions and practices
◇ Identification of the three strategies perceived to have the greatest impact on student retention
◇ Interventions and practices that differentiate community colleges with high first- to second-year retention rates from those with low retention rates

As WWISR data are reviewed, it is important to keep several caveats in mind. First, the data reported in this survey are based on the perspectives of the individuals who responded to the survey. Although in a few instances respondents indicated that institutional data supported their answers, survey responses were based primarily on the opinions of the respondents. In addition, the findings reported in this chapter represent only a small portion of that collected in the survey. Because it is not feasible to include the complete data set, the author made choices both about the survey items to report and the cutoff points for means and percentages to be included in the tables. Finally, the absence of information about a particular retention practice should not be interpreted as a negative qualitative statement. For example, for each intervention included in a table with a mean score greater than or equal to 3.8, there are several interventions rated 3.7 that are not included in the table.

### Coordination of Retention

An important aspect of the campus retention effort is the coordination of and accountability for retention programs. On the issue of identifying a person responsible for the coordination of retention programs, there was no significant change from the 2004 survey when 40.7% of the campuses indicated the existence of retention coordinators. In 2009, that percentage was 40.5%. For those campuses reporting an individual assigned to retention coordination, four titles accounted for just under two thirds of the titles cited. Those were chief student affairs officer (26.1%), chief academic affairs officer or dean (16.5%), coordinator (13.6%), and chief enrollment officer (11.4%). All of the remaining titles were cited at fewer than 7% of the campuses.

### Retention and Degree-Completion Goals

Although the pool of respondents varied between the 2004 and the 2009 surveys, each survey included responses from more than 300 colleges. Those in the 2009 administration were slightly more likely to establish goals for first-to-second-year retention and degree completion than they were in the previous survey. In 2004, just over 27% of campuses reported having a goal for retention as compared to 32.1% of campuses reporting in the 2009 survey. Between 2004 and 2009, the percentage of campuses reporting a degree completion goal increased from 19.9% to 23%. Table 3.1 displays the time frames established for achieving the identified retention and degree-completion goals.

Table 3.1

*Time Frames for Achieving Retention and Degree Completion*

| Time frame | Retention goal achievement percentage | Degree-completion goal achievement percentage |
|---|---|---|
| No specific time frame | 7.5 | 13.4 |
| One year | 25.8 | 10.4 |
| Two years | 10.7 | 8.9 |
| Three years | 32.3 | 37.3 |
| Four years | 8.6 | 10.4 |
| Five years | 14.0 | 19.4 |
| More than five years | 1.1 | 0.0 |

### Institutional Collaborations to Enhance Transfer

While institutional retention efforts are the focus of the WWISR survey, student enrollment patterns are becoming increasingly complex. Although many students remain enrolled in a single campus until transferring or until they complete an associate degree or certificate, others may enroll in more than one institution during a given term. Still others enroll in online courses taught by a variety of institutions. Although retention and degree completion are institutional issues, student success is a much broader concept requiring significant transparency as students move from institution to institution. For this reason, the WWISR survey asked respondents to report participation in common course numbering systems, articulation agreements, and course applicability systems across a range of sections. The results of that inquiry are reported in Table 3.2.

Table 3.2

*Participation in Transfer Enhancement Programs*

| Program | Selected colleges percentage | Group or consortium percentage | Systemwide percentage | Statewide percentage | None of these percentage |
|---|---|---|---|---|---|
| Common course numbering | 10.5 | 11.1 | 22.2 | 30.5 | 34.8 |
| Articulation agreements | 69.8 | 18.4 | 25.2 | 39.0 | 0.1 |
| Course applicability system | N/A | 31.1 | 20.0 | 34.8 | 3.9 |

*Note.* Multiple responses possible. Percentages do not tally to 100%.

Two factors are most notable among the findings in Table 3.2. First, virtually all community colleges participate in articulation agreements, with 69.8% reporting such agreements with selected colleges. Second, statewide application of common course numbering, articulation agreements, and course applicability systems are all reported by 30% or more of the institutions responding. While clearly designed to ease the transition to other institutions, such collaborations will need to be expanded so that all community college students are able to move seamlessly between and among institutions.

### Characteristics or Factors Related to Attrition

Respondents to the WWISR survey were asked to rate the degree to which each of the 42 student and institutional characteristics or factors had an impact on student attrition. Each characteristic was rated on a 5-point scale, with 1 = little or no affect on attrition and 5 = major effect on attrition. It should be noted that a high mean rating suggests that survey respondents believe that the characteristic or factor had a significant effect on attrition.

Table 3.3 identifies the 14 characteristics or factors that had a mean rating of 3.5 or higher. Campus respondents, as a group, felt that these characteristics were contributing to attrition. What is striking about Table 3.3 is that nearly all the characteristics, including the top eight, are rated as having greatest significant effect on attrition are student characteristics. While it is not surprising that respondents view student characteristics as significant factors in attrition, these characteristics also provide a clear focus for extensive and intensive interventions.

Table 3.3

*Characteristics or Factors Having the Greatest Effect on Attrition*

| Student or institutional characteristic | Mean |
|---|---|
| Level of student preparation for college-level work [a] | 4.27 |
| Student study skills [a] | 4.11 |
| Adequacy of personal financial resources [a] | 4.06 |
| Level of student commitment to earning a degree | 4.00 |
| Level of student motivation to succeed [a] | 3.92 |
| Student family responsibilities [a] | 3.91 |
| Level of job demands on students [a] | 3.83 |
| Student low socioeconomic status [a] | 3.81 |
| Amount of financial aid available to students | 3.63 |
| Student personal coping skills | 3.59 |
| Student educational aspirations and goals [a] | 3.57 |
| Level of certainty about career goals | 3.54 |
| Level of emotional support from family, friends, and significant others | 3.50 |
| Student first-generation status [a] | 3.50 |

[a] Also rated at ≥ 3.5 in WWISR 2004.

The 14 characteristics or factors that had a mean rating of 2.75 or below are identified in Table 3.4. Campus respondents, as a group, felt that these characteristics had only a limited effect on attrition. What is equally striking in Table 3.4 is that many of the factors cited as making the least contribution to attrition are institutional characteristics. As with the results of the 2004 survey, institutional respondents are far more likely to place responsibility for attrition on student characteristics while minimizing the impact of institutional factors on student success.

Table 3.4

*Characteristics or Factors Having the Least Effect on Attrition*

| Student or institutional characteristic | Mean |
|---|---|
| Ratio of loans to other forms of financial aid | 2.75 |
| Student peer group interaction | 2.68 |
| Student access to needed courses in the appropriate sequence [a] | 2.64 |
| Level of intellectual stimulation or challenge for students [a] | 2.63 |
| Relevancy of curricula [a] | 2.57 |
| Commuting or living off-campus | 2.49 |
| Student physical health issues | 2.30 |
| Extracurricular programs [a] | 2.25 |
| Cultural activities [a] | 2.15 |
| Distance from students' permanent homes | 2.10 |
| Rules and regulations governing student behavior [a] | 2.09 |
| Campus safety and security | 1.95 |
| Residence hall facilities [a] | 1.51 |
| Programs to support students' transition to residence hall living | 1.39 |

[a] These or very similar items were also rated at ≤ 2.75 in WWISR 2004.

## Retention Interventions

The most comprehensive section of the 2009 WWISR study included the rating and ranking of 94 retention interventions and two other options. The items were revised and expanded from the 84 interventions that were included in WWISR 2004. Respondents were asked to indicate whether each of the interventions was offered at the institution. The percentage of campuses offering interventions is called the incidence rate. If the intervention was offered, the respondents were then asked to rate the intervention on a 5-point scale, where a rating of 5 indicated that the practice made a major contribution to retention and a rating of 1 indicated little or no contribution to retention. Finally, individuals were asked to review all 94 practices and identify the three interventions that made the greatest contribution to retention. Table 3.5 lists the 13 most common retention interventions identified by community college respondents. These interventions are employed in at least 4 of 5 community colleges in the study. Table 3.6 lists the retention interventions that were used the least frequently by community colleges participating in the study.

Table 3.5

*Interventions With the Highest Incidence Rates*

| Intervention or practice | Incidence percentage |
|---|---|
| Faculty use of technology in teaching | 96 |
| Tutoring [a] | 95 |
| College-sponsored social activities | 89 |
| Mandated placement of students in courses based on test scores [a] | 89 |
| Remedial or developmental coursework (required) | 88 |
| Individual career counseling [a] | 88 |
| Faculty use of technology in communicating with students | 87 |
| Pre-enrollment financial aid advising | 84 |
| Assessing student performance | 83 |
| Student leadership development | 82 |
| Library orientation, workshop, and/or course | 81 |
| Instructional (teaching) techniques | 80 |
| Study skills course, program, or center | 80 |

[a] Also identified by ≥ 80% of the respondents to WWISR 2004.

Table 3.6

*Interventions With the Lowest Incidence Rates*

| Intervention or practice | Incidence percentage |
|---|---|
| Recognition or rewards for faculty academic advisors | 13 |
| Recognition or rewards for nonfaculty academic advisors | 12 |
| Extended first-year orientation (noncredit) | 12 |
| Degree guarantee program [a] | 12 |
| Community member mentoring | 8 |
| First-year seminar or university 101 (noncredit) [a] | 7 |
| Living/learning communities (residential) | 5 |
| Other student subpopulations | 5 |
| Required on-campus housing for first-year students [a] | 4 |
| Fraternities or sororities [a] | 4 |
| Freshman interest groups (FIGS) [a] | 3 |

[a] Identified by <12% of the respondents to WWISR 2004.

Table 3.7 reports the 15 retention practices/interventions with mean ratings of 3.8 or above among the community college respondents, suggesting that these initiatives were believed to have a significant impact on retention. Initiatives seen as effective by 2009 respondents are remarkably consistent with effective practices highlighted on the 2004 survey. Eleven interventions/practices were among the top rated interventions in both surveys. Of these 11 practices, seven focus on learning support and four on academic advising. The consistency of high ratings for advising and learning assistance provide a strong argument for reviewing and expanding those services at community colleges that seek to improve retention. Table 3.8 reports the retention practices with mean ratings of 3.0 or below, suggesting that respondents believed these initiatives had minimal impact on retention.

Table 3.7

*Highest-Rated Retention Interventions or Practices*

| Intervention or practice | Mean |
|---|---|
| Reading center or lab [a] | 4.14 |
| Comprehensive learning assistance center/lab [a] | 4.12 |
| Tutoring [a] | 4.11 |
| Mandated placement of students in courses based on test scores [a] | 4.11 |
| Remedial or developmental coursework (required) [a] | 4.08 |
| Increased number of academic advisors [a] | 4.01 |
| Writing center or lab [a] | 4.00 |
| Mathematics center or lab [a] | 4.00 |
| Program for first-generation students | 3.97 |
| Advising interventions with selected student populations [a] | 3.92 |
| Academic advising center [a] | 3.87 |
| Recommended placement of students in courses based on test scores | 3.87 |
| Integration of advising with first-year transition programs [a] | 3.87 |
| Supplemental Instruction | 3.84 |
| Remedial or developmental coursework (recommended) | 3.82 |

[a] Also rated ≥ 3.8 on WWISR 2004.

Table 3.8

*Lowest-Rated Retention Interventions or Practices*

| Intervention or practice | Mean |
|---|---|
| Personality assessment [a] | 3.00 |
| Programs for gay, lesbian, bisexual, or transgender students | 3.00 |
| Health and wellness course/program | 3.00 |
| Residence hall programs | 3.00 |
| Enhanced or modified faculty reward system | 2.98 |
| Freshman interest groups (FIGS)[b] | 2.89 |
| Degree guarantee program | 2.82 |
| Recognition or rewards for faculty academic advisors | 2.65 |
| Recognition or rewards for nonfaculty academic advisors | 2.61 |
| Fraternities or sororities | 2.40 |

[a] Also rated ≤ 3.0 in WWISR 2004.
[b] Rated among top practices (4.0) in WWISR 2004.

A clearer picture of successful interventions and one that provides guidance for future retention planning evolves when both the incidence rate and the mean rating are included in the analysis of data (see Tables 3.9-3.11). Table 3.9 identifies nine interventions or practices that are both very common and also highly rated. These practices exist for 60% or more of the community colleges surveyed and have an overall mean rating greater than or equal to 3.8. Table 3.10 identifies 10 interventions or practices that are moderately common and also highly rated. The range of incidence rates is 37% to 52% and have an overall mean rating greater than or equal to 3.7. Table 3.11 identifies five interventions or practices that are uncommon yet highly rated by respondents whose campuses employed them. These interventions have incidence rates less than or equal to 31% and an overall mean rating greater than or equal to 3.6.

Table 3.9

*Interventions or Practices With High Incidence and High Rating*

| Intervention or practice | Incidence percentage | Mean |
|---|---|---|
| Comprehensive learning assistance center or lab [a] | 73 | 4.1 |
| Tutoring [a] | 95 | 4.1 |
| Mandated placement of students in courses based on test scores [a] | 89 | 4.1 |
| Remedial or developmental coursework (required) [a] | 88 | 4.1 |
| Writing center or lab | 86 | 4.0 |
| Mathematics center or lab | 70 | 4.0 |
| Advising interventions with special populations | 73 | 3.9 |
| Academic advising center | 64 | 3.9 |
| Supplemental Instruction | 62 | 3.8 |

[a] Met similar criteria on WWISR 2004.

Table 3.10

*Practices With Moderate Incidence and High Rating*

| Intervention or practice | Incidence percentage | Mean |
|---|---|---|
| Reading center or lab [a] | 50 | 4.1 |
| Increased number of academic advisors | 36 | 4.0 |
| First-generation students | 39 | 4.0 |
| Recommended placement of students in courses based on test scores | 52 | 3.9 |
| Integration of advising with first-year transition programs | 36 | 3.9 |
| Remedial or developmental coursework (recommended) [a] | 45 | 3.8 |
| International students | 44 | 3.7 |
| Racial or ethnic minority students | 50 | 3.7 |
| First-year seminar or university 101 (credit) [a] | 52 | 3.7 |
| Summer bridge program | 37 | 3.7 |

[a] Met similar criteria on WWISR 2004.

Table 3.11

*Practices With Low Incidence and High Rating*

| Intervention or practice | Incidence percentage | Mean |
|---|---|---|
| Organized student study groups | 28 | 3.8 |
| Extended first-year orientation (credit) | 28 | 3.7 |
| Foreign language center or lab [a] | 24 | 3.7 |
| Peer mentoring | 31 | 3.7 |
| Staff mentoring | 20 | 3.6 |

[a] Met similar criteria on WWISR 2004.

As noted earlier, after respondents completed the rating of individual interventions or practices, they were asked to identify the three interventions that made the greatest contribution to retention. Table 3.12 below reports the percentage of institutions that selected an intervention as one of the top three.

Table 3.12

*Interventions Making the Greatest Contribution to Retention*

| Intervention or practice | Percentage |
|---|---|
| Mandated placement of students in courses based on test scores | 36 |
| Tutoring | 22 |
| Remedial or developmental coursework (required) | 20 |
| Comprehensive learning assistance center or lab | 14 |
| Academic advising center | 12 |
| Early warning system | 12 |
| First-year seminar or university 101 (credit) | 10 |
| Summer orientation | 10 |
| Training for faculty academic advisors | 10 |

An additional analysis focusing on the relationship between retention practices and first-to-second-year retention rates was conducted. Comparisons of the incidence rates of effective retention initiatives were made between high-performing institutions (i.e., first-to-second-year retention rates are in the top quartile for all participating community colleges) and low-performing institutions (i.e., first-to-second-year retention rates are in the bottom quartile for all participating community colleges). Table 3.13 lists those practices where the incidence rate for high-performing institutions is more than 10% above the low-performing incidence rate. While it is not possible to attribute higher retention rates solely to these interventions, institutions focusing on improved retention rates would do well to consider implementation of interventions linked to increased persistence.

Table 3.13

*Interventions Differentiating Between High- and Low-Performing Colleges*

| Intervention or practice | Percentage of high performing ($n = 66$) | Percentage of low performing ($n = 67$) |
|---|---|---|
| Pre-enrollment financial aid advising | 93 | 77 |
| Comprehensive learning assistance center or lab | 81 | 70 |
| Diagnostic academic skills assessment | 69 | 41 |
| Programs for racial or ethnic minorities [a] | 63 | 41 |
| Reading center or lab [a] | 61 | 48 |
| Center that integrates academic advising with career or life planning | 61 | 45 |
| Remedial or developmental coursework required | 51 | 37 |
| Increased number of academic advisors | 44 | 32 |
| Integration of advising with first-year transition programs [a] | 43 | 28 |
| Staff mentoring | 29 | 18 |

[a] Also differentiated high- or low-performing colleges in WWISR 2004.

## Recommendations for Increasing First-Year Student Success

The recommendations for increasing first-year student success presented in this section are organized into three categories: direction, implementation, and evaluation. These recommendations include many that are nearly universally accepted, yet are deserving of reaffirmation. Other recommendations are not as obvious but are supported by data from both the 2004 and the 2009 WWISR studies, and still others represent the (hopefully well-reasoned) opinions of this author.

*Direction*

◇ ***Designate an individual responsible for the coordination of retention initiatives.*** This recommendation, along with a few others, was also cited in the 2004 study. It is repeated here because there has been virtually no change in the percentage of campuses identifying a person responsible for the coordination of retention strategies. Nearly three of five community college campuses have not designated such an individual. While it is true that retention is everyone's business, the absence of coordination fosters multiple and individual interpretations of factors contributing to attrition that may undermine retention efforts. Without coordination, planning, implementation, and assessment, retention strategies are, at best, left to chance.

◇ ***Establish an overall retention goal.*** In spite of the fact that the percentage of institutions reporting the existence of a goal for first-to-second-year retention has increased from 27% (2004) to 32% (2009), it is nevertheless disappointing to note that more than two thirds of the community colleges surveyed have not established such a goal. It is equally disappointing to observe that ACT IDQ retention data suggest that the national retention rate for community colleges has been stagnant, hovering just above 50% for more than 25 years. That average is a gross statistic that includes all reporting campuses: those that are large and those that are small, those that are rural and those that are urban. The national rate also includes campuses with a highly variable mix of associate of arts, associate of applied science, and certificate programs. Each institution is unique, and as a result, an institutional retention goal should focus on improving the existing retention rate. Improvements based on individual institutional goals would most likely translate into an increased retention rate at the national level.

◇ ***Establish a set of goals that acknowledges that there are multiple definitions of student success.*** First-to-second-year retention and persistence-to-degree rates are only two measures of the broader construct of student success. Students enroll in community college for a variety of reasons, which cannot necessarily be measured through persistence or degree completion. Some students enter with the intent of transferring after one year while others enroll to take courses that will advance their careers. Still others enroll for personal enrichment or to explore the possibility of pursuing further education. Students in all of these categories can be successful in reaching these goals even though they do not return for a second year or earn degrees. Community college leaders should identify these multiple definitions of success and establish goals relative to them.

◇ ***Specify a realistic time frame for the achievement of retention goals.*** The majority (56%) of survey respondents at institutions that have established a retention goal expect to achieve the goal in three years or more. While there is no hard and fast rule for the length of time to achieve the retention goal, more ambitious goals require a longer timeline, and success should be measured by the achievement of incremental progress until the goal has been reached.

*Implementation*

◇ ***Focus on learning support, academic skills assessment, and academic advising.*** The 2004 and 2009 surveys are consistent in identifying the program clusters that respondents believe are most critical to retention efforts. Those program clusters are learning support, academic skills assessment, and academic advising. Clearly, it is not possible to identify and rate every retention intervention in each of these clusters. Yet, the surveys provide compelling evidence that these three clusters should be the focus of campus dialog.

◇ *Consider implementing or adapting the highly rated, low-incidence interventions.* Table 3.11 identifies interventions or practices that have not been widely implemented, but nevertheless, as indicated by high ratings, are seen as making a considerable contribution to retention. Although the establishment of a foreign language center or lab may not be appropriate for all campuses, organized study groups, peer and staff mentoring programs, and for-credit extended orientation experiences have broad applicability for all community colleges. It is, in fact, interesting to note that these practices have two things in common. First, all four practices connect students with each other and/or with institutional representatives. In addition, each of the practices occurs informally on virtually all campuses. The perceived effectiveness of these interventions on some campuses suggests that institutions should consider their role in fostering interpersonal relationships by formally structuring these interventions.

◇ *Consider reviewing or implementing the interventions cited as having the greatest impact on retention.* The interventions appearing in Table 3.12 also have high incidence rates (see Table 3.9). The rates range from 64% (academic advising center) to 95% (tutoring). It is interesting to note that the same interventions were highlighted as most effective in both 2004 and 2009. If any of these practices are not in place on campus, implementation or adaptation should be strongly considered. Campuses already employing these interventions should conduct ongoing program review to increase effectiveness and focus on assessing the impact these interventions have on student success.

◇ *Consider implementing or reviewing interventions that differentiate between high- and low-performing community colleges.* Since virtually all community colleges are open admission, the differences between high- and low-performing colleges are more likely to be attributed to institutional practices than the prior academic performance of entering students. These findings suggest that a reading center or lab, the integration of academic advising with first-year transition programs, and programs for racial or ethnic minorities are potential differentiators between high- and low-performing community colleges. If any of these differentiated practices are not in place on campus, implementation should be strongly considered. Campuses already employing these interventions need to conduct ongoing program review to increase effectiveness.

### Evaluation

Readers were cautioned earlier in this chapter to remember that, for the most part, the responses to this survey were based primarily on the opinions and perspectives of survey respondents. It is inappropriate to accept WWISR survey results as fact because the survey is based on what people think, not necessarily on what they know. A quality assessment program involves identifying the factors that make a difference in student success. The following recommendations are provided to support that contention:

◇ *Establish a comprehensive student information and tracking system.* It is impossible for an institution to make informed decisions without a well-designed tracking system. The system should do more than monitor academic progress and collect information on who enrolled, who continued to be enrolled, and who completed a degree or certificate. In addition to these data elements, the system needs to identify student goals at the time of first enrollment, use of services on campus, and participation in programs designed specifically to enhance student success.

◇ ***Study the impact of various interventions on retention goal achievement.*** Once the tracking system is in place, it becomes possible not only to identify students who have been (or continue to be) successful in achieving the goals they articulated at first enrollment but also to identify the specific programs and services that contributed to their success. While the singular most important question is Did the student succeed?, knowing which programs the student participated in has profound ramifications for the success of future students. Programs that provide evidence of contribution to goal attainment should be expanded; those that show modest contribution might be reconfigured; and those whose contributions are negligible need to be re-engineered or dropped.

◇ ***Collect information on student opinions and attitudes during the first year of enrollment.*** Students who enter college for the first time may experience transitional shock created by the dissonance between their expectations for and the realities of student life. It has been suggested that the first six weeks of enrollment are critical to the institution's retention efforts as a period when most of the antecedents of dropout behavior are manifested. The assessment of first-year student attitudes and opinions on programs, policies, people, and procedures can provide significant clues in unraveling the mystery of why some students stay and some students leave. While this first-year snapshot of opinions and attitudes can provide useful information, comparing the responses of persisters versus nonpersisters one year later can be even more revealing. Such a comparison may uncover causes of attrition that are not identified through other forms of assessment.

## Conclusion

While individuals may have differing opinions on the causes of student departure and the interventions that contribute to student success, there is little disagreement that student success is the ultimate goal of community colleges. Success takes on many definitions. It can be defined by degree completion, transfer, career advancement, or personal enrichment. Three clear themes emerge from this chapter. First, regardless of individual student goals, community colleges should focus on improving the number of first-year students who achieve their goals. In addition, student success is not an institutional accident. It is a result of intentional actions taken by the college. Those actions include coordinating retention activities, establishing goals, implementing appropriate intervention strategies, and assessing the impact of those strategies. Finally, there appears to be a growing body of evidence that learning support and academic advising are believed to be the most significant contributors to student success. Institutions that focus on these themes may very well reap the benefits of increased student success.

## References

ACT. (2010a). *Research and policy issues: College retention and graduation rates.* Retrieved from the ACT website: http://www.act.org/research/policymakers/reports/graduation.html

ACT. (2010b). *Research and policy issues: Policy reports.* Retrieved from the ACT website: http://www.act.org/research/policymakers/reports/index.html

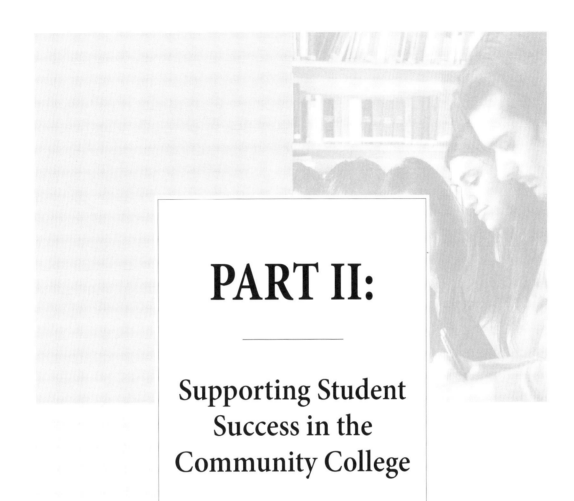

# PART II:

## Supporting Student Success in the Community College

# ▦ Chapter 4

## Reframing At-Risk to High-Potential: Supporting the Achievement and Success of Underprepared Students in the Critical First Year of College

Thomas Brown and Mario Rivas

"There are within each of us the seeds of who we might become. All we need is to find someone to water the seeds of our goodness." —Thich Nhat Hanh (2005), Buddhist Monk, 1967 Nobel Peace Prize Nominee

Nearly 30 years ago, Harold Hodgkinson (1985), a well-respected analyst of demographics and educational issues, predicted that increasing numbers of students would enroll in U.S. colleges unprepared for the academic, social, and psychological challenges of college life. Hodgkinson suggested that these students would only be successful if they experienced campus environments and encountered educators with the sensitivity necessary to support them. In this respect, two-year colleges are on the front lines of American higher education, providing access and opportunities to postsecondary education for students who would otherwise be denied them. These colleges serve an essential access function and enroll more than half of all first-year students entering public institutions, as well as significant percentages of first-generation, low-socioeconomic status (SES), and multicultural students. As truly democratic educational institutions, community colleges make winners out of ordinary people (Koltai, 1993).

However, the majority of community college students are academically underprepared to achieve success (Schuetz & Barr, 2008). According to the National Center for Education Statistics (2003), about 60% of first-year students at community colleges test into at least one remedial class, and many test into two or more. Among Black and Hispanic students, the numbers are even higher (Bradley, 2010). This chapter focuses on the challenges underprepared first-year community college students confront in their quest to move in, through, and out of college successfully—whether that be entering the workforce, transferring to a four-year institution, or obtaining certification or an associate degree. Understanding student qualities and the characteristics that place them at risk for not succeeding in college is essential. However, given that campus context makes a difference to student outcomes, it is equally important to define the roles and responsibilities that institutions and individuals have to create environments in which underprepared first-year community college students are more likely to achieve their goals. Therefore, this chapter will examine how being underprepared combines with institutional characteristics to influence first-year student engagement, learning, and persistence. A teaching and advising model will be presented that integrates both the student and institutional perspectives in an effort to define practices that are designed to increase underprepared students' success in the first year of college. Finally, the chapter will make recommendations about strategies two-year community and technical colleges can adopt to fulfill their promise of being the most democratic of all U.S. postsecondary institutions.

## Examining and Defining Underpreparedness

In chapter 1, Boggs points out that community colleges enroll disproportionately high numbers of nontraditional students who exhibit characteristics that put them at risk for not completing college, such as attending part time, being first-generation college students, not entering college directly after high school, balancing their lives as single parents, coming from low-income families, or being students of color. The National Center for Education Statistics (NCES, 2002) reported that three quarters of today's college students could be described as nontraditional. Given the fact that nearly half of students who enroll in two-year colleges drop out between the first and second year (ACT, 2009), it is easy to conclude that traditional students who come from middle to high socioeconomic backgrounds, have solid academic preparation, attend full time, and have high rates of success are the exception rather than the rule.

There can be no question but that community colleges continue to be the open door to postsecondary education for countless people seeking to improve their social, economic and occupational standing. Eighty percent of new jobs will require some postsecondary education, but only 42% of today's students leave high school with the necessary skills to begin college-level work. NCES (U.S. Department of Education, 2004) data indicate that 61% of community college students take at least one developmental course in either English or mathematics and that these students are much less likely to graduate or transfer to four-year colleges. NCES (2003) also indicates that since 1996, there has been a 33% increase in students who are underprepared in reading, writing, and/or math.

Maxwell (1997) describes underprepared students as having skills, knowledge, and motivation that are significantly below those of the typical student in the program or college in which they are enrolled. Students who attend two-year colleges typically have earned lower SAT and ACT scores, are less likely to have gone beyond Algebra I in high school, and are more likely to take at least one developmental course while in college than their peers in four-year institutions (McIntosh & Rouse, 2009). Ender and Wilkie (2000) suggest that being underprepared hinders a student's ability to compete academically with other students attending the same institution.

Drawing on extensive interviews with faculty at Paradise Valley Community College in Arizona, Rings (2001) defines underprepared students as those who are not ready for college-level work because of gaps in several areas:

◇ General knowledge (i.e., inadequate background knowledge in specific areas, such as history, civics, or literature)
◇ Skills necessary for college work (e.g., ability to read and write in English at college level, college-level computational skills)
◇ Computer skills and other technology competencies
◇ Study skills and self-management skills, including time management and the ability to organize and categorize information, distinguish important from unimportant information, and delay gratification
◇ Critical thinking and analysis
◇ Vision for the future that supports motivation and persistence in college
◇ Knowledge of behaviors and dispositions required for success in college

◇ Willingness to take instructors' advice related to improvement
◇ Understanding that learning is an active, shared responsibility with faculty

In sum, underprepared students have gaps in the knowledge, information, and skills necessary to understand and address the academic and procedural demands of college. From a psychological perspective, underpreparedness may also stem from low self-efficacy or the sense that one has little control over the thoughts, feelings, and actions (Bandura, 1985) that are conducive to success in college.

Many students come academically, socially, and motivationally underprepared for college because of experiences of poverty, marginalization, oppression, and discrimination. They may have graduated from high schools that do not offer the courses, curricula, or other resources to prepare them for college (Metropolitan Opportunity Project, 1987; National Council of La Raza, 1998; Tinto, 2004). These students can include

◇ Adult students who experience a lack of self-confidence and anxieties from previous learning situations that hinder their ability to learn (Bailey, 2007; Brookfield, 2006)
◇ First-generation students, for whom poor academic preparation poses severe challenges (Nunez & Cuccaro-Alamin, 1998) and whose adjustment may be complicated by ethnic minority and low-income statuses (Thayer, 2000)
◇ First-year students who often do not understand the demands of college and what is required to be successful
◇ International students, including refugees, who must enter and engage a new country, culture, and educational system that is often alien to their home-country experiences and requires the development of a new set of cultural competencies
◇ Lesbian, gay, bisexual, transgender, and queer or questioning (LGBTQ) students who confront and are concerned about an unsupportive campus environment, including harassment, and are hindered in their ability to focus on either academic or cocurricular learning (Rankin, 2003)
◇ Multicultural students (i.e., Aboriginal, Native American or First Nations People; African American or Black, Asian Pacific American; Hispanic or Latino/a; biracial or multiracial) who often experience being minorities for the first time on predominantly white campus, where they can encounter negative stereotypes; marginalization; and low expectations from faculty, staff, and peers (Brown & Rivas, 2004)
◇ Multilingual or ESL students, who may be well educated in their home countries but need help with English skills or students with basic literacy deficiencies (Crandall & Sheppard, 2004)
◇ Student athletes who have significant competing time and task demands, tend to be less academically prepared, and who report lower levels of growth in college than other students (Bok, 2003)
◇ Students from low-income backgrounds who are underprepared compared to those from high-income backgrounds (Tinto, 2004) and who work more, study less, and report lower GPAs than their high-SES peers (Walpole, 2003)
◇ Students with disabilities who are routinely stereotyped as damaged, helpless, and inferior human beings lacking the skills needed to succeed and who are routinely denied opportunities to develop their abilities fully (Johnson, 2006)
◇ Transfer students who need to be prepared to enter receiving campus environments that are often less supportive and require greater independence

◇ Undecided or exploratory students who frequently are less academically engaged due to confusion about and/or lack of commitment to a field of study
◇ Veterans who enter or return to college with vulnerabilities (e.g., feelings of alienation, strained family relationships, mental health problems) that require a wide range of support services to enable them make sense of and transition from wartime military service to civilian life and college

In fact, many students possess multiple risk factors. For example, a first-year student athlete with an undiagnosed learning disability may also be undecided about her program of study. A first-year African American adult student on a predominantly White campus may also be the first person in his family to attend college. A first-year ROTC student from a low-SES background may also be trying to come to terms with her sexual identity, even as she struggles to improve her ability to read and write English as a second language. Given all that many such students have had to overcome to make it to college, it might be more accurate to see them as high-potential rather than at-risk students.

For many, the open door of the community college has become a revolving door, with nearly half of students leaving in their first year (ACT, 2009). This may be particularly true for underprepared and other at-risk students, and Schuetz and Barr (2008) question whether community colleges are ready to help these students achieve their educational goals.

## The Responsibility of Serving Underprepared Students

As noted elsewhere in this monograph, two-year colleges have a distinctive mission and serve a very different population of entering first-year students than do four-year colleges and universities. While four-year institutions can select the students they will or will not educate, community colleges are open-admissions institutions that admit and strive to educate all who enroll.

The mission of community colleges presupposes that in order for first-year students to succeed, they must be engaged with educators who believe in the capacity of all students to develop and learn. This is a reality that bears mentioning because it undergirds any effort to improve the effectiveness of community colleges. Four in five community college professors believe their institutions take responsibility for educating underprepared students, and they are likely to agree that their values are congruent with the dominant institutional values where they work (Lindholm, Szelenyi, Hurtado, & Korn, 2005). Nonetheless, while faculty and staff feel deeply committed to supporting underprepared students, most institutions have a fragmented approach to responding to student needs (Sperling, 2009).

One reason for this fragmented approach may be that colleges are far more likely to attribute attrition to student rather than institutional characteristics (Habley & McClanahan, 2004). While it may be comforting to believe that students' precollege characteristics will determine whether they will succeed or fail, Tinto (1999) also suggests that what happens to students after they enter college is more critical than precollege attributes in determining whether students persist or leave before achieving their goals. Pascarella and Terenzini (2005) observe that some institutions seem to be more effective in promoting the achievement of students from a wide variety of backgrounds. These campuses recognize that what happens to students after they enroll is more important than what students bring to college. In short, success-oriented colleges communicate their belief that all students can succeed, and they demonstrate that everyone in the campus community is committed to facilitating student success (Community College Survey of Student Engagement, 2009).

Refocusing the college's mission and values on the learning process and putting students at the center of their work (O'Banion, 1999) is a hallmark of success-oriented colleges. Such a refocusing also calls for a broadened definition of teaching and those who are responsible for it. Good teaching takes place in classrooms, laboratories, and libraries; however, it also takes place in counseling, academic advising and career centers, in residence halls, as well as on athletic courts and playing fields. When students were asked to identify a critical incident that had changed them profoundly 80% identified an encounter or interaction beyond the classroom (Light, 2001). Northern Virginia Community College (Annandale, VA) employs the term *facilitators of learning* to highlight the fact that student learning takes place as students experience the entire campus and is a shared responsibility of faculty, staff, and administrators. Brown and Ward (2007) use the terms *instructional faculty* and *administrative faculty* to indicate that student learning takes place both inside and outside the classroom. Improving the success of underprepared students takes a campus community working together. It must be a shared, college-wide responsibility with leadership and commitment at every level (The Carnegie Foundation for the Advancement of Teaching, 2008).

Students do not have encounters with educational institutions. Rather, they have a series of interactions with individuals that comprise their college experiences. Rendón (1994, 2002) observed that even the most nontraditional students can be transformed into powerful learners through academic and interpersonal validation—inside and outside the classroom—by faculty and staff members who believe in them and can affirm their capacity to learn and perform at high levels. Ann Masten, distinguished professor at the University of Minnesota, concluded that students are more likely to persist and succeed when they have close relationships with competent, confident adults who believe in them (Brown, 2000). Yet, Spann, Spann, and Confer (1995) observe that the major inhibitor to possible success for underprepared students is the psychological distance that most faculty maintain between themselves and their students. Moreover, underpreparedness can manifest as a hesitancy and lack of trust on the part of students to become fully engaged with faculty and staff, who are often perceived to represent societal and institutional interests rather than those students (Brown & Rivas, 1994, 2004). McClenney (2009) advises that community colleges must act intentionally to better retain students and increase the likelihood that they will succeed, by promoting a culture of high expectations and instituting policies that encourage, if not require, faculty/student interaction and student engagement. She adds that engagement does not happen by accident; it happens by design.

## Empowering Students, Faculty, and Staff to Share the Responsibility for Learning and Success

Social cognitive theory (i.e., how individuals' beliefs and expectations influence behavior), and learning theory (i.e., how well students self-monitor and self-control their learning efforts) offer a powerful conceptual framework for understanding the challenges faced by underprepared first-year students and for supporting their success. In the area of social cognitive theory, Bandura (1985) argued that the beliefs people have about themselves, along with the effects of the beliefs of others that they encounter in the educational environment, are critical elements in the exercise of control and personal competence. Thus, individuals are viewed both as products and as producers of their own environments and social systems. This conception of human motivation meshes well with the framing of student achievement in college as being an interactive product of faculty and staff in the college environment partnering with students in promoting their success.

Applications of Skinner's (1953) behavior learning theory (e.g., Covington, 1992; Watson & Tharp, 2007) offer concrete strategies for guiding poor-performing students to develop greater effectiveness in monitoring the progress of their academic performance and for making changes to ensure improvement and success. Accordingly, individuals who are clearer about the goals they want to pursue and about the steps required to achieve success are more likely to realize their goals.

As with many college students, underprepared students are striving to develop their competency and self-efficacy related to the following developmental factors: identity and personality (Erikson, 1950; Madison, 1969); intellectual capacity (Perry, 1970); emotions, sense of autonomy, and ability to interact with others (Chickering, 1969); moral reasoning (Gilligan, 1982; Kohlberg, 1981); and ethnic identity (Cross, 1971; Sue & Sue,1999). Instructional faculty, academic advisors, counselors, and others on college campuses can support underprepared college students in learning to understand the various factors that influence the development of their sense of self and their confidence in their ability to think and to cope with the challenges of life (Branden, 1994). For underprepared community college students, the important challenges include moving from being undecided to choosing a program or major; assessing and responding to the need for skill development essential to college and career success; managing family, work, and other responsibilities; and facing the day-to-day psychological challenges associated with beliefs and expectations related to becoming a confident, competent, committed, and successful students.

What follows is a model of teaching, learning, and advising that incorporates social cognitive theory (i.e., how to support students to understand and change personal beliefs and expectations that undermine their effectiveness as learners) and learning theory (i.e., how to help students structure and monitor their development as learners especially with respect to defining and developing their competence and career development goals) into an intervention that can be used in and outside the classroom.

Initially developed as the 0-100% Competence Method (Rivas, 1988), the 0-100% Learning, Teaching, and Advising Method is a theoretically based model that helps the user to understand more clearly how to organize and structure development in the areas of general knowledge; learning and study skills; and socio-psychological skills related to motivation, development of academic competence, and the steps required to achieve academic goals. The model has been further developed over a subsequent 20-year span in the areas of counseling, administration, and teaching in community and four-year colleges. The 0-100% model asks the student or educator to assess current competence in a given area on a scale of 0-100. The same scale can be used to set goals and to monitor progress toward those goals.

Two developmentally focused theories undergird the use of the 0-100% Learning, Teaching, and Advising Method with students. The first is Weiner's (1985) Attribution Theory of Achievement and Emotion (Figure 4.1), which posits that beliefs about ability (i.e., attributions) and task-difficulty influence goal expectancies. Weiner noted that a student who believes she has low ability regarding a task she perceives as having high difficulty will likely have low goal-achievement expectancies. Weiner's theory also tied attributions to emotions, with low-ability attributions leading to feelings of shame and doubt and high task-difficulty attributions resulting in feelings of hopelessness and helplessness. Weiner argued that these emotions are powerful inhibitors with respect to applying effort to academic work.

Self-attributions of low ability (e.g., I can't do calculus), as well as low-ability attributions faculty and staff make about students (e.g., Those students can't do calculus) can adversely affect the extent to which students become fully engaged in a task, as well as the extent to which faculty and staff become fully engaged in supporting students to succeed at a task. When students and faculty make these kinds of attributions, they have internalized the notion that ability is the primary determinant of achievement and success. Furthermore, they are implying that ability is a fixed, unchangeable capacity, in this instance, one either has the ability to succeed in calculus or does not.

|          | Ability      | Task Difficulty   | Goal Expectancy           |
|----------|--------------|-------------------|---------------------------|
| **Belief**   | Low          | High              | Low                       |
| **Emotion**  | Shame/doubt  | Helpless/hopeless | Nonengagement/giving up   |

*Figure 4.1.* Weiner's Attribution Theory of Achievement and Emotion. Adapted from "Attribution Theory of Achievement and Emotion," by B. Weiner, 1985, *Psychological Review*, 92, p. 565. Copyright 1985 by the American Psychological Association.

This belief (or cognition) creates the aforementioned emotions of hopelessness and helplessness, with the result being withdrawal from the task. If, however, students and faculty shift their attributions from ability to background, and recognize that it is background rather than innate ability that is the primary determinant of academic achievement, there can also be a shift in their expectancies of success, followed by a deeper level of engagement.

Nicholls' (1984) theory of Task Versus Ego Involvement is also at the core of the 0-100% Learning, Teaching, and Advising Method. Nicholls hypothesized that in any achievement situation a student can either be task or ego involved. Ego-involved students focus on social comparisons (i.e., how he or she rates in comparison to others). In contrast, a task-involved student focuses on task mastery rather than achieving an idealized standard of excellence.

With regard to social comparison, schools in the United States could be considered fear factories, places where students of color may learn to associate fear and self-doubt with learning. If students (e.g., low-performing, ethnic minority, low-SES students) compare themselves to so-called bright or fast learners (i.e., those from wealthier schools and more privileged backgrounds), they may see having difficulty learning as a sign of inferiority and intellectual weakness. Therefore, if a student, especially a low-skilled individual, compares him or herself to an idealized norm, her or his thoughts, feelings, and behaviors will be negative and detract attention from mastering a task and may lead to feelings of helplessness and hopelessness (Rivas, 2005). Such ego-involved comparisons serve to undermine motivation, leading to decreased effort and persistence to task completion. Other students overestimate their preparedness for academic work, perform less well than expected in their classes, become discouraged, and either lower their academic sights or drop out (Driscoll, 2007; Nicholls, 1984).

Rivas (1988) combined Weiner's (1985) and Nicholls' (1984) theories to develop the 0-100% competence scale as a way to explain the developmental challenges many underprepared students confront in college. The more developed 0-100% Learning, Teaching, and Advising Method (Rivas, 2009) offers developmentally appropriate ways for educators to support students in organizing and monitoring their development. It also provides simplicity, structure, and organization to learning and growth (Brown & Rivas 1994). Rivas uses the 0-100% Teaching, Learning, and Advising Method to help shift these students from being ego involved to being task involved (Figure 4.2).

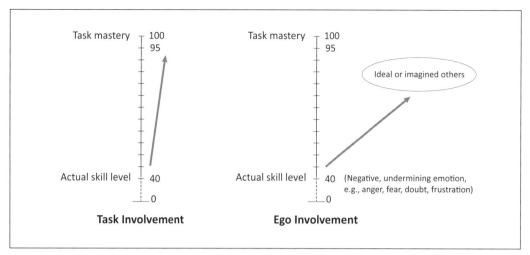

*Figure 4.2.* Task versus ego involvement.

Using the 0-100% scale, Figure 4.2 illustrates how a student's motivation toward a task can be lessened if she focuses on comparing herself to others rather than on improving her skills. In the figure, a student rates herself low on a skill (i.e., 40) while comparing herself to other high-skilled students. The arrow on the ego-involvement scale shows the focus on comparison to others versus task mastery, which can result in negative feelings, such as anger, fear, doubt, or frustration. These feelings can undermine motivation, in the face of the many other factors that influence goal persistence (Atkinson & Feather, 1966). Conversely, if a student focuses on task involvement (i.e., the arrow on this scale points to skill goal and the steps required to achieve the goal), she is more likely to be aware of making incremental progress toward goal achievement and may be more likely to persist in pursuing the goal (Nicholls, 1984; Weiner, 1985).

In this same vein, it is important for those working with first-year students to know about research related to *stereotype threat* (Aronson & Steele, 2005), which suggests that the academic performance of students can be harmed when a negative stereotype exists regarding their capacity for success in particular areas. Stereotype threat has been found to harm the academic performance of Black students (Aronson & Steele), Hispanics (Gonzalez, Blanton, & Williams, 2002), students from low socioeconomic backgrounds (Croizet & Claire, 1998), women in math (Good, Aronson, & Harder, 2008), and even White males when confronted with the specter of Asian superiority in math (Aronson et al., 1999). A primary result of stereotype threat is that students are likely to limit their range of majors, programs, and professions, and, in many cases, withdraw from courses or leave college altogether. Challenging and changing negative, undermining, ego-involved attributions, stereotypes, and expectations into positive, realistic assessments and strategy development are among the primary tasks of educators seeking to enhance the engagement, learning, and success of at-risk, first-year college students.

## Employing the 0-100% Method

The 0-100% scale (Rivas, 2009) has been used in advising, teaching, and learning assistance to guide students to organize their step-by-step development and achievement. This approach emphasizes task versus ego involvement, wherein students increase hope and motivation as they progressively improve skills. In counseling and academic advising, the scale has been used to help students self-assess their skills level in areas needed to succeed in a course, major, program (e.g., public speaking, writing, quantitative reasoning).

When students and faculty focus on ability as a primary determinant of success, the role of time, effort, and effective strategies are undervalued. In the classroom, students are challenged to assess their level of learning efforts (i.e., On a scale of 0-100%, how much effort are you applying in your coursework?), knowledge acquisition (i.e., On a scale of 0-100%, how well do you understand a particular concept or topic?), and confidence in being able to participate in class (i.e., On a scale of 0-100%, how confident are you that you can paraphrase what you have learned?). Beyond the classroom, the method can enable students to understand and assess strategies that can improve academic performances (i.e., Are you studying in groups, using tutorial services, meeting with your instructor?).

Developmental English students have used the 0-100% method to (a) understand the different skill demands related to becoming competent writers (e.g., On a scale of 0-100%, where are you in your ability to understand and use grammar concepts?) and (b) to monitor whether they are—task- versus ego-involved—in their efforts to improve their writing skills (personal communication, J. Quintero, September 4, 2009). The method has also been employed to help students gauge their degree of learning, and Rivas (2009) found that Latino/a students perceived their level of knowledge (0-100%) as significantly lower than non-Latino students. Rivas has also noted that using the think-pair-share reading method (Lyman, 1981), where students read and discussed material with their classmates as part of a group learning exercise, helped Latino/a students raise their perception of what they understand on a classroom topic to a level equal to non-Latino students.

In homework assignments, students are asked to note their level of understanding on work that they do in order to help them monitor their ongoing level of learning as they read and complete homework assignments (i.e., On a scale of 0-100%, how much understanding do you have of each part of the homework you completed?). Finally, in the area of learning assistance, the 0-100% method has been used to help students structure and monitor their level of skill development as they work with tutors in a learning center to improve specific content and learning skills (Destandau, Ingmier, van Dommelen, & Wiederholt, 2000).

Brown (2010) has used the 0-100% in professional development work with faculty and staff to assist them in becoming task involved in establishing individual and programmatic goals and outcomes and has employed the method with campuses, administrators, and department or program chairs to establish outcomes for accreditation. At an individual level, faculty, counselors, academic advisors, and others are asked to establish competence goals (e.g., 85 on a 100-point scale) and to assess their current level of competence in a particular area. For example, in active listening, understanding, and responding to the needs of specific first-year student populations (e.g., LGBTQ, international, multicultural students) or knowledge of campus referral services. Once they have engaged in a task-involved assessment of their current levels of competence or effectiveness (e.g., 60 on a 100-point scale), they use the method to identify concrete tangible actions they will take to advance toward their goals and to assess their progress.

At a programmatic level, the method can enable academic and student affairs programs administrators and staff in areas such as academic advising, career counseling, or service for students with disabilities to establish goals, outcomes, or standards of effective practice. Administrators, faculty, and staff collaborate to assess the current level of program effectiveness, again being task involved, and develop action plans with timelines for goal achievement and strategies for assessing effectiveness in achieving the established outcomes.

## Recommendations

Following are areas where the 0-100% Teaching, Advising, and Learning Method can be used to structure colleges efforts to improve work with underprepared students:

◇ Mandate assessment and placement, with a focus on having faculty, counselors, and advisors using the 0-100 % method to help students understand how developmental courses can close learning gaps and increase their opportunities to achieve their academic, vocational, and personal goals. For example, if students are to succeed in calculus, they need to have taken the appropriate courses (e.g., basic math, algebra, trigonometry, precalculus) and achieved an appropriate level of competence in each preceding course (e.g., 80+ on the 0-100% scale). If placement tests reveal that students are inadequately prepared, community colleges can then offer the sequence of developmental (basic math), introductory (algebra), intermediate (trigonometry), and advanced courses (precalculus) that can bridge the gap between where students are and where they to need to be in order to succeed in calculus.

◇ Require participation of underprepared students in programs and services known to increase learning, persistence, and graduation, including mandatory assessment, placement, and orientation; required meetings with instructors and academic advisors at specific times in the first semester; mandatory use of tutorial services and Supplemental Instruction; and required study groups. Emphasize the use of the 0-100% method to help students identify and monitor the development of competency in success-related skills and to help programs monitor how effectively they are supporting the success of underprepared students.

◇ Employ intrusive or active outreach advising, which means that faulty and staff (e.g., counselors, academic advisors, academic support services personnel) take the initiative throughout the first year to schedule meetings with students and advisees, especially for those who encounter academic difficulties, are enrolled in developmental courses, are un-decided about a program or major, or are otherwise determined to be at risk due to being underprepared. Many at-risk students make inadequate use of academic support services because they have difficulty recognizing that they have a problem and may not reach out for assistance in time for support services to be of greatest benefit. Encouraging faculty to be proactive in connecting students to services can enhance their opportunities for success.

◇ Encourage faculty and staff to take the initiative in connecting students to campus and community resources that can enhance their opportunities to achieve their goals. This requires that institutional professional development programs provide guidance regarding what programs offer, how students should be referred, and the nature of effective follow-up with referred students and referral resources. Use the 0-100% Method to structure areas of focus to assist students as well as to monitor progress toward success.

◇ Professional development for faculty and staff must be aligned with the goals of increasing the achievement and success of underprepared students. This includes preservice and in-service professional development programs that emphasize integration of theory and practice

◇ Encourage and facilitate collaborations between academic or instructional and student affairs units, including the development of early warning systems that advise faculty and student affairs personnel (e.g., counseling, career services, equal opportunity programs, international student programs, disability services) of students who are at risk and/or en-countering difficulties, so these areas can act collaboratively to intervene. Have faculty and student affairs staff collaborate to develop and assess orientation and transition programs. Invite the staff of programs serving special populations (e.g., disability services, minority student programs, student athlete programs) to visit first-year student success courses to explain their services, how students can access them, and the benefits accruing to students who have previously used the services.

◇ Employ culturally relevant academic advising, support programs, and services that are responsive to the needs of specific populations (e.g., academically underprepared, international, multicultural, LGBTQ students).

## Conclusion

While students may be underprepared academically, they often have the determination, motivation, and resilience to succeed. Yet, they need the support of caring educators in finding the alignment among their previous experiences, strengths, and educational goals. They also need help in realistically assessing their own limitations and putting those limitations into perspective as they set goals for the future. The 0-100% method described in this chapter provides both students and educators a useful framework for accomplishing this.

The 0-100% method is also a useful guide for helping educators visualize how to improve practices that can support underprepared students to achieve their personal, educational, and career goals. Readers are encouraged to make a regular audit of their own work and the campus environment by using the 0-100 scale to respond to these and similar questions:

1. How well do I understand the characteristics underprepared first-year students commonly share or exhibit? To what extent do these characteristics adversely affect their ability to succeed in college?
2. How would I assess my knowledge, skills, attitudes, and behaviors regarding support for underprepared first-year students? In what areas do I need to improve to serve these students more effectively?
3. How well are existing programs, offices, services, and people on my campus collaborating to support first-year students who are underprepared?
4. How effective are existing initiatives in supporting underprepared first-year students? What new initiatives or interventions might need to be developed to serve these students on my campus?

## References

ACT. (2009). *National collegiate retention and persistence to degree rates.* Retrieved from http://www.act.org/research/policymakers/pdf/retain_2009.pdf

Aronson, J., Lustina, M. J., Good, C., Keough, K., Steele, C. M., & Brown, J. (1999). When White men can't do math: Necessary and sufficient factors in stereotype threat. *Journal of Experimental Social Psychology, 35,* 29-46.

Aronson, J., & Steele, C. M. (2005). Stereotypes and the fragility of human competence, motivation, and self-concept. In E. Elliot & C. Dweck (Eds.), *Handbook of competence and motivation* (pp. 436-456). New York, NY: Guilford Press.

Atkinson, J. W., & Feather, N. T. (1966). *A theory of achievement motivation.* New York, NY: Wiley.

Bailey, C. A. (2007). Advising adult learners. In L. Huff & P. Jordan (Eds.), *Advising special populations* (Monograph No. 17, pp. 11-26). Manhattan, KS: National Academic Advising Association.

Bandura, A. (1985). Model of causality in social learning theory. In S. Sukemune (Ed.), *Advances in social learning theory.* Tokyo: Kaneko-Shoho. [Reprinted in Bandura, A. (1985). Model of causality in social learning theory. In M. J. Mahoney & A. Freeman (Eds.), *Cognition and psychotherapy* (pp. 81-99). New York, NY: Plenum Publishing Corporation.]

Bok, D. (2003). *Universities in the marketplace: The commercialization of higher education.* Princeton, NJ: Princeton University Press.

Bradley, P. (2010, May 31). Playing catch up. *Community College Week.* Retrieved from http://www.ccweek.com/news/templates/template.aspx?articleid=1875&zoneid=7

Branden, N. (1994). *The six pillars of self-esteem.* New York, NY: Bantam.

Brookfield, S. (2006). *The skillful teacher: On technique, trust, and responsiveness in the classroom* (2nd ed.). San Francisco, CA: Jossey-Bass.

Brown, P. (2000, June 14). The pomp of graduation after overcoming difficult circumstances. *The New York Times.* Retrieved from www.nytimes.com

Brown, T. (2010, January 10). *Student learning outcomes: Enhancing teaching, learning, and student success.* A keynote address. Northern Virginia Community College Faculty Cross Campus Day. Alexandria, VA.

Brown, T., & Rivas, M. (1994). The prescriptive relationship in academic advising as an appropriate developmental intervention with multicultural populations. *NACADA Journal 14*(2) 108-111.

Brown, T., & Rivas, M. (2004). Advising students of color. In M. Houland, E. C. Anderson, W. McGuire, & D. Crockett (Eds.), *Academic advising for student success and retention: Participant book/resource guide* (pp. 223-234). Iowa City, IA: Noel-Levitz.

Brown, T., & Ward, L. (2007). Preparing service providers to foster student success. In G. L. Kramer & Associates, *Fostering student success in the campus community* (pp. 302-317). San Francisco, CA: Jossey-Bass.

The Carnegie Foundation for the Advancement of Teaching. (2008). *Strengthening pre-collegiate education in community colleges: Project summary and recommendations.* Stanford, CA: Author.

Chickering, A. (1969). *Education and identity.* San Francisco, CA: Jossey-Bass.

Community College Survey of Student Engagement (CCSSE). (2009). *Making connections: Dimensions of student engagement* (2009 CCSSE Findings). Austin, TX: The University of Texas at Austin, Community College Leadership Program.

Covington, M. V. (1992). *Making the grade: A self-worth perspective on motivation and school reform.* Cambridge, MA: Cambridge University Press.

Crandall, J., & Sheppard, K. (2004). *Adult ESL and the community college.* New York, NY: Council for the Advancement of Adult Literacy.

Croizet, J., & Claire, T. (1998). Extending the concept of stereotype threat to social class: The intellectual underperformance of students from low socioeconomic backgrounds. *Personality and Social Psychology Bulletin, 24,* 588-594.

Cross, W. F., Jr. (1971). The Negro-to-Black conversion experience: Towards a psychology of Black liberation. *Black World, 20,* 13-27.

Destandau, N., Ingmier, P., van Dommelen, D., & Wiederholt, K. (2000). *Assessment, performance, and retention* (Learning Assistance Center Report). San Francisco, CA: San Francisco State University, Department of Undergraduate Studies, .

Driscoll, A. K. (2007). *Beyond access: How the first semester matters for community colleges students' aspirations and persistence.* Retrieved from http://gse.berkeley.edu/research/pace/reports/PB.07-2.pdf

Ender, S. C., & Wilkie, C. J. (2000). Advising students with special needs. In V. N. Gordon, W. R. Habley, & Associates. *Academic advising: A comprehensive handbook* (pp. 118-143). San Francisco, CA: Jossey-Bass.

Erikson, E. (1950). *Childhood and society*. New York, NY: Norton.

Gilligan, C. (1982). *In a different voice. Psychological theory and women's development*. Cambridge, MA: Harvard University Press.

Gonzales, P. M., Blanton, H., & Williams, K. J. (2002). The effects of stereotype threat and double-minority status on the test performance of Latino women. *Personality and Social Psychology Bulletin, 28,* 659-670.

Good, C., Aronson, J., & Harder, J. A. (2008). Problems in the pipeline: Stereotype threat and women's achievement in high-level math courses. *Journal of Applied Developmental Psychology, 29,* 17-28.

Habley, W. R., & McClanahan, R. (2004). *What works in student retention*. Iowa City, IA: ACT.

Hanh, T. N. (2005, September 25). Untitled dharma talk at Deer Park Monastery, Escondido, CA.

Hodgkinson, H. (1985). *All one system: Demographics of education, kindergarten to graduate school*. Washington, DC: Institute for Educational Leadership.

Johnson, A. G. (2006). *Privilege, power, and difference*. New York, NY: McGraw-Hill

Kohlberg, L. (1981). *The meaning and measurement of moral development*. Worcester, MA: Clark University Press.

Koltai, L. (1993). Community colleges: Making winners out of ordinary people. In A. Levine (Ed*.), Higher learning in America:1980-2000* (pp. 100-113). Baltimore, MD: The Johns Hopkins University Press

Light, R. *(2001). Making the most of college: Students speak their minds*. Cambridge, MA: Harvard University Press.

Lindholm, J. A., Szelenyi, K., Hurtado, S., & Korn, W. S. (2005). *The American college teacher: National norms for 2004-2005*. Los Angeles, CA: UCLA Higher Education Research Institute.

Lyman, T. (1981). The responsive classroom discussion: The inclusion of all students. In A. Anderson (Ed.), *Mainstreaming digest* (pp. 109-113). College Park, MD: University of Maryland Press.

Madison, P. (1969). *Personality development in college*. Reading, MA: Addison-Wesley.

Maxwell, M. (1997). *Improving student learning skills*. Clearwater, FL: H&H Publishing.

McClenney, K. (2009, April 25). Helping community-college students succeed: A moral imperative. *Chronicle of Higher Education*, p. A60.

McIntosh, M. F., & Rouse, C. E. (2009). *The other college: Retention and completion rates among two-year college students*. Washington, DC: Center for American Progress.

Metropolitan Opportunity Project. (1987). *Minority and low-income high schools: Evidence of educational inequality in metro Los Angeles* (Working Paper #8). Chicago, IL: University of Chicago.

National Center for Education Statistics (NCES). (2002). *Special analysis: Nontraditional undergraduates*. Washington, DC: U.S. Department of Education.

National Center for Education Statistics (NCES). (2003). *Remedial education at degree-granting postsecondary institutions in fall 2000*. Washington, DC: U.S. Department of Education.

National Council of La Raza. (1998). *Latino education: Status and prospects*. Washington, DC: State of Hispanic America.

Nicholls, J.G. (1984). Achievement motivation: Conceptions of personality, subjective experience, task choice, and performance. *Psychological Review, 91,* 328-349.

Nunez, A.-M., & Cuccaro-Alamin, S. (1998). *First-generation students: Undergraduates whose parents never enrolled in postsecondary education* (NCES 98-082). Washington, DC: U.S. Department of Education, National Center for Education Statistics.

O'Banion, T. (1999). *Launching a learning-centered college*. Mission Viejo, CA: League for Innovation in the Community *College.*

Pascarella, E. T., & Terenzini, P. T. (2005). *How college affects students: A third decade of research, volume 2.* San Francisco, CA: Jossey-Bass.

Perry, W. (1970). *Forms of intellectual development in the college years.* New York, NY: Holt, Rinehart & Winston.

Rankin, S. (2003). *Campus climate for sexual minorities: A national perspective.* New York, NY: National Gay and Lesbian Task Force Policy Institute.

Rendón, L. (1994). Validating culturally diverse students: Toward a new model of learning and student development. *Journal of Innovative Higher Education, 19*(1), 33-51.

Rendón, L. (2002). Community college puente: A validating model of education. *Educational Policy,16*, 642-667

Rings, S. (2001). *The underprepared student initiative at Paradise Valley Community College.* Retrieved from the Paradise Valley Community College website: http://www.pvc.maricopa.edu/usi/old/usiResearch.doc

Rivas, A. M. (1988). *An exploratory study of a group intervention for underprepared minority university students.* Unpublished Doctoral Dissertation. University of Minnesota, Minneapolis, Minnesota.

Rivas, M. (2005). Gestalt educational counseling. In T. L. Bar-Yoseph's, *The bridge: Dialogue across cultures* (pp. 113-134). Cleveland, OH: Cleveland Gestalt Press.

Rivas, M. (2009, November). *Strategies to promote Latino student success in the classroom.* (Webinar). Thornton, CO: Innovative Educators.

Schuetz, P., & Barr, J. (Eds.). (2008). *Are community colleges underprepared for underprepared students?* (New Directions for Community Colleges No. 144). San Francisco, CA: Jossey-Bass.

Skinner, B. F. (1953*). Science and human behavior.* New York, NY: Macmillan.

Spann, N. G., Spann, M. G., & Confer, L. S. (1995). Advising underprepared first-year students. In M. L. Upcraft & G. L. Kramer (Eds.), *First-year academic advising: Patterns in the present, pathways to the future* (Monograph No. 18, pp. 101-110). Columbia, SC: University of South Carolina, National Resource Center for The Freshman Year Experience and Students in Transition.

Sperling, C. (2009, June 30). *Massachusetts community colleges developmental education best policy and practice audit* (Final Report). Boston, MA: Massachusetts Community College Executive Office.

Sue, D., & Sue, D. W. (1999). *Counseling the culturally different: Theory and practice* (3rd ed.). New York, NY: John Wiley and Sons.

Thayer, P. B. (2000). *Retention of students from first-generation and low-income backgrounds.* Washington, DC: Council for Opportunity in Education. (ERIC Reproduction Services No. ED 446 633)

Tinto, V. (1999). Taking retention seriously: Rethinking the first year of college. *NACADA Journal, 19*(2), 5-9.

Tinto, V. (2004). *Student retention and graduation: Facing the truth and living with the consequences.* Washington, DC: Pell Institute.

U.S. Department of Education. (2004). *The condition of education* (NCES 2004-077). Washington DC: U.S. Government Printing Office.

Walpole, B. (2003). Socioeconomic status and college: How SES affects college experiences and outcomes. *The Review of Higher Education, 27*(1), 45-73.

Watson, D. L., & Tharp, R. G. (2007). Self-directed behavior: Self-modification for personal adjustment. In W. Weiten, M. Lloyd, D. Dunn, & E. Hammer, *Psychology applied to modern life* (pp. 132-137). Belmont, CA: Wadsworth.

Weiner, B. (1985). Attribution theory of achievement and emotion. *Psychological Review, 92*, 548-573.

# Chapter 5

## Developing and Engaging Educators to Support First-Year Student Success

Thomas Brown and Christine Johnson McPhail

Changing student demographics and increasing numbers of academically underprepared students are driving community colleges to find new and better ways to improve the first-year student experience. Many new students face a variety of challenges as they transition to college. This is often even more so the case for community college students, who are much more diverse than their four-year peers with respect to age, personal and social background, socioeconomic status, academic preparation, and career aspirations. These students are also more likely to be at risk for dropping out. Clery and Topper (2008) found that 14% of students who began community college credit classes in the fall term did not complete a credit in their first term, and another study found that nearly half of the students who enter two-year colleges dropped out before commencing their second year of study (ACT, 2009). Part of being successful requires that students adapt to the environment of the colleges in which they enroll. Students who leave in the first term never really "arrive," as they do not complete the transition from their prior academic, personal, and cultural experiences to the new campus cultures of the institutions they attend.

Students rely on faculty and staff to inform them about what they must do to succeed in the first year of college and beyond. Farrell (2009) concludes that faculty and staff significantly influence students' decisions to persist or drop out and suggests that colleges can teach faculty and staff to improve the quality of their interactions with students. She specifically highlights the importance of informed, professionally developed staff to facilitate student retention and indicates that such programs are an important part of first-year student initiatives. However, many campuses are ill-prepared to support first-year and other students to achieve success due to the lack of preservice and in-service training or professional development, training efforts that are sporadic or lacking in focus, or professional development targeting only full-time instructional faculty. Increasing student success requires the education, commitment, and engagement of all members of the campus community—new and experienced full-time and adjunct faculty, administrators, coaches, academic advisors, and classified professionals.

Professional development cannot be left to chance, and it should emphasize what educators must understand, know, and do in order to support students as they move into, through, and out of college. Rather than allowing such programs to be optional, campuses should offer and require preservice and in-service programs that define roles and responsibilities; set expectations (i.e., institutional, program, and student); and provide opportunities for the development and enhancement of the attitudes, skills, and behaviors essential to creating optimal learning environments for first-year students in particular and all students in general.

This chapter expands the lens of professional development to include the understanding that it is an essential factor in promoting student success in the critical first-year of college, especially in the community college. It describes the conceptual, relational, and informational skills that constitute comprehensive professional development (Brown, 2008; King, 2000) and considers how these might be integrated into effective professional development programs. The chapter also emphasizes the importance and use of principles to create comprehensive professional development programs, identifies core competencies, and suggests standards for developing educators so they can employ strategies and techniques that can produce increased student success in the first year and beyond.

## Challenges Presented by First-Year Community College Students

Community college students are more likely to enter college with risk factors, including parents with lower levels of education, delayed entry into postsecondary education after high school, part-time enrollment, full-time employment, dependents at home, single parent status, and lack of adequate academic preparation (National Center for Educational Statistics, 2003). As such, increasing student engagement, persistence, and success is an ongoing challenge for two-year institutions. When instructional faculty and academic advisors in two-year colleges were asked if students understood what was required to be successful, less than 15% agreed this was the case (Brown, 2009). Furthermore, when asked how many hours they studied during a typical week, only 12% of community college students reported studying more than 21 hours a week, while 67% reported spending 10 hours a week or less preparing for class (CCSSE, 2008). Thus, first-year students need to be taught the attitudes, skills, and behaviors essential to personal, academic, and career goal achievement, including effective time management, goal setting, planning and decision making, study skills, and knowing and using campus and community resources.

Similarly, McClenney (chapter 2) indicates that students are often surprised or discouraged when they learn they have to take a developmental course, although those who persist later acknowledge the value of such courses to their success. Students may need help reframing placement in precollege-level courses so that they see it as a bridge to their long-term goals rather than a step backward. First-year students also need to understand that there is a difference between getting good grades and acquiring skills that will enable them to be successful in college, in their careers, or in life. When students complete their studies and move on from community college, future employers are unlikely to be interested in the grades they received. What will matter is whether or not students have the skills needed to perform well in a subsequent course or program, or on the job. First-year students need to understand that the learning process is just as important, if not more so, than the product of educational experiences (e.g., getting the right answer or a making a good grade; Conley, 2003).

First-year students, some of whom may have been outstanding high school students, may also need help understanding that failure is a part of learning—that every wrong attempt discarded is another step forward. Palmer (1998) writes that students are afraid to fail and look foolish in front of their peers; however, successful students understand that falling down is not failing as long as they persist in applying themselves to a task and use campus resources that can support increased levels of understanding and achievement. First-year students should also be encouraged to view criticism as essential to effective teaching and learning because successful students understand that receiving constructive feedback and making adjustments based on such feedback is a critical part of learning and development (Conley, 2003).

### A Model for Ensuring Student Success

While students encounter many challenges as they enter college, they must be actively involved in finding ways to overcome those challenges if they are to succeed. Figure 5.1 offers a model of shared responsibility for student success, which can be adapted for a wide range of campus educators, and is based on the work of Brown (2008), Brown and Rivas (1994), Creamer (2000), and Lynch (1989).

This model proposes that student needs and responsibilities evolve as students move in, through, and out of college (Lynch, 1989). Creamer (2000) suggests that students initially need information and guidance; however, as they transition effectively into college, their needs shift from seeking information to wanting feedback from and/or consultation with faculty, counselors, and advisors, who they then use as sounding boards. Brown and Rivas (1994) contend that educators often need to take the lead and be more prescriptive in their interactions with some students (e.g., first-generation, multicultural, international students), especially during the first year, when

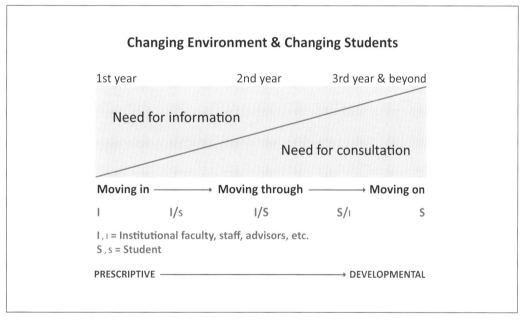

*Figure 5.1.* A model of shared responsibility. Adapted from "Critical Concepts in Advisor Training and Development," by T. E. Brown, 2008, in *Academic Advising: A Comprehensive Handbook* (2nd ed.), p. 314. Copyright 2008 by Jossey-Bass; "The Prescriptive Relationship in Academic Advising as an Appropriate Developmental Intervention With Multicultural Populations," by T. E. Brown & M. Rivas, 1994, *NACADA Journal, 14*(2), pp. 108-111. Copyright 2004 by the National Academic Advising Association; "Use of Theory in Academic Advising," by D. G. Creamer, 2000, in *Academic Advising: A Comprehensive Handbook*, p. 29. Copyright 2000 by Jossey-Bass; and "Moving In, Moving Through, and Moving On," by A. Q. Lynch, 1989 in *Improving Higher Education Environments for Adults*, Copyright 1989 by Jossey-Bass.

many such students need and expect a more directive approach. As students gain experience and confidence, their interactions with teachers, advisors, or counselors become more developmental, meaning students assume greater responsibility for goal setting, planning, and decision making. As students move through college and prepare to move on, they turn to others for advice and feedback, rather than for direction.

Faculty and staff, as representatives of the institution, (the *I* in the model) must take the initiative to establish relationships with first-year students. As students make effective transitions (moving through), they come to share responsibility with faculty and staff (*I/S*), and eventually bear the primary responsibility (*S*) as they prepare to move on to the world of work or transfer to four-year institutions (Brown, 2008). Because hope (Snyder et al., 1991) and optimism (Seligman, 1991) are better predictors of first-year college success than prior grades or test scores, faculty and other campus professionals should be encouraged to interact with students in ways that lead students to be hopeful and optimistic about their chances to achieve their personal and educational goals.

## Linking Professional Development to Student Success

Chickering (1994) suggests that helping students move into college effectively is the most important work for educators. Yet, Driscoll (2007) indicates that many first-year community college students do not fully understand the academic challenges and do not anticipate the time and effort required to succeed. As such, students are dependent on faculty and staff to inform them about what they must do to be a successful during the critical first year of college, particularly for students who are first-generation, academically underprepared, or from other backgrounds that put them at greater risk for dropping out. However, when students drop out, two-year college educators are more inclined to place the blame on student shortcomings, rather than examining institutional factors that contribute to student attrition (Habley, Bloom, & Gore, in press: Habley & McClanhan, 2004). These attitudes persist in spite of evidence that suggests what happens to students after they enroll is often more critical to their persistence than their prior academic records (Pascarella & Terenzini, 2005; Tinto, 1993). In order to support increased student persistence, community colleges must shift from a student deficit perspective to one that considers institutional influences on attrition (Schuetz & Barr, 2008).

Yet, changing this perspective may not be easy. Grubb (1999) observed that most community college instructors enter the teaching profession with inadequate training, and many receive little or no support to improve their teaching skills. More recently, the Carnegie Foundation for the Advancement of Teaching (2008) concluded that most community college faculty have received little or no training to engage the increasing numbers of underprepared students coming to their campuses and classrooms. Tinto (2006-2007) noted that while faculty interactions are critical to institutional retention efforts, college faculty, unlike primary and secondary school instructors, are the only teachers who are not trained to engage their students inside and outside the classroom. As a result, faculty have been placed at risk for being ineffective teachers because they lack the instructional theories and practices and, of greater importance, the guidance to address a wide range of challenges that extend beyond classroom teaching (Grubb). For example, Habley and Mc-Clanahan (2004), as well as Habley et al. (in press) found academic advising to be among the most effective retention strategies for two-year colleges. However, Brown (2009) reported that fewer than one third of community college faculty indicate they had adequate preparation and training before they began advising students. Specifically, professional development programs will need to teach faculty, including adjuncts, to address the needs of increasingly diverse student populations.

Faculty, staff, and administrators are expected to have relevant competencies in their areas of responsibility (e.g., subject area knowledge, technical skills, program development experience, or competence in counseling or academic advising) before commencing their work with students. However, other key competencies (e.g., knowledge of campus resources, relational skills) are developed only after educators arrive on campus (Brown & Ward, 2007). Laursen and Rocque (2009) suggested that faculty development could address the needs of today's college students by providing opportunities for personal growth, career reflection, and long-term professional development needs of individual faculty members. Diamond (2002) identified four major outcomes of faculty development: (a) demonstration of the institution's concern for the individual, (b) improvement in the productivity of individual faculty members through increased teaching effectiveness, (c) facilitation of focused change with more emphasis on what students learn and less on what the faculty member covers, and (d) improvement of faculty attitudes toward teaching.

Yet, Gordon (1992) observed that professional development has too often been viewed as a one-time event at the beginning of the academic year, and she concluded that effective professional development requires more extensive, ongoing engagement that can be viewed as rites of renewal. Rather than a single activity or series of events, professional development is a process that should be viewed as being integral to the work of community colleges and for individual faculty and staff members. Instructional faculty, in particular, must take appropriate responsibility for their first-year students' learning, bringing the most effective practices to their work and collaborating with others to improve those practices, both inside and outside the classroom. The Carnegie Foundation (2008) strongly recommended that colleges provide "more powerful occasions for educators to learn about what works for students" (p. 8) and concluded that professional development must be more than occasional programs or workshops.

Students, however, do not make distinctions between faculty, administration, and staff or between full-time, part-time, or adjunct status when they encounter a problem or need referral to sources of assistance. For this reason, professional development is essential for all members of a campus community seeking to increase first-year student engagement, satisfaction, and persistence. Furthermore, as increasing numbers of senior faculty, staff, and administrators move toward retirement, there will be even greater need for effective professional development, especially at upper leadership levels. Programs must be designed specifically to ensure that first-year success remains a high priority for community colleges and must focus on the engagement and development of all constituent groups in support of this goal. For example, Cuyahoga Community College (Cleveland, OH) offers ongoing professional development for maintenance staff. As President Jerry Sue Thornton observed, "They often are the first line for students. Some of our friendliest, most helpful people are those who have nothing to do with classroom teaching. But they want students to be successful..." (CCSSE, 2009, p.14).

## Standards for Comprehensive Professional Development Programs

Professional development programs must have clear goals and outcomes that are directly linked to student learning, development, and success. When community colleges plan professional development activities, they should consider standards for designing and implementing programs that take context, process, and content into account (NSDC, 2005).

## Context Standards

In planning professional development programs, it is important to consider the context in which the activities are being offered. It is essential to align professional development with the mission, vision, core values, and strategic plans of the institution. A comprehensive professional development program does not occur in silos. Rather, it requires leadership support for resources and a campus climate that encourages collaboration across all units of the institution. Among the questions to ask to provide the context for the program, How will the professional development programs be organized? Who will lead the programs? What stakeholders need to be involved? What resources are available to support learning and collaboration throughout the college?

Efforts to engage and develop community college educators in student success agendas must start by defining student success. A consistent definition of the college's student success agenda should be shared with all constituent groups, which makes it more feasible to develop training programs that will help educators support students in achieving college-defined success goals.

## Process Standards

A comprehensive faculty development program designed to engage and empower faculty to support student success will offer multiple approaches. Key processes include (a) conducting needs assessments; (b) providing general and targeted programs for specific constituent groups, such as first-year students, multicultural, international, and underprepared students; (c) using multiple formats and delivery systems; and (d) using student and institutional data to determine program priorities. Community college leaders should establish a culture of evidence wherein decisions about student success interventions are supported by data. As community colleges seek new ways to achieve their missions, comprehensive professional development programs can be a useful tool to engage and develop the entire campus community to support student success.

## Content Standards

If professional development activities are to engage and develop community college educators to support student success, the training curriculum must reflect the skills and knowledge necessary for all members of the campus community to understand, embrace, and support the institution's student success agenda. Questions that should guide the content of professional development include (a) What do community college educators need to understand, know, and do in order to promote student success? and (b) How do we know? This requires more than having colleagues participate in a single event or complete a required number of hours. "Seat time" is not an indicator of professional development; rather, efforts should be made to assess competencies achieved as a result of having participated in specific learning experiences.

Despite the increased attention to student success and calls for faculty development, what many community colleges lack is a set of commonly accepted competencies that effective faculty and staff should possess. An examination of the literature pertaining to training programs reveals common elements regardless of the setting or audience (Brown, 2008; Habley, 1986; King 2000). These can be grouped into three categories—conceptual, relational, and informational—described in greater detail below.

***Conceptual elements*** are what faculty and staff need in order to understand the students they serve, as well as about their work as teachers, counselors, academic advisors, and support staff. These include how first-year student/faculty and staff interactions inside and outside the classroom impact learning and persistence, factors that contribute to students' being underprepared, and an overview of student development and how this influences student engagement and willingness to connect to campus support services and to take responsibility for their own learning. Conceptual elements also include supporting educators to understand their roles and responsibilities for assisting students, as well as helping students understand their own roles and responsibilities. Specific conceptual competencies include understanding

◇ The distinctive mission of community colleges
◇ Student demographics (e.g., age, gender, ethnicity, socioeconomic status) on a particular campus
◇ Theories of student development, learning, and persistence
◇ Challenges to first-year student persistence
◇ Effective strategies to support first-year student learning and engagement
◇ Challenges facing specific at-risk cohorts (e.g., first-generation students, LGBTQ students, student athletes, adult or re-entry students, undecided students, students with disabilities, underprepared students, veterans, international students)
◇ Theories of career decision making and career development

*Informational elements* include specific details regarding institutional policies, procedures, and programs that must be grasped in order to provide timely and accurate information, advice, and referral to first-year students. For example, informational competencies encompass knowledge about institutional policies, procedures, and programs; classroom, support, and administrative functions; campus and community resources and referral mechanisms; and technology resources and how to use them.

*Relational elements* are the skills, attitudes, and behaviors that faculty and staff should use to engage first-year students in academic goal setting, planning, and decision making. These include rapport building and interviewing skills, active listening, developing cultural competencies to respond to broad issues of diversity, and employing effective referral skills. Relational competencies also involve the belief in the capacity of all students to learn, develop, and achieve at high levels; a willingness to advocate for students as appropriate; and the ability to support students' exploration of alternative goals or programs. While these skills are frequently employed in one-on-one encounters with students, they also involve developing effective teamwork and collaboration skills for partnerships with other educators in designing programmatic supports for students.

These three elements can be applied to establish a common knowledge base for faculty and staff, in general, and for those working with first-year students, in particular. Community colleges may advance their first-year student success agendas by identifying specific core competencies (conceptual, informational, and relational) that members of the campus community should possess—whether they are instructional faculty, counselors, academic advisors, student services staff, or classified professionals. These competencies can form a central curriculum that unifies what may have been perceived as disconnected events and activities.

### Program Leadership

*The role of central administration.* The campus leadership team frequently makes key decisions about the structure of professional development at many community colleges, and it is not uncommon for the content of such activities to be determined at the leadership level, as well. Tinto (2006-2007) recommends that institutions invest resources and promote behaviors that reflect their proclaimed commitment to student success. Establishing, implementing, and maintaining effective professional development requires commitment, leadership, and involvement of stakeholders throughout the college. To ensure that professional development supports student success, community college leadership teams should

◇ Ensure that the content of the professional development curriculum is an appropriate balance between employee-determined and institution-determined needs
◇ Select a program coordinator with personal and professional qualifications and credibility to engage and collaborate with all constituent groups
◇ Allocate sufficient resources, including facilities and technology to support the program
◇ Provide ongoing support
◇ Require an evaluation of the impact of professional development activities
◇ Provide rewards, incentives, and recognition of activities that demonstrate change in employee behavior resulting from participation in professional development programs
◇ Introduce the first-year professional development plan to the college as a major priority to promote collegewide buy-in

***The role of the professional development coordinator.*** The program coordinator plays a critical role in the professional development process at the institution. On an increasing number of campuses, this role is assumed by the person responsible for the teaching and learning center (e.g., Tacoma Community College, Tacoma, WA; Middlesex County College, Edison, NJ; Southern Maine Community College, South Portland, ME). The coordinator's visibility and engagement collegewide is essential for fostering collaboration among departments, divisions, and various campus constituencies. Professional development coordinators should

◇ Involve all stakeholders in the planning and implementation of the professional development process
◇ Link professional development to student success, mission, core values, and strategic plans
◇ Develop learning communities for program and departmental units
◇ Collect and report information in a routine and consistent manner
◇ Direct and support evaluation activities
◇ Use outcomes to guide improvements in behaviors, practices, and policies
◇ Recognize and celebrate participants (e.g., advising their supervisors) in professional development programs

## Implementing Comprehensive Professional Development Activities

This section expands on the previous recommendations related to the roles and responsibilities of campus leadership and program coordinators for professional development initiatives. While all professional development activities must be guided by their unique institutional context, the following are some recommended steps in the process of implementing or expanding a professional development plan to support first-year student success.

### Step 1 - Form a Professional Development Planning Committee

This representative planning group can identify important collegewide student success issues, focused on what faculty and staff need to know to promote first-year student success. It can be particularly effective to have the group appointed by the president, instructional vice president, and/or commissioned within the existing governance structure (King, 2000) to ensure its standing and credibility. Members of the planning group should include representation from faculty, staff, and administrators.

### Step 2 - Align Definitions of Student Success With the College Mission

The work of the planning committee must be guided by local and national definitions of first-year student success. The institutional research office can be instrumental in collecting and sharing national and institutional data on student success in clear and concise terms. The mission of the college should be also revisited so that the planning committee can align first-year student success definitions with the overall institutional mission. Professional development programs that are directly related to the college's mission to support student engagement, learning, and persistence are more likely to receive financial and administrative support.

### Step 3 - Conduct a Needs Assessment

A needs assessment to identify collegewide first-year student success issues to be addressed in the professional development program should be performed as an initial planning step. Needs assessments could list a number of conceptual, relational, and informational issues and ask employees what they need to learn more about in order to support student success. Such assessments ensure that programs correspond to real needs and increase the sense of buy-in that is critical to the success of any campus initiative. Needs assessments also allow institutions to design programs for subgroups of first-year students, for example international students, re-entry students, veterans, or students with disabilities, as well as for faculty and staff involved with specific cohorts.

### Step 4 - Establish Goals and Objectives

Goals and objectives of the training program should be linked to the student success agenda and the mission of the college and be drawn from the results of the needs assessment. Each objective must be written so that it is "specific, measurable, achievable, realistic, and tangible" (King, 2000, p. 292). For example, objectives for many Achieving the Dream campuses include specific student outcomes, such as

◇ Successfully completing remedial or developmental instruction and advancing to credit-bearing courses
◇ Enrolling in and successfully completing the initial college-level or gatekeeper courses in subjects, such as math and English
◇ Completing courses with grade *C* or better
◇ Improving persistence from one term to the next
◇ Completing a certificate or associate degree or transferring to four-year institutions

When objectives follow these guidelines, the outcomes of the training program and its effectiveness can be measured. Moreover, such an approach makes ongoing assessment of the professional development program more sustainable.

*Step 5 - Select Appropriate Content, Strategies, and Methods*

A comprehensive professional development program offers multiple approaches and activities. Professional development activities are also offered at a variety of times to accommodate the schedules and needs of all constituents—many of whom may work evenings and weekends to facilitate delivery of the college's learning opportunities. For example, the Loudon campus of Northern Virginia Community College has offered Saturday professional development programs to accommodate adjunct faculty members, while Danville Community College (Danville, VA) and College of the Sequoias (Visalia, CA) have offered similar programs in the evening.

Effective programs provide opportunities for constituents to reinforce their knowledge and skills and practice what was learned in the professional development experience. College-wide professional development days or retreats provide opportunities for faculty and staff to meet to identify, discuss, and respond to specific professional development needs in a systematic manner with an internal facilitator and/or external consultant. Activities might also take the form of learning communities, scenarios and role playing, simulations, job shadowing, and departmental showcasing of exemplary practices. The Center for Innovative Teaching and Technology at Hillsborough Community College (Tampa, FL) provides an environment that fosters the development and delivery of engaging, innovative instructional strategies and technologies promoting successful student learning opportunities. The Academic Excellence Center (AEC) at Cuyahoga Community College (Cleveland, OH) also seeks to improve the use of new and emerging instructional technologies by providing faculty access to equipment and software used to enhance teaching and learning in traditional and online classroom settings. Workshops are conducted throughout the year covering a variety of topics ranging from course design to emerging technologies. One-on-one consultations are provided as well as small-group instruction. Similarly, The Professional Development Institute at Wayne County Community College District (Detroit, MI) provides employees and staff with opportunities to develop their skills and support the District's ongoing commitment to student success, community outreach, and economic development.

The structure of many community colleges simply does not lend itself to spontaneous collaborative efforts; therefore, extra efforts need to be employed to create interaction between various departments and divisions. The curriculum of the professional development program must contain content that will facilitate collaboration to support student success. The Teaching and Learning Center (TLC) at the College of DuPage (Glen Ellyn, IL) has been noted by Troller (2002) as a place where faculty and staff come together to learn. The TLC has a highly visible centralized office that offers workshops as well as courses. All college personnel attend course offerings during sessions that focus on key issues to the college, such as diversity, academic advising, time management, teaching and learning, and wellness.

*Step 6 - Seek Support From Institutional Leaders*

Leadership support for professional development to enhance first-year success begins at the top. Committed community college leaders are increasingly interested in a more integrated service delivery system leading to student success. Chairpersons, deans, instructional vice presidents, and others should communicate that professional development is mandatory and a critical link to the success of students, in general, and first-year students, in particular. Why mandatory? Because many faculty and staff are not likely to volunteer to attend more meetings without some directive from supervisors unless they already have a commitment and understanding of their role in increasing student learning, engagement, and success.

On campuses with collective bargaining agreements, it is essential to involve faculty and staff representatives at every stage of the planning process in order to gain their input about how to best engage their colleagues in professional development activities that are consistent with contracts and other guidelines. Participation may be a matter for negotiation, and recognition and reward must be considered as part of this process.

Tinto (2006-2007) suggests that most colleges do not align their reward systems to their expressed goal of increasing student persistence and success. If faculty and staff are to be fully engaged in efforts to increase first-year student success, colleges must finds ways to recognize and reward those who participate in professional development programs (e.g., in promotion and tenure processes, reassigned time, stipends). Patrick Henry Community College (Martinsville, VA) offers additional compensation to adjunct faculty who attend professional development workshops. North Hennepin Community College (Brooklyn Park, MN) acknowledges faculty and staff who participate in their LGBT Ally Training program by providing printed Ally Certificates. Campuses receiving support from Title III, Title V, and Achieving the Dream initiatives can use a portion of grant funds to support professional development. South Texas College (McAllen, TX), Odessa College (Odessa, TX), Pima Community College (Tucson, AZ), and Porterville College (Porterville, CA) are among the campuses that have used Title V grants to support professional development, and Jefferson College (Hillsboro, MO) has used some Title III funding for this purpose. The fact that a campus recognizes and rewards participation in professional development matters much more than the nature of the recognition itself.

### Step 7 - Design Effective Programs

Successful professional development programs integrate the content and format of professional development with the experience, skill level, and willingness of constituents to participate (Brown, 2008; King, 2000; McPhail & Costner, 2004). Table 5.1 presents a professional development model that integrates participant characteristics (e.g., experience levels, willingness to participate, needs) with content and delivery techniques (Brown, 2008). Originally designed for use with academic advisors, this model can be adapted to plan professional development programs for other members of the campus community.

Experienced faculty and staff often have a firm grasp of informational issues and may be reluctant to participate in professional development programs. However, findings from needs assessments may suggest deficits in their understanding of students and their individual role and responsibility to support student success. Student satisfaction surveys may also indicate a need for faculty and staff to strengthen the skills essential to developing effective relationships with students, which ultimately correlate with increased learning, satisfaction, and persistence.

On the other hand, newer, less experienced, faculty and staff may be more willing to participate in professional development programs because they recognize the need to increase their knowledge of programs, policies, and resources. While in-service programs for experienced participants may focus more on conceptual and relational issues, preservice programs for inexperienced participants could address conceptual, relational and informational issues.

The model suggests that newer faculty and staff may be more likely respond to programs involving internal presenters, while external presenters might be more attractive and effective with experienced participants. Both groups could use readings, simulation exercises, and video vignettes, with case studies being shared for experienced participants and more extensive question, answer, and discussion provided for newer faculty and staff.

Table 5.1

*Structuring Programs to Respond to Participant Needs*

|  | **Experienced educators** | **Inexperienced educators** |
|---|---|---|
| Skill level | Moderate | Low |
| Experience | High | Low |
| Willingness to participate | Moderate | High |
| Conceptual needs | Moderate | High |
| Informational needs | Low | High |
| Relational needs | Moderate | High |
| Program techniques and formats | External presenters<br>Readings/discussions<br>Panel presentations<br>Simulations/role plays<br>DVD/Video vignettes<br>Group discussions<br>Case studies | Internal presenters<br>Reading/discussions<br>Pretest knowledge<br>Brainstorming needs and issues<br>DVD/Video vignettes<br>Group discussions<br>Questions and answers |

Institutions should also consider creating a cycle of professional development programming, wherein priorities and goals are identified and addressed over a two- or three-year period. This approach emphasizes the fact that increasing competence is the result of a well-conceived process rather than events that are sporadic and lacking in focus.

### Step 8 - Assess and Evaluate Professional Development Programs

Despite the current discussions in the literature about data-driven decision making, assessment of professional development activities is a weak link in many of the nation's community colleges. For example, one professional development coordinator noted that assessment was not an institutional priority:

> there is no relationship between the assessment of what I do with the professional development programs and what faculty really do in the classroom. I just offer the programs, and my evaluation is based on how good the participants feel. The program is not connected to any goals. If I have the seats filled, I'll get the nod of approval from my senior level administrators.

Yet, assessments that are grounded in satisfaction and participation rates are inadequate for program improvement and maintenance. Community college faculty development programs must be agenda driven—focused primarily on student success. Outcomes should indicate what participants will understand (affective), know (cognitive), and do (behavioral) more effectively as the result of their involvement in professional development activities.

To ensure that the assessment is linked to student success, it must document reactions to the professional development experience, knowledge or skills gained, and anticipated changes in behavior resulting from the experience. For example, the assessment process should include an opportunity for participants to provide feedback on how the activity equipped them to improve teaching, learning, academic advising, and other student support efforts. An interview or survey prompt may read, How did this activity help you improve learning outcomes for your students? or How will you use the knowledge gained in this workshop to improve teaching and learning outcomes for students? The status and effectiveness of professional development can be raised when participants are required to apply the knowledge gained from the activity to their discipline.

Ongoing and systematic assessment and evaluation activities are essential to effective professional development. The processes should be considered throughout the planning and implementation of the professional development program and tied directly to measuring progress toward meeting the stated goals and outcomes. As noted elsewhere in this volume, community colleges are facing unprecedented challenges (e.g., increasing enrollments, record numbers of underprepared students, declining fiscal and human resources). Thus, it is an especially critical time to emphasize assessment of programs and services, in response to omnipresent demands for accountability and in order to provide data for informed decision making with regard to allocating limited resources.

## Conclusion

It would be impossible in one chapter to discuss all of the variables that affect the engagement of educators to promote student success. Both Grubb (1999) and Tinto (2006-2007) have suggested that most community college educators commence their work with inadequate training, and many receive little or no support to improve their teaching skills. It is critical for faculty and other community college educators to develop the knowledge and skills to support first-year student success. In order for two-year colleges to realize their promise to enhance student success, professional development must play a pivotal role in the improvement of teaching and learning in these institutions. More specifically, if professional development initiatives are to have a meaningful impact on first-year student success, the activities must not only change participant behavior, but they must also be used by the college to improve programs and services. The significance of a comprehensive program is that all constituents are involved in professional development activities. A single employee who learns and uses strategies for student success will not significantly change classroom experiences, programs, and services. Yet, when all employees understand and support student success, meaningful campus transformation is possible.

Community colleges cannot assume that faculty and staff will become more effective in their work to support first-year student success without comprehensive preservice and in-service professional development programs. Campuses must examine the quality and scope of their current professional development efforts (McPhail & Costner, 2004) and make ongoing professional development an institutional responsibility and part of the job description for all part-time and full-time campus members. They should also create incentives for participation, linking it to institutional recognition and reward systems. Finally, they need to create institutional structures that provide opportunities for faculty and staff to reflect together on their experiences to be more effective in their work with students inside and beyond the classroom (The Carnegie Foundation for the Advancement of Teaching, 2008). Community colleges must seek to systematically enhance and expand the ways they provide professional development in order to improve the first-year learning experience.

## References

ACT. (2009). *National collegiate retention and persistence degree rates.* Retrieved October 5, 2010, from http://www.act.org/research/policymakers/pdf/retain_2009.pdf

Brown, T. E. (2008). Critical concepts in advisor training and development. In V.N. Gordon, W. R. Habley, & Associates, *Academic advising: A comprehensive handbook* (2nd ed., pp. 309-322). San Francisco, CA: Jossey-Bass.

Brown, T. E. (2009). *Questionnaire on academic advising.* Unpublished study. St. Helena, CA: Thomas Brown & Associates.

Brown, T. E., & Rivas, M. (1994). The prescriptive relationship in academic advising as an appropriate developmental intervention with multicultural populations. *NACADA Journal, 14*(2), 108-111.

Brown, T. E., & Ward, L. (2007). Preparing service providers to foster students. In G. L. Kramer (Ed.), *Fostering student success in the campus community* (pp. 302-317). San Francisco, CA. Jossey-Bass.

The Carnegie Foundation for the Advancement of Teaching. (2008). *Strengthening pre-collegiate education in community colleges: Project summary and recommendations.* Stanford, CA: Author.

Chickering, A. W. (1994). Empowering lifelong self-development. *NACADA Journal, 14*(2) 50-53.

Clery, S., & Topper, A. (2008, October/November). Students earning zero credits. *Data Notes, 3*(4), 1-4.

Community College Survey of Student Engagement (CCSSE). (2008). *High expectations and high support.* Austin, TX: The University of Texas at Austin, Community College Leadership Program.

Community College Survey of Student Engagement (CCSSE). (2009). *Making connections: Dimensions of student engagement* (2009 CCSSE findings). Austin, TX: The University of Texas at Austin, Community College Leadership Program.

Conley, D. T. (2003). *Understanding university success: A report from standards for success.* Eugene, OR: Center for Educational Policy Research.

Creamer, D. G. (2000). Use of theory in academic advising. In V. N. Gordon, W. R. Habley, & Associates, *Academic advising: A comprehensive handbook* (pp. 18-34). San Francisco, CA: Jossey-Bass.

Diamond, R. M. (2002). Faculty, instructional, and organizational development: Options and choices. In K. H. Gillespie (Ed.), *Guide to faculty development: Practical advice, examples, and resources* (pp. 2-8). Bolton, MA: Anker Publishing.

Driscoll, A. K. (2007). *Beyond access: How the first semester matters for community colleges students' aspirations and persistence.* Retrieved from http://gse.berkeley.edu/research/pace/reports/PB.07-2.pdf

Farrell, P. (2009). Investing in staff for student retention. In *2009 almanac of higher education* (pp. 85-92). Washington, DC: National Education Association.

Gordon, V. N. (1992). *Handbook of academic advising.* Westport, CT: Greenwood Press.

Grubb, W. N. (1999). *The economic benefits of sub-baccalaureate education: Results from the national studies* (CCRC Brief, Number 2). New York, NY: Columbia University, Community College Research Center. (ERIC Document Reproduction Services No. ED 441 549)

Habley, W. R. (1986). *Advisor training: Whatever happened to instructional design?* ACT workshop presentation. Iowa City, IA: ACT.

Habley, W. R, Bloom, J. L., & Gore, P. (in press). *Increasing student persistence: Integrating theory, research, and practice to enhance student success.* San Francisco, CA: Jossey-Bass.

Habley, W. R., & McClanahan, R. (2004). *What works in student retention.* Iowa City, IA: ACT

King, M. C. (2000). Designing effective training for academic advisors. In V. N. Gordon, W. R. Habley, & Associates, *Academic advising: A comprehensive handbook* (pp. 289-297). San Francisco, CA: Jossey-Bass.

Laursen, S. L., & Rocque, B. (2009, March/April). Faculty development for institutional change: Lessons from an ADVANCE project. *Change,* 18-26. Retrieved from http://www.changemag.org/Archives/Back%20Issues/March-April%202009/full-advance-project.html

Lynch, A. Q. (1989). Moving in, moving through, moving on. In N. K. Schlossberg, A. Q. Lynch, & A. W. Chickering (Eds.), *Improving higher education environments for adults*. San Francisco, CA: Jossey-Bass

McPhail, C. J., & Costner, K. (2004). Seven principles for training culturally responsive teachers. *Learning Abstract, 7*(12). Retrieved from http://www.league.org/istreamSite/abstracts_index.cfm?url=learning/lelabs0412.html

National Center for Educational Statistics (NCES). (2003). *Community college students: Goals, academic preparation, and outcomes*. Washington, DC: U.S. Department of Education.

National Staff Development Council (NSDC). (2005). *Learning to lead, leading to learn: Improving school quality through principal professional development*. Retrieved March 15, 2005, from http://www.ndsc.org/library/leaders

Palmer, P. (1998). *The courage to teach*. San Francisco, CA: Jossey-Bass.

Pascarella, E. T., & Terenzini, P. T. (2005). *How college affects students: A third decade of research*. San Francisco, CA: Jossey-Bass.

Schuetz, P., & Barr, J. (Eds.). (2008). *Are community colleges underprepared for underprepared students? (*New Directions for Community Colleges No. 144). San Francisco, CA: Jossey-Bass.

Seligman, M. (1991). *Learned optimism*. New York, NY: Knopf.

Snyder, C. R., Harris, C., Anderson, J. R., Holleran, S. A., Irving, L. M., Sigmon, S. T., . . . Harney, P. (1991). The will and the ways: Development and validation of an individual-differences measure of hope. *Journal of Personality and Social Psychology, 60*, 570-585.

Tinto, V. (1993). *Leaving college: Rethinking the causes and cures of student attrition* (2nd ed.). Chicago, IL: The University of Chicago Press.

Tinto, V. (2006-2007). Research and practice of student retention: What next? *Journal of College Student Retention, 8*(1), 1-19.

Troller, K T. (2002). College of DuPage Teaching and Learning Center: A comprehensive professional development program. In G. E. Watts (Ed.), *Enhancing community colleges through professional development* (New Directions for Community College No.120, pp. 67-74). San Francisco, CA: Jossey-Bass.

# Chapter 6
## Creating Effective Transfer Initiatives

Thomas J. Grites and Susan Rondeau

Transfer is the key success criterion for close to half of today's 12 million community college students. They intend to begin their education at a community college, perhaps earning an associate degree, and then move on to a four-year institution. A major concern of every transfer student is how their previous courses and credits will transfer and apply to the degree requirements at their new institution, along with the natural concerns about making the overall transition to a new institution. Yet, the bachelor's degree is a goal within the reach of every transfer student, provided effective transfer initiatives are in place. This chapter presents initiatives that originate from outside the institution, those that are specific to community colleges and receiving institutions, and cooperative efforts. Strategies for assessing transfer initiatives are also addressed.

The need for these initiatives becomes paramount as a continually increasing number of community college completers seek admission to baccalaureate programs. During any economic downturn, laid-off workers return to school en masse to upgrade skills and train for new careers. When men and women complete military service, many select the community college as the place to use their educational benefits. Not only is the community college a cost saving alternative to most four-year institutions, it is often a first choice for many because of its traditionally smaller class sizes and faculty who are committed more specifically to teaching. The recent surge, however, has been so large that students have even been denied admission to traditionally open-door community colleges (Mullin & Phillippe, 2009).

Transfer students are commonly defined as students who earn credits at one school and move on to another, including students transferring from one community college to another. A large number of first-year community college students define themselves as transfer students when they begin their studies, even before they have earned any transferable credits. Community colleges refer to these students as intending to transfer or prospective transfer students. Typically, effective transfer initiatives place a focus on students transferring from a community college to a four-year institution. Most four-year institutions will not consider incoming transfer students for admission unless they have met specific criteria (e.g., successful completion of a minimum number of transferable credits, minimum GPA). In an effort to increase first-year student success, this chapter stresses the importance of accepting transfer students with or without earned degrees and understanding that programs and services must be made available in the student's first year at the community college and continue until a complete and effective transition to the four-year institution has been made.

In recent years, a new type of transfer student has emerged: the *swirling* student. These students exhibit a rather involved pattern of attendance, which might include multiple transfers, going back and forth between schools, attending two schools simultaneously, and/or stopping out of school for a brief time. The proliferation of online coursework readily available to students makes it easy for them to search beyond their home institution to fulfill unmet academic needs. Certainly, access to online education increases the numbers of swirlers, and institutions need to recognize the attendance patterns of this new breed of transfer student (Bailey, 2003).

While there are many benefits to being a transfer student, there are also challenges. For example, students may experience transfer shock, which is typically described as the tendency for community college transfers to see an initial drop in their GPAs during their first term of enrollment at a four-year institution. The shock results from the cumulative effect of all the differences students encounter between their previous school(s) and their new one. It is the overwhelming feeling students have as they begin processing all the changes occurring as they transition to a new academic environment. The more variations there are to the students' expectations, the greater the discomfort they are likely to experience (Rewey, 1998; Thurmond, 2007).

In fact, some of this shock might even be the residual effect of an emerging condition observed in community college students. Cox (2009) identified a fear factor that may be present in many students when they first enroll in community colleges. She found that simply becoming a college student precipitated feelings of academic inadequacy, especially in writing and math; of intimidation, based upon their perceptions of the super-knowledgeable faculty members they would encounter; and the nature of college courses and subject matter. Once community college students have overcome these fears and anxieties, many transfer into yet another new academic environment, only to face the transfer shock syndrome.

Most transfer students either expect the new institution to be much like the first or expect that they will acclimate quickly and easily to the new environment. Variations in campus culture and climate, classroom locations, academic options and course availability (including potential work and class schedule conflicts), living and commuting arrangements, and extracurricular activities may produce enough stress to create transfer shock, especially when combined with changes in magnitude—larger city, campus, and class sizes. While most transfer students experience some degree of transfer shock, institutions can help alleviate it by including helpful information in those initiatives that are designed specifically for transfer students, such as a course, workshop, or orientation designed to help students in the actual transfer process and beyond. Effective transfer initiatives originate from a variety of sources. Individuals responsible for transfer students at both sending and receiving institutions must take advantage of all the resources and initiatives that are already in place to facilitate successful transfer processes and to assist transfer students.

## External Initiatives

Not all initiatives that facilitate successful transfer efforts and programs originate on college campuses. A variety of external sources influence the nature and scope of the two-year to four-year transfer process, as well as those that evolve on the affected campuses.

### *Legislated Initiatives*

The Education Commission of the States (2001, 2009) reports that at least 38 states now have some form of legislation that addresses the transfer of credit. The conditions included in these statutes, bills, or resolutions range from initial pilot programs to determine the feasibility and potential effectiveness of such mandates to full guarantees of credit in specific and/or prescribed curricula, and annual tracking and reporting of student participation and success in the programs.

Campus personnel who work with both sending and receiving transfer students, curriculum development initiatives, and academic policies certainly need to be aware of these legislative initiatives and the updates that may occur. More importantly, they must be clear as to the intent and interpretation of the details and nuances of the conditions included in them vis-à-vis their own institutional policies and practices in order for students to be most successful. Some institutions maintain articulation offices that provide a centralized communication link with other institutions to facilitate compliance with legislated initiatives.

### Transfer Websites

National, regional, and statewide resources have been created as means for potential transfer students to review their course acceptability and, in some cases, their applicability to multiple institutions they are considering. Examples of course equivalency databases, statewide articulation agreements, common core curricula, and common course numbering systems are described below.

*College Source Online, Inc.* The Transfer Evaluation System component of this service is the most ambitious of these resources available. Transfer students at subscriber institutions are able to seek assistance from an academic advisor to identify course acceptability at hundreds of institutions across the country.

*u.select.* Formerly known as the Course Applicability System (CAS), this online resource includes course equivalencies between and among hundreds of institutions in 14 states across the country. Students can create free accounts and access the member schools to determine the course acceptability and applicability of the courses they have completed and/or might plan to take. Individualized modifications and enhancements can also be made by participating states.

*State initiatives.* Many states, often as part of the legislation enacted, have comprehensive resources available for transfer students within their state systems. Most of these state resources include complete course equivalency databases. Others have more comprehensive information relating to admission criteria; academic programs; financial guidance; available student services; user chat groups; and other transfer tools and services that assist students, administrators, and faculty in developing a productive and seamless transfer process. For example, Minnesota Transfer and AZ Transfer are online resources that include separate links to comprehensive sets of information, including course equivalencies through u.select for students, transfer specialists (advisors), and educators (administrators of transfer programs). NJ Transfer also has separate links for students and parents and for educators, which contain a database of course equivalencies and program articulations within the state. PA TRAC (the Pennsylvania Transfer and Articulation Center) is maintained through an outside provider (AcademyOne, Inc.) and includes links for students, faculty, and administrators to be able to manage the transfer process more efficiently.

## Community College Initiatives

### Adopting a Philosophy of Transfer

Prior to planning any specific transitional program at a sending institution, there must be an underlying philosophy that includes the possibility of transfer for each enrolled student. Every academic advising and career counseling session should be conducted mindfully, understanding any student attending a community college may someday decide to transfer and pursue a bachelor's degree. The most important community college initiative is to adopt this philosophy and incorporate it into conversations with students during their first year.

The philosophy is best illustrated through the selection and completion of general education coursework. In some occupational degrees, technical writing and math classes that may not transfer are sufficient for the general education requirements of a program. When transferable English and math credits can be used in the occupational program, the student is making a future investment by selecting courses that definitely apply, perhaps at a later date, to the general education requirements of a baccalaureate program. Skilled academic advisors and counselors play a key role in presenting these options and strategies to students.

Using the philosophy of transfer, effective programming for first-year community college students geared toward preparing them for transfer needs to be developed. Many entering community college students may require assistance in understanding a large university structure, in becoming familiar with the various colleges and schools within that structure, in discovering which programs and degrees are offered, and where key resources are located. They may also need to know about their options regarding smaller colleges, public and private, and the other avenues open to them for a bachelor's degree. This is particularly true for first-generation college students, who may lack the familial and social network connections to make them aware of these options. Information about a range of transfer options can be provided in initial advising sessions or in a more formal setting, such as orientation.

*Designing Initiatives*

Once community colleges adopt a philosophy of transfer and commit to using skilled transfer counselors, additional initiatives should be created, such as orientations, workshops, and classes. Ideally, most students entering the community college will attend a new student orientation session, preferably a traditional in-person event or, at a minimum, the more recent and convenient online variety. Creating a specialized orientation designed to address the needs of students planning to transfer and earn bachelor's degrees is an economical method of introducing general transfer information. Such an orientation can focus on the selection of general education coursework for typical bachelor's degree pathways, popular transfer institutions and programs in the area, articulation agreements, and all of the transfer resources available to students, including how to select a major. Such an orientation has the potential to create learning communities because many students will find themselves enrolling in the same sections of general education classes. By providing this level of service, students often leave the orientation program with clear direction and a degree plan.

Many community colleges also provide some sort of electronic degree evaluation for students. Curriculum, Advising and Program Planning (CAPP) and Degree Audit Reporting System (DARS) are two popular examples used with the Banner and PeopleSoft student information systems, respectively. Electronic degree evaluators create reports that compare a student's academic history to the requirements of a selected degree program and identify courses needed to complete the program. These systems typically include what-if scenarios, allowing students to apply their completed coursework to different majors and view their progress made toward degrees in those fields. Yet, electronic degree audit systems may only be used for what-if scenarios when the community college degrees are articulated with the four-year institution, either course to course or as a block. While electronic degree evaluations can be used for any degree or certificate program at a community college, they are particularly helpful in supporting undecided transfer students who have accumulated general education and liberal arts credits.

In an effort to reduce the number of undecided transfer students, Pima Community College (Tucson, AZ) developed the University Transfer Preparation (STU107) course, one of several

Student Success (STU) courses available districtwide. It is a one-credit, elective course that transfers to all three state universities. Components of the course include clarification of degree and major based on career and academic interests; introduction to and utilization of transfer resources, financial resources, and college payment plans; and general transition planning.

Assignments in STU107 typically include taking an interest inventory, a personality test, and a values assessment in order to select a compatible program of study. Students research and explore possible connections between majors and careers by collecting and organizing pertinent information. They also develop a financial plan to pay for college, beginning with estimating the complete cost of attendance, identifying the financial resources they have, and creating strategies to acquire what they will need.

Additionally, students complete exercises demonstrating their competency with the electronic transfer resources found at AZTransfer.com and use the college website to develop their academic plan. Many assignments can be completed in small groups, giving students the opportunity to work together, form small communities, and carry connections into the next term.

Any community college with a significant number of undecided transfer students can benefit by offering a course like STU107. Pima Community College provides a second course to transfer students typically taken during their last semester. Information about this course is found in the section on cooperative efforts.

## Four-Year College Initiatives

No matter how well the sender has prepared its students for the transition, if the receiving institution is not well prepared, the process may be subject to failure. Perhaps one of the reasons why four-year institutions have not systematically addressed the needs of transfer students is that this rapidly growing population has been ignored in the institutional success criteria that matter to administrators and legislators and, ultimately, in the public perception of the quality of institutions. The primary criterion that has driven institutional efforts is the college ratings systems, such as those published in *U.S. News and World Report*. These perceptions, other rankings, and even funding formulas are primarily based on the entry characteristics (e.g., ACT, SAT scores), the third-semester persistence rates, and the six-year graduation rates of first-time, full-time, first-year students. Transfer students are excluded from these ratings; they simply do not matter.

One new effort, the Access to Success Initiative (A2S), may be paving the way to remedy this exclusion in the future. Under the auspices of the National Association of System Heads (NASH) and supported by The Education Trust, 24 public college systems have proposed that the calculation of graduation rates begin to include part-time and transfer students within each state system of higher education. It is estimated that graduation rates now based only on cohorts of first-time, full-time students would nearly double under this formula (Engle & Lynch, 2009). Implications for state funding could also result, and efforts to recruit, retain, and graduate transfer students would become much more meaningful. Transfer students would matter.

Clearly, individual institutions have developed programs and initiatives that ease the transitions for their transfer student populations. Every institution needs to examine the best practices that are available and adapt them in order to provide their own transfer populations the best opportunities for success—at least the same graduation (rate) that is so carefully monitored for first-year cohorts.

## Pretransfer Initiatives

There are a few common efforts made by institutions that serve potential transfer students prior to their actual transfer. These initiatives also better equip institutions to facilitate the transfer for incoming transfer students.

*Maintenance of databases and articulation agreements.* These two types of enhancements are most likely to facilitate the academic course and program aspect of the transfer process, at least on the macro level. However, they are only as effective as they are current and updated or revised. This is no easy task since the databases frequently extend to multiple institutions, especially within states, and new courses, programs, and curricula are constantly being created or modified. Nevertheless, such ongoing updating is necessary in order for the transfer of academic credit to occur seamlessly.

*Outreach efforts.* The easiest and most obvious way to connect with potential transfer students is through electronic means (i.e., the Internet). Applications, frequently asked questions (FAQs), key contact personnel, and even orientation programs for transfer students are included on many institutional websites. Since these are available 24/7, a specific site for transfer students is one of the best ways to introduce, inform, and include new transfer students in the transition process.

Another common outreach effort, especially when nearby or primary feeder community colleges send a substantial number of their students to a local four-year institution, is the onsite visit at the community college. Admissions personnel normally conduct these visits, but many also include academic advisors, who help provide the prospective student with a more specific analysis of how their credits will transfer and what they will need in order to complete their bachelor's degree. A critical feature in this effort is the ability to specify or recommend preferred electives to students—that is, courses that would serve the student better in the context of his or her intended four-year program.

Other campus personnel are sometimes included in these site visits as well, such as residential life, financial aid, and student activities staff. Perhaps the most important people to include are students who have already made the transition between the two schools.

*Onsite initiatives.* Most four-year institutions host a series of open houses for potential new students, but these normally target high school students. Although transfer students are rarely excluded from these events, neither are they specifically invited. Transfer Days demonstrate to potential transfer students the importance and uniqueness they bring to the institution. These can be offered prior to the student's application, such as Instant Decision or Early Admit programs, or after the student has been admitted, but has not yet committed to attend.

*Financial aid.* Most students transferring from community colleges realize that the costs of attending a four-year school will be higher. What they may not know, however, are the specific required policies and procedures or the opportunities that may be available to them. This information can be offered via the Internet, community college visits, or open houses, but it definitely needs to be provided in a systematic way. Although it is yet another way in which transfer students tend to be neglected, scholarships that are specifically made available to this population need to be publicized. If they do not exist, institutions should endeavor to develop them.

## Posttransfer Initiatives

Once transfer students have made the commitment to attend their new institution, any number of efforts might ensue. Since not all transfer students come from the community colleges, the following initiatives would benefit all transfer students.

*Orientation programs.* Most institutions have some type of orientation program, including registration, for new transfer students. However, the extent of these efforts is often diminished from what first-year students receive. New transfer students need to be as fully informed about the campus as new first-year students. Providing anything less is a disservice to a group of students who pay the same tuition and fees as first-year students.

Part of this deficiency results from certain assumptions that both students and institutions make in this process. Since transfer students have already been in college, they may assume that things will essentially operate in the same manner as they did at their former institutions and that they do not need as much, if any, orientation to the new institution. Similarly, orientation planners often feel that these are experienced college students and, therefore, need less orientation to the campuses. Also, staff tend to plan programs as though all transfer students have the same needs, skills, and expectations. These assumptions are fraught with inaccuracies and undocumented generalizations.

One way to curtail some of these assumptions is to develop an online pre-orientation module for transfer students. In developing such a module, campus staff can use the real-time information students are providing as they complete the program to address any preconceived or inaccurate beliefs held about transfer students. The module can also be used to inform new students about the purpose and value of orientation.

*Additional orientation efforts.* Once they are on campus, transfer students may lack the confidence needed to become part of their new institution. They observe that everyone else seems to know what to do, where to go, and who to see. Thus, they may be less likely to become engaged in the milieu of the institution (Thurmond, 2007).

Specific programs for these students can help alleviate preconceived notions, fears, and uncertainties they may have. Transfer Fairs where the membership and active participation of new transfer students is sought, small-group meals and other social events, group discounts for tickets to athletic or theatrical events, and other give-away efforts are some of the ways to inform these students of the opportunities available and engage them in the campus.

*Peer mentors.* Currently enrolled transfer students who are satisfied with their experiences on a campus are the best ambassadors and advocates for new and potential students. If each new transfer student were assigned or paired with a current transfer student as a mentor, the new student would be more likely to have a positive experience. Since many transfer students are commuters, formal meeting times may be difficult, but phone and e-mail contacts can be readily established. This approach can be especially effective for community college transfers, since they often attend schools in the local area and where a substantial number of students from the same institution probably already attend. Each mentor might be responsible for 5-10 new students, thus increasing the potential to reach all new transfers every term.

*Academic advising and other support personnel.* Perhaps the most important person for the new transfer student on a new campus is an academic advisor or a counselor who is especially skilled in working with transfer students. The academic advisor typically has a broad knowledge of the institution, but advisors who work with transfer students should periodically review and update their knowledge in all areas that affect new transfers. They also need to be engaged in planning activities for new transfer students.

A relatively new type of support position is the transition facilitator. In 2007, the University of Arizona (UA) and Pima Community College jointly launched the Transition Facilitator Program to enhance the retention and four-year degree completion for all transfer students attending UA. The facilitator is a Pima Community College counselor, housed at the UA campus, to assist transfer students in their transition to the university and also to support university students taking classes at Pima. The facilitator helps connect students to academic advisors, tutoring services, career services, the university learning center, and other student support services.

*The transfer student seminar.* The best way to assist transfer students in their transition to a new environment is in a more systematic, ongoing, and sustained way. The classroom format (i.e., a course) provides the optimal opportunity to deliver such an effort through a variety of possible strategies. For example, GSS 2642 Contemporary American Education is a course in the general studies curriculum at Richard Stockton College of New Jersey (Pomona, NJ). The four-credit class is elective and examines current issues in K-12 and higher education. The unique feature is that only new transfer students are permitted to enroll. Students are required to complete six to seven short writing assignments, several of which require them to engage in the campus in some way; a group and an individual research project; and a final paper. By having only new transfers in the course, students quickly and naturally form a network and support group among themselves. They, in fact, become a learning community.

This course-based approach can be adapted in any discipline at any institution and without additional curricular approvals. Costs are minimal when using existing courses/sections, although additional expenses would be incurred if new sections must be added. To date, approximately 20 different courses have been adapted for this effort at Stockton, with three to six offerings each semester. Different delivery models for such courses are used at Rutgers University (New Brunswick, NJ), the University of Maryland at Baltimore County, the University of Oregon (Eugene, OR), SUNY – Stonybrook, the University of Southern Mississippi (Hattiesburg, MS), Limestone College (Gaffney, SC), and others.

It is critical to the success of transfer students, especially those from the community colleges, that their transition be as smooth, seamless, and supportive as possible. Initiatives at four-year institutions need to become a regular part of the transfer process.

## Cooperative Initiatives

Clearly, the transition between institutions is most seamless and productive when the institutions make intentional efforts to support transition. Some of these efforts are described in greater detail below.

### *Degree Completion Program (One Site)*

This type of cooperative effort has grown significantly in the last decade. Community college students complete an associate degree and remain at the same campus location to complete a bachelor's degree offered by a (relatively) local four-year institution. The proliferation of online course delivery has enabled students to complete their degrees in much more convenient ways, especially where time, distance, employment, and personal circumstances might otherwise prevent this achievement. One-site initiatives include very specifically articulated degree programs (e.g., business administration, criminal justice, social work) offered by both the community college and the four-year institution and/or very generic degree programs (e.g., self-designed interdisciplinary studies, humanities, behavioral sciences). Whatever the degree program, however, there are advantages and disadvantages to such arrangements.

Clearly, the largest advantage to the student in such programs is the ability to complete a four-year degree program at times and at a place that is much more convenient to their personal lives. Other advantages include decreased time and expense of travel, reduced need for temporary residential accommodations, guaranteed transfer of credit, and a limited disruption of lifestyle. Working parents, adults returning to complete their degrees after long interruptions, and even the more traditional college students take advantage of these opportunities.

Certain disadvantages might also exist, notably in the overall quality of the degree and experience. For example, many of the courses provided in these programs are more likely to be taught by adjunct faculty. There is no inherent deficiency in adjunct faculty, but if the students never have face-to-face contact with a regular faulty member from the degree-granting institution, something is lost.

Also, the courses made available to students in these programs are considerably limited. Students are able to enroll only in those courses (and degree programs) that the four-year institution provides, either online or face-to-face. They will not have the opportunity to choose from among the same variety of options they would likely have if they were enrolled on the four-year campus. Such limitations can diminish the breadth (and depth in some cases) of what the on-campus option provides.

Further, the campus experience is sacrificed. Not every student who takes advantage of these programs would join a sorority, or perform in a play, or become president of the student senate, but not having exposure to these opportunities limits the overall value of what the four-year institution provides. Students may also lose the opportunity for informal conversations with peers and faculty, which can enhance the classroom learning experience.

The more recent iteration of the single site option is not really cooperative per se in that the community college actually provides and awards the baccalaureate degree. Russell (2010) reported that 465 such degree programs are offered in 54 different institutions across 18 states. These programs are primarily approved in particular geographic areas (usually rural) and in high-demand fields, such as nursing, education, and specialized technologies.

## Degree Completion Programs (Multiple Sites)

The development of articulation agreements has proliferated over the last several decades. These agreements were often conceived as the panacea for ensuring the transfer of credit (or at least preventing the loss of it), especially before legislatures began regulating the transfer process. The most common form of agreement is the simple one-to-one, course-to-course set of equivalencies from one institution to another. This form of articulation increased significantly when computer databases were able to store large volumes of information and to provide easy update capabilities.

Another form of articulation is the institution-to-institution agreement in which common sets of curricular requirements are agreed to have been fulfilled under certain conditions managed between the institutions. One type of articulation that has gained acceptance in some states is that of common course numbering, where all similarly titled courses are assigned the exact same course number at each institution participating in the agreement.

Probably the most effective type of articulation agreement is between specific academic programs. The faculty of a sending institution consults with the faculty of the receiving institution, and the two plan (and agree) that the completion of certain courses and experiences at the first institution will fulfill certain requirements at the second. In Arizona, for example, discipline-specific Articulation Task Forces (ATFs) provide institutions with a forum to exchange articulation information in a timely and cooperative manner in order to participate in the Arizona transfer support systems (AZTransfer.com). Designated faculty members represent their institutions and specific academic areas to discuss course competencies. These community college and university faculty realize they share the same goals and have the same expectations for their students, allowing cross-institutional collegiality to develop.

The proliferation of articulation agreements, however, might not always produce the desired effects. Grites (2004) argued that some of these pacts might be overrated since they often limit the goals of general education, are not systematically reviewed for their effectiveness, and are too often simply used for recruitment and public relations reasons. Further, Anderson, Sun, and Alfonso (2006) found no significant differences in transfer rates in states that had mandated articulation agreements. Rather, they found that students whose aspirations were to acquire a bachelor's degree, who were dependent on parental income, and who were enrolled full-time were more likely to transfer, irrespective of mandated articulation agreements in their states.

More recently, Smith, Miller, and Bermeo (2009) reported that a structured academic pathway, including articulation agreements, was one of three common characteristics among six Texas community colleges that produced higher than expected transfer rates. Other characteristics were a student-centered campus culture that focused on transfer through its support services, flexible scheduling, and culturally sensitive leadership.

Well-planned articulation efforts between and among institutions can be very effective and efficient. When all transfer elements are in place, understood, advocated, and implemented, the seamless transfer process need not be so elusive. One example of this effort exists in Arizona, where three levels of transfer and articulation occur.

◇ *Level 1: Two-tiered building block concept.* The first tier includes completion of one of three prescribed Arizona General Education Curricula (AGEC), and the second tier consists of additional transferable courses that enable students to graduate with their choice of associate degrees.
◇ *Level 2: Between institutions.* Pima Community College and Arizona State University employ a Transfer Admission Guarantee (TAG), which includes admission, curriculum articulation, and potential tuition incentives.
◇ *Level 3: In the classroom.* The third level occurs in the two-credit, transferable Transfer Strategies course, which includes discussion and use of college or university resources, transition procedures and policies, completion of applications, and participation in other transfer activities that lead to a detailed academic plan. Several class meetings are held at the university where students meet representatives from dozens of student support offices, ranging from parking and transportation to career services. A campus tour, led by student ambassadors, is always included. The course provides more in-depth knowledge than students typically receive in an orientation, thereby, greatly reducing their transfer shock.

## Initiatives to Assess Transfer Programs and Services

With the multiple student characteristics and programmatic options presented here, each institution needs to determine which combinations of programs and services will result in the highest levels of student success on its own unique campus. Regular assessments of current programs and predicted outcomes of anticipated changes should be well documented.

### Pretransfer Initiatives

The ability to predict which students will transfer, and exactly when they might do so, is much greater for community college students. Community colleges would do well to assess the effectiveness of their orientations, workshops, courses, and services offered to their transfer students. Retention and graduation data of students in transfer degree programs would also prove useful. Because these students will most likely transfer to four-year institutions within a fairly close geographical area, four-year institutions should know all they can about them in order to prepare the best programs to ensure their continuing success. This can be achieved in two ways.

*Review articulation agreements.* These agreements can be very effective when exercised with their fullest intent and potential. Too often, however, agreements are developed, signed, and publicized, but not regularly reviewed for their effectiveness. It is incumbent upon both institutions that enter into an agreement to review periodically the number of students who actually enroll under the conditions of the agreement and their subsequent successes.

*Know who the transfer students really are.* Not all transfer students are alike; in fact, there is likely a much larger diversity in an institution's new transfer population than in its first-year students, both in the variety of institutions from which they transferred and reasons for their transfer. Few assumptions can be made about all transfer students, so careful analyses need to be made to identify what each entering transfer student brings to the new campus.

### Posttransfer Initiatives

Once transfer students have committed to an institution, it becomes important to know what actually leads to academic success and persistence to a degree. Again, few generalizations can be made as to what will work for this diverse population. Some areas that should routinely be examined are described here.

*Orientation efforts.* The most common transition program for transfer students is a single orientation program, which can range from a limited individual appointment to a full-day academic and social program. The most common assessment strategy is the satisfaction survey, but focus groups or end-of-term surveys might also be considered. Whatever formats are used, some systematic review of its effectiveness is necessary.

*Retention and graduation data.* As noted earlier, these institutional data are rarely collected on transfer students by four-year institutions, typically because the data are not normally included in the required external statistical reports. However, nearly 60% of all students in the United States are transfers, and nearly 75% of all who graduate each year have some transfer credit (Adelman, 2006). These figures alone should demonstrate the value of collecting these data at the institutional level.

Additionally, community college transfer students normally have completed many of their general education and lower-level course requirements, which enable them to enroll in upper-level courses. The retention and graduation of transfer students is as important to the vitality of an institution as of those who start their college careers at the same institution.

Efforts to gather retention and graduation data on transfer students in the same ways as with first-year students may benefit four-year institutions, if they use these data to improve programs and services. Knowledge of such success by community college personnel can be important to planning the successful transfer of future students.

*Progress data.* Other means of determining whether transfer students are successful between admission and graduation are also possible and reflect what many institutions already do for first-year students, namely, reviewing four-, five- and especially six-year graduation rates. This is an assessment of students' length of time to earn a four-year degree. Similarly, two- and three-year graduation rates are being used to determine the success of community colleges. This time-to-degree factor is being more closely monitored and more strongly advocated by many state legislatures as a means to exercise fiscal responsibility. This factor should be calculated for cohorts of new transfer students to determine what conditions might foster (or prohibit) a logical time-to-degree for transfer students. Community college personnel could also review these data to determine conditions that might facilitate their own improved graduation rates.

*Major changes.* One way four-year institutions can assess the compatibility of their transfer students with their own academic programs is to monitor the number of changes of major that students enact, along with the rationale or need for the change. Such information can highlight the necessity for clearer expectations with respect to rigor, the need for course availability and sequencing, and potential career outlooks for both two- and four-year institutions.

*Engagement.* Two popular assessment measures used by two- and four-year institutions are the Community College Survey of Student Engagement (CCSSE) and the National Survey of Student Engagement (NSSE). These tools are intended to assist institutions in learning how well their students are involved academically and socially in the institution. The most recent results and analyses (Terris, 2009) indicate that transfer students are less likely to take part in high-impact activities, such as participation in study abroad, internships, research with faculty, and senior capstone experiences. Specifically, those who transfer vertically (i.e., community colleges to four-year institutions) are even less likely than those who transfer horizontally (i.e., four-year to other four-year institutions).

Of even greater concern is that, while beginning community college students reported that they felt welcome, they did not always receive information critical to their success and/or have opportunities to outline their academic goals. Further, within the first three weeks of classes, they tended to lapse into risky academic behaviors, such as not using campus resources outside the classroom and submitting assignments late or not at all (Moltz, 2010). Furthermore, the Center for Community College Student Engagement (2010) reported that community college students tended not to be engaged in deep learning that would promote broadly applicable higher level cognitive skills. Creating more intentional engagement strategies needs to be a priority for these students in order to prepare them for success as fully and as quickly as possible.

Finally, exit surveys of transfer students can provide another dimension of assessment regarding the quality of the transfer process at both two- and four-year institutions. Irrespective of the reason for leaving (e.g., withdrawal, dismissal, another transfer, or graduation), such data can inform both sending and receiving institutions and future transfer students of the experiences they are likely to have.

Assessment is the pervasive process driving much of what institutions do to improve their status, their enrollment, their financial stability, and the quality of their enterprise. To neglect or minimize the value that transfer students add to these overall dimensions weakens the institution as a whole. Since most college students will be transfer students at some point, assessment efforts need to be honed to capitalize on the merits of this growing population.

## Conclusion and Recommendations

The next steps in attempting to plan for the future of the transfer process will not be easy, since the economic conditions in higher education are anything but stable. State funding is dwindling for public institutions, yet demand for enrollments continues to grow. The demand is even more evident in the traditionally open-door community colleges. Therefore both two- and four-year institutions need to plan more intentionally how they will attempt to meet these enrollment demands and expectations and still provide the best environment for the quality education and success of their transfer students. To that end, we offer a few suggestions.

### Improve Data-Driven Decision Making

The systematic and inclusive collection of data about transfer students must begin at all levels. Although certain efforts have been suggested on a national level (e.g., a student unit record system), and many states collect and use data on a statewide basis, the information about transfer students that is collected and used by individual institutions, beyond what is required, is minimal. As with any assessment effort, the purpose of such data should always be for the quality improvement of programs and services that enable transfer students to achieve at their highest levels. If institutions want to improve their images and increase their transfer enrollments and the overall success of these students, they need to create and foster positive elements throughout the transfer process. By assessing the current status of the transfer process, they will be better able to meet the coming enrollment demands in ways that are most productive.

A broad set of examples of community colleges that have begun such efforts is reported by the Center for Community College Engagement (2009a; 2009b; 2010). The key element in these reports is that of building connections—among all administrators, faculty, and staff and with other students. Specific efforts highlighted in the institutional programs include required orientation courses, mentoring programs, use of social networking, online learning options, and highly engaged classroom environments.

## Extend Orientation Programs

The transfer shock phenomenon need not be as dramatic as it seems. The transition from one institution to another must be as seamless as possible not only in the transfer of credits, but also in the social aspects of transfer. For community college transfers, this transition should begin prior to the actual physical presence on the new campus. Yet, it is in the four-year (receiving) institution that these efforts need to be addressed more directly and with greater emphasis.

Receiving institutions should examine their transfer orientation and transition programs, especially as they compare to those provided for first-year students. The latter often extend over several days, have entire staffs dedicated to planning and implementing them, include faculty mentors, require specific transition courses (e.g., first-year seminars), and generally allocate a much larger budget to accommodate this new student population. These efforts continue to dominate the first-year student population, in spite of the fact that historically 25-30% of these students leave their institutions before beginning their second year (ACT, 2010).

Any of the models described above could be considered to improve the transition of transfer students, but we clearly advocate for the course-based approach, at both two- and four-year institutions. A sustained effort over an extended period of time prepares each new transfer student to adjust to the new environment as confidently as new first-year students.

## Examine Transfer Policies

Most academic curricula and policies are designed with first-year students in mind. However, certain aspects of some policies and/or procedures might actually have an adverse effect on the ultimate success of an institution's transfer student population and should be reviewed periodically for their accuracy and effectiveness. Do the articulation agreements allow for flexible course selection and scheduling? Are there appeals processes in place to provide responses in a timely manner? Are the registration priorities equitable for transfer students? Are transfer students eligible for honors courses, programs, and awards? Do student clubs and organizations actively recruit transfer students or allow them to participate prior to transfer? Are any of the credit acceptance policies arbitrary, or have they been documented as fulfilling the expectations that are assumed? Are prerequisite courses actually fulfilling the competency expectations for which they are intended? Are these questions being asked on the two-year campus in order to prepare students for a successful transition? These and other questions need to be reviewed for every policy that is already in place or being developed so that transfer students have the equivalent opportunities and support for their success as native students.

*Promote a Culture of Transfer*

Adelman (2008a, 2008b) argued for institutions to develop and foster a culture of transfer in order to accommodate transfer students into their new environment more successfully. Unless all constituents of the institution are committed to this concept these students will be more prone to a lack of integration, engagement, and the fulfillment of their greatest potential.

Administrators, faculty, academic advisors, student development personnel, and career counselors must become aware of the needs and expectations of transfer students. They should extend their programs, services, and resources to transfer students to achieve the same outcomes targeted for first-year students—confidence, a sense of welcome and comfort, and academic and personal success.

## References

ACT, Inc. (2010). *2010 retention/completion summary tables*. Retrieved November 21, 2010 from http://www.act.org/research/policymakers/pdf/09retain_trends.pdf

Adelman, C. (2006). *The toolbox revisited: Paths to degree completion from high school through college*. Washington, DC: U.S. Department of Education.

Adelman, C. (2008a, February). *Transfer success summit 2008*. Summit conducted by the Texas Higher Education Coordinating Board, Austin, TX. Retrieved from http://www.thecb.state.tx.us/index.cfm?objectid=803A288A-B1CC-E2F6-81169752912BB0B1

Adelman, C. (2008b, February). *Turning nomads into transfers*. Presentation at the AACRAO Transfer Conference, Washington, DC. Retrieved from http://www.aacrao.org/transfer/Cliff_Adelman.pdf

Anderson, G., Sun, J., & Alfonso, M. (2006). Effectiveness of statewide articulation agreements on the probability of transfer: A preliminary policy analysis. *The Review of Higher Education, 29*(3), 261-291.

Bailey, D. S. (2003, December). "Swirling" changes to the traditional student path. *Monitor on Psychology, 34(*11), 36. Retrieved from http://www.apa.org/monitor/dec03/swirling.aspx

Center for Community College Student Engagement. (2009a). *Making connections: Dimensions of student engagement* (2009 CCSSE findings). Austin, TX: The University of Texas at Austin, Community College Leadership Program.

Center for Community College Student Engagement. (2009b). *Benchmarking & benchmarks: Effective practice with entering students*. Austin, TX: The University of Texas at Austin, Community College Leadership Program.

Center for Community College Student Engagement. (2010). *The heart of student success: Teaching, learning, and college completion* (2010 CCCSE findings). Austin, TX: The University of Texas at Austin, Community College Leadership Program.

Cox, R. D. (2009). *The college fear factor: How students and professors misunderstand one another*. Cambridge, MA: Harvard University Press.

Education Commission of the States. (2001). *Transfer and articulation policies* (Policy paper). Retrieved November 7, 2009, from http://www.ecs.org/ecsmain.asp?page=%2Fhtml%2FIssuesbyLetter%2Easp%3Fs%3Dg%26e%3Dz%26l%3Dp

Education Commission of the States. (2009). *Recent state policies/activities* (Policy paper). Retrieved November 7, 2009, from http://www.ecs.org/ecs/ecscat.nsf/WebTopicPS?OpenView&Count=-1&RestrictToCategory=Transfer/Articulation

Engle, J., & Lynch, M. (2009). *Charting a necessary path: The baseline report of the Access to Success Initiative*. Washington, DC: National Association of System Heads and The Education Trust.

Grites, T. J. (2004). Redefining the role: Reflections and directions. In T. J. Kerr, M. C. King, & T. J. Grites (Eds.), *Advising transfer students: Issues and strategies* (Monograph No. 12, pp. 123-132). Manhattan, KS: Kansas State University, National Academic Advising Association.

Moltz, D. (2010, March 29). Missed connections. *Inside Higher Ed.* Retrieved from http://www. insidehighered.com/news/2010/03/29/sense

Mullin, C. M., & Phillippe, K. (2009). *Community college enrollment surge: An analysis of estimated fall 2009 headcount enrollments at community colleges* (American Association of Community Colleges, Policy Brief 2009-01PBL). Washington, DC: American Association of Community Colleges.

Rewey, K. L. (1998). Transfer shock in an academic discipline: The relationship between students' majors and their academic performance. *Community College Review, 65,* 1-13. Retrieved from http://www.thefreelibrary.com/Transfer+Shock+in+an+Academic+Discipline%3a+The+R elationship+between+...-a063323085

Russell, A. (2010, October). Update on the community college baccalaureate: Evolving trends and issues. *Policy Matters.* Retrieved from the AASCU website http://www.congressweb. com/aascu/startpage.htm

Smith, C. T., Miller, A., & Bermeo, C. A. (2009). *Bridging the gaps to success—promising practices for promoting transfer among low-income and first-generation students: An in-depth study of six exemplary community colleges in Texas.* Washington, DC: The Pell Institute for the Study of Opportunity in Higher Education. Retrieved from http://www.pellinstitute.org/pdf/ COE_Pell_Report_layout_3.pdf

Terris, B. (2009, November 8). Transfer students are less likely to take part in "high impact" activities. *The Chronicle of Higher Education.* Retrieved from http://chronicle.com/article/ Transfer-Students-Are-Less-/49070/

Thurmond, K.C. (2007). *Transfer shock: Why is a term forty years old still relevant?* Retrieved from NACADA Clearinghouse of Academic Advising Resources website: http://www.nacada.ksu. edu/Clearinghouse/AdvisingIssues/Transfer-Shock.htm

# PART III:

A Comprehensive
First-Year Experience
in the Community
College

# Chapter 7

## Building Paths to Student Success:  Planning and Implementing for Effective Student Transition

Betsy O. Barefoot, Paul Arcario, and Ana Guzman

Throughout 2009 and 2010, headlines from newspapers across the nation reported local and regional variations of the same basic theme: Community colleges are bursting at the seams. The college that was once the safety net, the Plan B institution for many students has suddenly become Plan A. The reasons are primarily economic:  The American community college is the best educational bargain available. Community colleges also offer convenience and promise an outstanding quality of teaching delivered in small classes. There is every reason to believe that increasing numbers of students from all age categories and socioeconomic strata will continue to choose the community college as the ideal place to begin higher education. In addition, democracy's colleges, as two-year public institutions are aptly known, have also gained the attention of federal policy makers. The ideal of increasing the educational attainment rates of students across the nation is, more than ever, dependent on a strong community college system.

The attention and notoriety community colleges are receiving focus a public spotlight on the colleges themselves and the degree to which they are currently meeting the needs of entering students. In a two-year, open-admissions educational environment that is often a revolving door for many students, the difficulties of implementing successful transition programs are legion.

The purpose of this chapter is to explore both the challenges and opportunities for community colleges in designing and implementing successful new student transition programs. The chapter opens with a discussion of common issues these colleges face in ensuring effective student transitions, and the most frequently used types of transition programs:  preterm orientation and first-year seminars. Institutional case studies of successful transition initiatives at LaGuardia Community College in Queens, New York, and Palo Alto College in San Antonio, Texas, are the centerpiece of the chapter. Both colleges have designed unique first-year programs that meet their students' particular needs. The chapter concludes with a synthesis of lessons learned and recommendations for others who are working to help new students make the right start toward academic and personal success.

### Challenges to Successful Transition Programming

An initial challenge faced by community colleges is that the vast majority of their students are commuters; therefore, their time on campus is limited. Finding opportunities for face-to-face communication between faculty, staff, and students is so difficult that many community colleges have resorted to online placement, orientation, advising, and registration. Whether online methods support, or are barriers to, successful transition is an open question. But the sheer numbers of students entering two-year public institutions will likely result in more, not fewer, online initiatives in the near future.

Another concern is that many community college students leave well before the end of the first semester. Scholars at the University of Texas's Community College Leadership Program are focusing their attention on students' earliest transition experiences (i.e., what happens in the first three weeks) because of this phenomenon of early departure from college. Through the Survey of Entering Student Engagement (SENSE), campuses are encouraged to evaluate students' perceptions of preterm orientation, intake processes, and initial classroom experiences in an attempt to understand why many students leave almost as soon as they start (Center for Community College Engagement, 2008).

As community colleges enroll students across a wide spectrum of age and academic abilities, the colleges must also find a way to determine which students need particular kinds of assistance. Some students might need only to learn their way around campus. Others might benefit from a brush-up workshop in math or English. Many students benefit from extended orientation in the form of a first-year seminar or college success course that focuses not only on general topics, such as study skills or time management, but also on self-esteem and awareness of personal strengths. Still others need far more academic assistance in the form of developmental or remedial coursework. Students who begin their college experience in developmental education present a special transition challenge: They often have difficulty maintaining their interest and academic momentum when the dream of being a "real" college student seems so far away. The range of students attending community colleges and the issues they present mean that a one-size-fits-all approach to transition programming is almost never sufficient.

As there is no way to generalize about needs of community college students, so there is also the related challenge of determining the specific mix of transition programs that is most cost-effective. While some public two-year institutions have sufficient resources to offer multiple best-practice initiatives for new students, others will select one or two initiatives as their focus, the most common being preterm orientation sessions delivered face-to-face and/or online and first-year seminars.

## Preterm Orientation

Although the overwhelming majority of two-year institutions offer some sort of preterm orientation, designing on-campus programs that students will attend and value is a significant challenge. Many two-year campuses long ago abandoned a full-day or several-day orientation sessions in favor of one that lasts only a few hours (Policy Center on the First Year of College, 2000). In spite of strong recommendations from community college researchers and practitioners for required orientation (McClenney & McClenney, 2007), only about 50% of community colleges currently have such a requirement (Policy Center, 2000). Findings from the 2008 SENSE suggest that community college students "consistently recommend mandatory orientation . . . but their comments are retrospective. They understand the value of orientation long after the useful time to participate in it has passed" (Center for Community College Engagement, 2008, pp. 9-10). In fact, this 2008 survey finds that "fewer than half of entering [community college] students (44%) attended an on-campus orientation prior to the beginning of classes, and one in five students (21%) report that they were unaware of college orientation" (p. 10). Because of the difficulty in getting students to attend orientation sessions on campus, there has been recent exponential growth in online orientation used either as an alternative or a complement to on-campus orientation activities.

There is no reliable source for information on the number of two-year public institutions that offer online orientation, but anecdotally, providing this option has become common practice.

An ongoing topic of interest and some debate is how the time allocated to orientation, even limited time, should be used—whether it should be devoted to processing students through placement testing or registration or to celebrating students' arrival on campus through convocations; academic activities, such as common readings; and interactions with faculty, staff, and other students. Currently, there is no research-based best way to do orientation, and community colleges find themselves experimenting with various strategies to provide orientation experiences that are an essential part of successful college transition (Lenning, Sauer, & Beal, 1980; Rode, 2000; Mullendore & Banahan, 2005).

## Extended Orientation: The First-Year Seminar or College Success Course

While the majority of community colleges offer one or more first-year seminars or college success courses for some students, fewer than 20% require all students to take such a course (Policy Center, 2002). Often, the first-year seminar at a community college will be designed only for developmental students or those who are part of an Educational Opportunity Program. Generally, these courses place a heavy emphasis on study skills in addition to helping students learn about campus resources, time management, and career exploration. In 45% of community colleges, a first-year seminar carries only one semester or quarter hour of credit; however, three-credit hour seminars are employed at 36% of these institutions (Tobolowsky & Associates, 2008).

On some campuses, first-year seminars are one course of two or three that constitute a learning community. Research conducted in 2002 by the Policy Center on the First Year of College (Swing, 2002) found that students' perceptions of seminar effectiveness on a number of desired outcomes are higher for those seminars that are embedded in learning communities.

A number of institution-specific studies performed at two-year institutions found that students who participated in first-year seminars were more likely to be retained than similar nonparticipants. Some, but not all, studies also found that participants earned higher grades (Barefoot, Warnock, Dickinson, Richardson, & Roberts, 1998; Tobolowsky, Cox, & Wagner, 2005).

In addition to retention and improved grades, first-year seminars can address many other areas of student success. Upcraft, Gardner, and Barefoot (2005) write that student success includes the following eight dimensions: developing academic competence, establishing interpersonal relationships, exploring identity development, deciding on a career, maintaining personal health, considering faith and spirituality, developing multicultural awareness, and understanding civic responsibility. These eight dimensions offer a valuable template for the creation of first-year seminars in the community college.

## Institutional Stories

To put flesh on the bones of this chapter topic—designing effective transition experiences—two community college leaders and practitioners share their stories. Their accounts illuminate inherent challenges and opportunities in creating environments that foster student success in the first year. Paul Arcario works as academic dean at LaGuardia Community College in Queens, New York. LaGuardia enrolls a highly international student body representing diverse academic abilities. LaGuardia's approach to preterm orientation is supplemented by several programs that provide continuing or extended orientation. Ana "Cha" Guzman leads Palo Alto College, a midsized community college in San Antonio, Texas, where the centerpiece of the first year is a first-year seminar specifically designed to meet the needs of Hispanic students, especially women, who constitute the majority of the student population.

## The Transition to College Life at LaGuardia Community College

### The Institution

LaGuardia Community College's mission focuses on providing access to higher education, particularly for traditionally underserved students, and translating that access into success. Located in Queens, the most diverse county in the nation, LaGuardia has been a gateway to college for thousands of students—immigrant, Hispanic and other minorities, low income, and first generation. As one of 17 undergraduate colleges in the City University of New York (CUNY), LaGuardia serves more than 17,000 degree students and more than 65,000 students in noncredit and outreach programs. Among degree students, nearly 60% are immigrants, representing more than 150 countries and speaking 117 different languages. The majority (80%) of degree students are minorities, and 60% are female. About 80% require at least one basic skills course to prepare them to do college-level work (LaGuardia Community College, 2009).

### The Importance of the First-Year Experience

As they begin their first year of college, LaGuardia's students are transitioning across complex and multiple boundaries: immigrant students negotiating a new culture, first-generation college students entering an academic world with unfamiliar norms and expectations, and underprepared students attempting to meet new intellectual challenges. At LaGuardia, first-year transition and orientation are viewed as a process of guiding students in developing key connections during their entire first year. The Opening Sessions orientation program immediately connects students with faculty; the common reading program connects them to the importance of text; learning communities not only create connections among peers, but also enable students to make connections between basic skills courses and courses in their majors; the ePortfolio guides students in seeing the connections between coursework and their broader lives; and a recently developed second-semester career development course connects students' initial aspirations to longer term educational goals and careers.

At the time of this writing, LaGuardia's first-year transition programs are changing. After a program has been in existence for six or seven years, revision is often needed to generate a sense of renewed excitement and commitment. In addition, circumstances change, and what once worked might no longer be as effective. For example, as this chapter later describes, significant increases in new student enrollment over the past few years necessitated rethinking Opening Sessions and the Common Reading, while advances in Web 2.0 technology are enabling the college to envision new ways to create learning communities.

### The First-Year Academies

To create a holistic and comprehensive transition year, LaGuardia needed an umbrella that would help link orientation, student development activities, and curricular offerings. Thus, First-Year Academies were created to focus all aspects of the first-year transition experience around the discipline areas that constitute the college's majors. Incoming students now enter one of three

Academies (i.e., business/technology, allied health/science, and liberal arts). The Academies combine a range of activities including a beginning-of-semester orientation day (Opening Sessions), discipline-specific New Student Seminars, learning communities, a second-semester career development course (Fundamentals of Professional Advancement) offered by the Cooperative Education department, student electronic portfolios (ePortfolios), and discipline-relevant cocurricular activities.

### Opening Sessions and the Common Reading: The Original Model

Students begin their Academy experience a few days before the start of classes at Opening Sessions for New Students, an orientation event collaboratively offered by the Divisions of Academic Affairs and Student Affairs. The Opening Sessions program was created to orient students to the nature of the college experience. To set an academic tone, the event was designed to resemble an academic conference, with a plenary session; faculty-led, small-group seminars to discuss the common reading; and concurrent workshops on topics such as leadership, study skills, communication, student success stories, and diversity. Although some changes have been made in Opening Sessions, students still attend a session with their Academy Coordinators who give students just-in-time information needed to navigate the opening week of the semester and begin the process of introducing students to their discipline areas. As a result, students are able to identify their Academy Coordinator as a go-to resource person for their first year at the college. Academy Coordinators build on the process begun at Opening Sessions by continuing to facilitate connections to the major for first-year students. For example, the health science Academy Coordinator works with nursing faculty to set up Orientation to the Nursing Major workshops for students who are in the preclinical phase of the nursing program in their first year and would otherwise have little contact with the nursing faculty and their intended discipline area.

Opening Sessions was originally designed to include students' first encounter with the common reading, an activity established to create a shared intellectual experience among students and impress upon them the importance of reading as a key to academic success. The common reading, selected by a faculty committee, was distributed free to all incoming students each year. At Opening Sessions, 30-40 faculty volunteered each semester to meet informally with students and discuss the book over lunch. Faculty who have chosen to use the common reading in their classes have had access to a resource website (LaGuardia Community College, 2010a) and study guide with links, resources, and suggested assignments assembled each summer by a paid faculty team. For the 2009-2010 selection, *Dreams From My Father* (Obama, 2004), the site included a number of resources, such as a study guide with discussion, introspection, and research questions.

LaGuardia also has held an annual series of events related to the common reading for both students and faculty. For example, in 2009-2010, the Office of Student Life hosted a Global Conversation in which students and staff listened to, discussed, and analyzed two speeches on international topics given by President Obama.

Survey evaluations of Opening Sessions indicate that students find the day valuable. For the fall 2009 event, 90% responded yes when asked, "Did you benefit from the event in the way you wanted or expected?" The majority (85%) agreed that they learned something to help them feel more prepared for college. Based on experience and student feedback, the Opening Sessions team is constantly trying to improve the day for students. At the fall 2009 event, in an effort to guide students in taking greater responsibility for their own success, faculty and staff prompted students to articulate particular commitments and actions by stating what they would do during their first semester to help ensure their own success. Survey questions were designed to correspond with this push toward action, asking students, "Did today's program motivate you to take certain actions during your first semester?" and "What actions will you take?" Eighty-two percent of the survey respondents identified specific actions. The three most commonly cited actions were (a) obtain tutoring assistance (24% of students saying they would do so), (b) meet with my advisor before the spring 2010 semester (23%), and (c) attend Academy study skills workshops (17%).

*Opening Sessions and the Common Reading: The Revised Model*

The Opening Sessions program has faced challenges, however. From the start, the day has been voluntary for students, but increased communication about the event during new student registration, coupled with recent enrollment growth, doubled the number of students attending the event to more than 1,400. The overwhelming logistical and staffing demands in holding a one-day event for that many people forced us to redesign the event in spring 2010 by spreading it over two days. Anticipating that greater student attendance might translate into too few faculty volunteers to run the small discussion groups, several sessions were piloted in fall 2009 using advanced students as leaders. Each student leader was joined by a staff or faculty member. Based on the success of existing peer programs at the college (i.e., advising, Supplemental Instruction, technology assistance in building ePortfolios) connecting incoming students with successful advanced students had the potential to be a powerful experience. These sessions, led by peer advisors, were rated very highly by new students.

While these sessions focused on the common reading, students' written feedback frequently revealed that, as one student put it, "the discussion of the book led to a conversation about how to be a success." Similar comments included: "I will apply information gained from the book to school;" "I learned about how I should conduct myself;" "I learned I need to be disciplined and responsible;" and "I learned about attitudes and behaviors than can interfere with success." The majority of students (93%) agreed it was helpful to have a fellow student speak to them about their experiences, and as one new student said, "Having students speak brings a level of security knowing that someone near my own age did the same things and can help me in my college years."

Students were also asked what they would want to hear from advanced students at future orientations. New students generally wanted to hear three things from their peers: (a) strategies for success (e.g., overcoming challenges, adjusting to college, connecting with campus resources and other students), (b) information (e.g., preparing for transfer to a four-year college, student life, and activities), and (c) other students' academic goals and plans.

Based on this feedback, Opening Sessions for the spring 2010 semester piloted a new approach to the discussion groups led by faculty and advanced students. Rather than using the common reading as the basis for discussion, students' own educational and career goals became the focus. Students were in discussion groups based on their Academies, so that faculty in the corresponding discipline areas were able to guide students in articulating their goals and understanding what it would take to achieve those goals. Students began to see the connections between their goals and the courses they need to take and the careers to which they aspire.

While faculty and staff were reluctant to lose the common reading at Opening Sessions, questions about the cost-effectiveness of the program given enrollment increases (more than 7,000 books were distributed free to new students in the 2009-2010 academic year) and strategies for assessing how many students were actually reading the book were impossible to ignore. Instead, the common reading is now being offered on a subscription basis; faculty who commit to using the book in any of their first-year classes will receive free copies for their entire class. While the reading will be somewhat less common in that all first-year students will not have a copy, substantial numbers of incoming students will still use the book in class. For the initial semester of the subscription model (fall 2010), 37 faculty signed up to use the common reading in 58 class sections.

*Academy Learning Communities*

As is the case for most, if not all, community colleges, a significant aspect of the education provided at LaGuardia involves developmental or basic skills courses. At many institutions, basic skills are precollegiate in that they consist of a set of courses that students must complete before being allowed to take courses in the major. At LaGuardia, for example, basic writing, reading, math, and English as a Second Language (ESL) are noncredit prerequisites to most introductory courses in the majors. Not surprisingly, incoming students often feel that basic skills courses are not connected to their primary reason for coming to college in the first place—that is, to study a particular major. Thus, students in developmental courses often do not feel connected to the college, their classes, or their academic aspirations.

LaGuardia believes that a community college transition program needs to address this issue by finding ways to connect students to the disciplines while they are still in basic skills courses. The approach of contextualizing skills development within disciplinary coursework is based on the belief that students learn best when they can apply their developing skills to the academic subject matter at hand, rather than experiencing skills instruction that is separate from and prior to discipline-area instruction. Learning communities thus link developmental courses with discipline-area courses in the first semester, allowing students to earn credits toward the major or general education requirements. For example, ESL has been paired with introductory courses in accounting, business, computers, and sociology, among others. The College's required New Student Seminar is often linked to these learning communities as well, along with a Studio Hour where students begin constructing their ePortfolios. Over the years, students in learning communities have consistently experienced higher learning outcomes, including higher course grades and pass rates.

Yet, the major challenge in regard to learning communities has been getting the program to scale. While more than 1,000 students registered for learning communities in fall 2009, more than 4,000 students entered the college in that semester. One way the college has been able to increase the number of traditional learning communities (i.e., two or more linked courses) has been to incorporate mathematics courses into learning communities for the first time. Funded by FIPSE and Title V, LaGuardia's Project Quantum Leap seeks to make developmental math instruction more engaging and meaningful by placing it in the context of compelling social issues: the environment, health, and the economy.[1] These themes became the way to link math to other courses, such as first-year composition and critical thinking, where the themes could be explored in greater depth while also focusing on how mathematical knowledge contributes to one's ability to understand the complexities of these issues.

Another exciting possibility for expanding learning communities arose when a professor in the English department described how students in his basic skills writing courses were communicating online with students in his advanced English classes. Expanding on this idea, in the spring 2010 semester a completely new learning community model—dubbed learning networks—was piloted. Using Web 2.0 technologies, learning networks created what could be considered vertical learning communities, that is, linking incoming students with advanced students in higher level classes. Thus, for example, faculty linked basic skills writing courses virtually with advanced courses taught by other professors in various discipline areas. By communicating with each other via blogs and other social networking technologies, the students completed a number of assignments that called for them to respond to each other's work. For example, incoming students in one developmental writing class wrote business-themed papers that students in an advanced business management class were asked to critique. Not only do learning networks provide another opportunity to connect new students with their more advanced peers, but from an administrative viewpoint, learning networks also obviate the need for scheduling blocked courses—something that has always been a limiting factor in terms of trying to expand the program. Initial student reaction has been very positive; 93% of the students say they found it helpful to interact online with students from other classes. As one student put it, "Getting opinions and feedback from other classmates helped shape our ideas and provided another perspective that we might have missed."

### ePortfolios

LaGuardia students are able to collect and showcase their academic work and learning via their electronic portfolios (LaGuardia Community College, 2010b). Students begin their ePortfolios during their first year and have the opportunity to develop and refine them throughout their time at LaGuardia. Work representing student academic and professional growth (e.g., writing, original art, oral interviews, résumés, and class projects) can be found in student ePortfolios.

In the first year, ePortfolios place particular emphasis on defining and clarifying academic and career goals, prompting students to take responsibility for and reflect on their learning. All sections of the second-semester career development course, Fundamentals of Professional Advancement, include an attached Studio Hour for intensive ePortfolio work. Studio Hour presents another opportunity for first-year students to work with advanced students: Successful upper-level students who are trained in technology and in mentoring serve as ePortfolio consultants. Once again, this kind of peer mentoring experience has proven to be extremely powerful, allowing new students to connect with successful peer guides and role models. As one first-year student describes her experience, "It's like getting help from your friend, because they're about your age. The Consultants are always so patient and everything, respectful. They've been through things and they help you a lot."

### Concluding Observations

LaGuardia views the entire first year as transitional for students and has sought to connect first-year students to faculty, their disciplines, and their advanced peers, and to connect the curricular with the cocurricular. Because LaGuardia students are so diverse and have so many pressures and demands, they respond best if offered multiple opportunities to connect over the course of their first year. Many find value in Opening Sessions; for some, the common reading strikes a chord, and others thrive in learning communities. In all cases though, the goal is to foster early connections to academic disciplines and to create multiple communities that support students in making successful transitions across varied and complex boundaries.

## Building a Successful First-Year Seminar at Palo Alto College

### The Institution

Palo Alto College (PAC) in San Antonio, Texas, is one of four publicly funded, independently accredited colleges in the Alamo Community College District. It was established in 1983 as a federally designated Hispanic-Serving Institution and is fully accredited by the Commission on Colleges of the Southern Association of Colleges and Schools. Originally expected to peak at an enrollment of 2,500 students, the college currently enrolls a record high of 8,300 students. Palo Alto offers 55 certificates and 77 degrees and also provides the first two years of a baccalaureate degree. Historically, two thirds of students at the College are part-time, Hispanic, and female. Their average age is 24, and more than half are under 21. Forty-nine percent are economically disadvantaged, and 74% are first-generation college students.

*The Importance of the First-Year Experience*

In 2002, the institution was in desperate need of stable leadership and predictable funding. Over the previous 15 years (since 1987), 13 presidents had come and gone, and the college had been underfunded for more than a decade. Few services were available to students through the student services division and, moreover, the available services were not coherent; rather, they were administered in functional silos throughout the college. Counselors served as directors for various student service offices, which left them little time to advise or counsel students. Faculty and staff were highly dissatisfied with the available services for students, but they believed that the existing resources were all PAC could afford. Through the years, faculty, staff, and administrators had experimented with various piecemeal retention strategies; however, these had been suspended for one reason or another. The College had been losing enrollment for seven years, and it was imperative to improve both recruitment and retention in order to survive and achieve institutional stability.

In 2003, the College began to put in place a coherent set of research-based retention strategies. First, the myriad silo offices that supported very few students were disbanded and a welcome and advising center was created where all new students would experience a small-group, two-hour orientation and obtain registration assistance. Because of the demonstrated positive impact of an existing three-day, voluntary orientation program on students' academic success and retention, a required student orientation course was proposed, and funding was secured to create a semester-long first-year seminar. In the fall of 2003, SDEV 0170: Strategies for Succeeding in College was implemented and made mandatory for all students.

No required program can be put in place without some initial challenges. The problems encountered in implementing this course and their solutions were as follows:

⬥ *Problem:* Because there are five colleges for students to select from within the Alamo Community College District, faculty and staff feared that an additional mandatory PAC course might encourage students to go to another college without the requirement.

*Solution:* The course was offered at no cost to students, and during registration, students and their parents were counseled regarding the importance of this course to student success.

⬥ *Problem:* Given limited financial resources and no tuition revenue for the course, paying an instructional team made up of only faculty members presented a funding obstacle.

*Solution:* At Palo Alto, counselors are classified as nonteaching faculty. The faculty senate considered whether counselors could teach course sections as part of their workload based on the argument that all faculty should teach and that the term nonteaching faculty was a misnomer. An agreement was reached among all stakeholders allowing counselors to teach three sections of a one-credit course per semester as part of their load.

⬥ *Problem:* The counselors were already working at capacity, and finding time to teach the course was an issue.

*Solution:* Counselors examined their work loads and methods (primarily one-on-one contact) and decided to try a group, rather than individual, advising approach as a way to allocate more time for teaching. Group advising was determined to be more cost-effective not only in time and dollars but also student satisfaction. The group format allowed counselors to reach a greater number of students and be more efficient by not repeating the same basic information to individuals. Other benefits were more peer bonding, including students helping each other during the meetings, and a greater level of student comfort in the group environment than in one-on-one sessions.

◇ **Problem:** Palo Alto College did not have an information technology system in place to monitor course enrollment.

**Solution:** Enrollment was monitored by hand, which was a time-consuming but worthwhile solution. At the end of the first year, only 500 students had taken the course, and yet there were 1,200 first-time-in-college (FTIC) students enrolled at the institution. In analyzing this discrepancy, it was discovered that a significant number of students either dropped or were exempted from the course as a result of the system not preventing withdrawal and some advisors not understanding the importance of the seminar. Data demonstrating significant improvement in retention and grade point averages of course participants were shared with faculty and staff, and the annual review of course and FTIC student numbers has since shown a steady increase in seminar enrollment.

Due to an enrollment surge at PAC, each counselor currently teaches 15 one-credit sections of the seminar per year (i.e., eight in one semester and seven in the next) with approximately 26 students per section. In addition, counselors are the official advisors for students in their classes. Prior to SDEV 0170 becoming the site for advising, contacts between students and counselors were sporadic at best. Because the seminar is required, more students are now aware of and have easier access to advising services as counselors help them commit to a major and enroll for the next semester. Most importantly, the counselors have an opportunity to develop deeper relationships with students.

Another by-product of the initiative is that faculty now value counselors' involvement in teaching, and counselors feel they are strategic partners with students, faculty, and administration. There are also clear financial benefits. In an environment where the financial support for higher education is diminishing, this approach allows counselors to produce contact hours, which are the basis for funding in Texas.

### Expanding the Course Curriculum to Include Culturally Relevant Information

The seminar has continued to evolve and has been adapted to serve the needs of the largely Hispanic student population by providing both extended orientation and culturally relevant information. Initially, the course was structured around a typical first-year seminar textbook that addressed a variety of strategies to help students succeed in college. In sharing feedback on the course, counselors expressed concern about cultural issues that were not addressed in the textbook. Some of these topics were specific to first-generation students—for instance, families who feared that the college experience would make students look down on relatives who had not attended college. One student shared her husband's concern that she would leave him for a "man with a varsity letter jacket." Other students repeated family members' statements such as, "Just because you are going to college doesn't mean that you know everything now," or "You think you are better than we are."

Textbook cost was also an issue, and many students were not purchasing the book. To address the cultural and cost concerns, PAC hired a writer and graphic artist to create its own seminar textbook, *¿Que Pasa? What's Up at Palo Alto*, for the fall of 2005. The book fits in a three-ring binder and is priced under $20. The text has been favorably received by both faculty and students, with several instructors purchasing the book for their own college-bound children and students requesting that the book be translated into Spanish to share with their parents.

The first chapter includes the history of the institution, highlighting PAC's contribution to cultural understanding in San Antonio's Hispanic southside community and the neighborhood's involvement and input in establishing the College. It also addresses the basis for the campus' mission-style architecture. This history encourages PAC students to take pride in their college and strengthens institutional engagement.

While many students arrive at PAC with great hopes and dreams, many also enter academically underprepared, requiring developmental education. These courses give students the essential skills for college success, but they can also become an impediment to persistence. PAC students, especially those who begin in developmental courses, need to discuss repeatedly their fears of not being able to be successful in college as well as the ingrained belief that they may not be worthy of success. *¿Que Pasa?* includes many examples of others who, like themselves, overcame adversity and achieved success. Students find these stories reassuring and empowering. The first-year seminar addresses the deep need that many students have to realize that their past is not their future. Whatever they have done or left undone, they have the power to change their personal story to one that is positive and uplifting.

In SDEV 0170, personal development is addressed through culturally relevant stories. Time management is presented within the context of the annual Fiesta Celebration, where planning for the next year's celebration begins as soon as the current celebration ends. The balance that must be achieved between time devoted to school and to personal life and the financial sacrifices a college education can demand are discussed at length, especially since many students are also parents or have families.

## Other Topics for the First-Year Seminar

Students are introduced to the Personalized Access to Learning and Services (PALS) system, an Internet homepage that gives them access to e-mail and other communication systems at the college. The seminar also addresses the services available for students with learning disabilities, while highlighting many stories of famous people who have such disabilities and stressing that a disability is not a prediction for failure but simply a reality to take into account in studying and learning how to succeed.

Both choosing a major and planning for a career are of utmost importance in SDEV 0170. Many students arrive at the College without a plan for the future. While high school counselors in the San Antonio area emphasize the importance of college, discussions rarely focus on going to college for a defined purpose. One of the reasons students are taking longer to complete college may be a failure to help them envision a future and determine how to use college as a vehicle to that future. As such, the first-year seminar devotes time to helping students visualize their options and develop an educational plan or major that will accomplish their goals. Before the end of the first semester, PAC students are required to choose a major and enroll for the next semester using that major's course of study.

## Where PAC Is Today

In the past few years, enrollment in the seminar has ranged from 1,200 to 1,400, mirroring PAC's FTIC population. And, since 2005, the course has been adapted for students who are on academic dismissal, on financial aid probation, or who place in the lowest level of three remediation areas.

*Course Outcomes*

In reviewing course outcomes, differences in retention and academic performance are apparent for participants who complete SDEV 0170 with a *C* or above compared to those who earned a lower grade and to the entire FTIC population.

*Within-course retention.* In 2003, seminar participants had an overall within-course retention rate (i.e., completion of the class within an academic term, regardless of retention to the next term) equal to the entire FTIC population. By 2006, the within-course retention rate for all students at the College was 81%, and the rate for seminar students was 94%, representing a 13-point difference. This increase is likely attributable to the content of SDEV 0170, the relationships developed within this course, and the use of a campus-specific textbook.

*FTIC retention.* In 2006, PAC's overall FTIC fall-to-spring retention rate was 68%, and the fall-to-fall rate was 44%. However, seminar students who earned a productive grade rate (PGR) of a *C* or above in the course had a fall-to-spring retention rate of 92% and a fall-to-fall rate of 66%.

*PGR in other courses.* In the fall of 2006, research was conducted to determine whether earning a *C* or above in the seminar correlated with the likelihood of maintaining a PGR in the students' other courses taken during the same semester. A direct correlation was found between a PGR in SDEV 0170 and the likelihood of earning a *C* or above in other courses. While the percentage of successful seminar students who maintained a PGR in other classes declined slightly over the four semesters that students were tracked (i.e., fall of 2005 through the spring of 2007), the data indicated that seminar participants still consistently outperformed those students who were either unsuccessful or did not enroll in the course.

Providing a first-year seminar is not a panacea. Data from the FTIC cohorts indicate that the high persistence and PGRs initially demonstrated by seminar participants begin to decline after three semesters in college. To counteract this decline in performance, a strong faculty advising system has been implemented, which is designed to provide continued support to students as they make the transition from the seminar and work toward graduation.

*Concluding Observations*

Over the past eight years, PAC has grown into a thriving and vibrant institution with a 134% increase in graduation rates and significant campus facility improvements. The Strategies for Succeeding in College seminar has been an instrumental part of this accomplishment. Working together, faculty, counselors, and administrators have built a course for a student population with a high risk for college failure and demonstrated that these students can and will succeed.

## Considering Both Institutional Stories: Lessons Learned and Recommendations

As anyone who observes first-year initiatives in community colleges across the United States will surely agree, there is no one best method for helping new students make a successful transition to college. As these stories demonstrate, colleges must create the approach that works best in their unique contexts. But no matter what the size or makeup of a community college, there are lessons to be learned from these stories.

First, in order for orientation or transition programming to be sustained, it must be considered essential by senior campus administrators. Unfortunately, that is not always the case. Some community colleges are so overwhelmed by the sheer numbers of new students seeking admission, that the notion of supporting them takes a back seat. In addition, some two-year colleges seem reluctant to encourage or require students to do anything that might be perceived as a barrier to their attendance. Students are therefore allowed to enroll without being guaranteed, or even offered, experiences that would increase the likelihood of their success and retention. As these institutional profiles demonstrate, transition programming has not been considered a low-status activity. Rather, senior administrators, in one case a president and in another case the chief academic officer, have participated actively in the design, evolution, implementation, and maintenance of these programs.

Although there are many successful boutique programs for small student subpopulations, in order for differences to be realized in overall retention, the number of participants should reach a critical mass, ideally 75% or more of new students. In the case of Palo Alto College, the intent is that all new students should enroll in a first-year seminar. LaGuardia Community College reaches a large percentage of its new students through a variety of initiatives, most of which are administered through its First-Year Academies.

These two profiles are evidence that change takes time. No program will be perfect in its first year of implementation; the best programs grow and evolve over a number of years and occasionally have to be revisited and refreshed. After the initial offering of the required first-year seminar, Palo Alto College learned that the course was not meeting the needs of Hispanic students who make up the overwhelming majority of students at Palo Alto. Therefore, changes were made to assure that the course was culturally relevant to new students. At LaGuardia Community College, a highly successful common reading program that was part of the Opening Sessions orientation program essentially sank under its own weight. As the program attracted more and more students, the expense of providing free books could not be justified. Program costs have now been reduced by providing free books only to students in first-year courses taught by instructors who intend to link the reading to course content.

A final lesson from these institutional stories is that successful student transition and orientation programs have effects beyond their original intent. Involving faculty, staff, administrators, and students in designing and implementing student transition programs generates institutional enthusiasm, commitment, and excitement. Partnerships develop across units that generate understanding and respect for everyone's role at the institution. At Palo Alto College, counselors, formerly considered nonteaching faculty, took on important teaching roles. Virtually all of LaGuardia's initiatives require the involvement and mutual support of units across the campus.

Community college educators ignore the importance of student transition experiences at their own peril. Accountability for new student success is absolutely essential if these institutions are to reach their potential to transform students and the wider communities. The nation is watching as these institutions take their position on the front line of fulfilling democracy's promise of educational opportunity for all people.

## Notes

[1] Project Quantum Leap adapts the SENCER (Science Education for New Civic Engagements and Responsibilities) model funded by the National Science Foundation. SENCER initially focused on advanced science and math courses; LaGuardia was the first community college to adapt the approach for developmental mathematics instruction.

## References

Barefoot, B., Warnock, C., Dickinson, M., Richardson, S., & Roberts, M. (1998). *Exploring the evidence: Reporting outcomes of first-year seminars, Volume II.* (Monograph No. 25). Columbia, SC: University of South Carolina, National Resource Center for The First-Year Experience and Students in Transition.

Center for Community College Engagement. (2008). *SENSE, Survey of Entering Student Engagement, 2008 field test findings.* Retrieved November 15, 2009, from http://www.ccsse.org/sense/survey/SENSE_2008_National_Report_March_18.pdf

LaGuardia Community College. (2009). *Institutional profile.* Retrieved May 3, 2010, from http://www.lagcc.cuny.edu/facts/facts03/PDFs_profile/Complete.pdf

LaGuardia Community College. (2010a). *Common readings.* Retrieved May 3, 2010, from http://www.laguardia.edu/stuinfo/firstyear/commonreading.aspx

LaGuardia Community College. (2010b). *ePortfolios.* Retrieved May 3, 2010, from http://www.eportfolio.lagcc.cuny.edu

Lenning, O. T., Sauer, K., & Beal, P. E. (1980). *Student retention strategies* (AAHE-ERIC Higher Education Research Report No. 8). Iowa City, IA: American College Testing Program.

McClenney, K., & McClenney, B. (2007). *Starting right: Inventory of entering student experiences.* Austin, TX: University of Texas, Center for Community College Engagement.

Mullendore, R. H., & Banahan, L. A. (2005). Designing orientation programs. In M. L. Upcraft, J. N. Gardner, B. O. Barefoot, & Associates, *Challenging and supporting the first-year student: A handbook for improving the first year of college* (pp. 391-409). San Francisco, CA: Jossey-Bass.

Obama, B. (2004). *Dreams from my father.* New York, NY: Three Rivers Press.

Policy Center on the First Year of College. (2000). *National Survey of First-Year Co-Curricular Practices.* Retrieved from the John N. Gardner Institute for Excellence in Undergraduate Education website: http://www.jngi.org/uploads/File/co-curricular_Final_Summary.pdf

Policy Center on the First Year of College. (2002). *Second National Survey of First-Year Academic Practices.* Retrieved from the John N. Gardner Institute for Excellence in Undergraduate Education website: http://www.jngi.org/uploads/File/2002_2nd_Nat_Survey_Responses_ALL.pdf

Rode, D. (2000). The role of orientation in institutional retention. In M. J. Fabich (Ed.), *Orientation planning manual.* Pullman, WA: National Orientation Directors Association.

Swing, R. (2002). *The impact of engaging pedagogy on first-year seminars.* Retrieved from the National Resource Center for The First-Year Experience and Students in Transition website: http://www.sc.edu/fye/resources/assessment/essays/swing-8.28.02_pdfs/introduction.pdf

Tobolowsky, B., & Associates. (2008). *2006 National Survey of First-Year Seminars: Continuing innovations in the collegiate curriculum* (Monograph No. 51). Columbia, SC: University of South Carolina, National Resource Center for The First-Year Experience and Students in Transition.

Tobolowsky, B., Cox, B., & Wagner, M. (2005). *Exploring the evidence, volume III: Reporting research on first-year seminars* (Monograph No. 42). Columbia, SC: University of South Carolina, National Resource Center for The First-Year Experience and Students in Transition.

Upcraft, M. L., Gardner, J. N., & Barefoot, B. O. (2005). Introduction. In M. L. Upcraft, J. N. Gardner, B. O. Barefoot, & Associates, *Challenging and supporting the first-year student: A handbook for improving the first year of college* (pp. 1-12). San Francisco, CA: Jossey-Bass.

# Chapter 8

## Academic Advising Models to Support First-Year Student Success

Margaret C. King and Rusty N. Fox

While many definitions of academic advising exist, the one offered by Crockett (1984) nearly four decades ago continues to be the most comprehensive: "Academic advising is a developmental process, which assists students in the clarification of their life/career goals and in the development of educational plans for the realization of these goals" (p. *i*). He goes on to acknowledge that academic advising is both a decision-making and ongoing communications process between advisors and students to help students realize their maximum educational potential. The advisor facilitates communication, coordinates learning experiences through course and career planning and academic progress review, and serves as a referral agent to other campus units as necessary (Crockett). Thus, rather than viewing academic advising as one in a constellation of programs and services, Habley (1995) suggests that academic advising is "the hub of the wheel" with connections to all of the other support services on campus as well as to the academic programs and departments. At the community college level, it is the only structured activity in which all students have the opportunity for ongoing, one-to-one interaction with a concerned representative of the institution (Habley, 1995).

As such, advisors play a critical role in responding to first-year student needs as well as ensuring that they are connected to other areas of the campus. In fact, next to the quality of instruction, students consistently indicate that academic advising is the most important area of the college experience (Noel Levitz, 2005). Students in two-year colleges rank academic advising slightly behind instructional effectiveness and registration effectiveness (Noel Levitz, 2009, p. 1). Despite the relative importance of academic advising, students may not always avail themselves of this resource. The 2009 Community College Survey of Student Engagement (CCSSE) found that "90% of students say that academic advising/planning is *very important* or *somewhat important*, but only 56% of students use this service *sometimes* or *often*. More than one third (35%) say they *rarely* or *never* use it" (Center for Community College Student Engagement, 2009, p. 14). Helping students understand the value of academic advising is a key strategy for increasing first-year student engagement and success. And given the diversity of community college students and the fact that many of them are first-generation students, designing effective advising programs and ensuring that students access them is critical for the community college.

This chapter explores strategies for using academic advisors to introduce students to higher education and guide them as they pursue coursework toward certificate, degree, or transfer. It opens with a discussion of developing a mission for academic advising that aligns with the larger institutional mission and using that mission as a framework for establishing program goals and learning outcomes. Yet, the bulk of the chapter focuses on a discussion of different strategies for organizing and delivering academic advising, with special attention paid to advising for first-year community college students.

## Connecting Advising to the Institutional Mission

Many two-year college mission, vision, or values statements express strong commitments to supporting student learning and success. The mission of Schenectady County Community College (n.d.), for example, advocates the use of "innovative practices and contemporary technology" to foster "success through excellence in teaching and support services" (para. 1). Academic advising is clearly one of those key support services, and advising programs need individualized mission statements, which describe their unique purposes and goals while aligning them with the larger institutional mission statement.

A mission statement for the advising program typically includes a list of beliefs about students and describes the nature of the program, its organizational structure, expectations of advisors and advisees, and goals. The National Academic Advising Association (NACADA, 2005) Statement of Core Values and the Council for the Advancement of Standards in Higher Education (CAS) Professional Standards in Higher Education (Dean, 2006) should serve as guides for the decisions that need to be made about what to do and how to do it. The mission statement also provides the roadmap for the achievement of goals, objectives, and learning outcomes.

Even though the advising mission statement reflects the work of a single program, its development should be the result of institution-wide discussions on what works best in student learning, success, and retention—especially if the advising program is to have more than a limited impact on the institution. A wide variety of constituents, including student development specialists and instructional faculty should be involved in the creation of the advising mission statement. When mission statements are viewed as a tool or a process, rather than a final product, they invite collaboration; compromise; and creative planning from faculty, staff, and students. Such a view also suggests that mission statements are not static documents. They are instruments to guide growth, assess direction, and document progress—both of individual student success and overall program effectiveness. As such, mission statements must be regularly reviewed and, if necessary, revised.

## Identifying Learning Outcomes for Academic Advising

The advising program must be guided by a set of written goals and objectives that are directly related to its stated mission. Examples of such objectives might include promoting student growth and development; discussing and clarifying educational, career, and life goals; assisting students in understanding the institutional context or environment; evaluating and monitoring student progress; and referring students to appropriate campus or community resources. Examples of specific goals and evidence of achievement include

◇ *Intellectual growth.* The student understands the requirements of an academic degree plan as well as institutional policies and procedures.
◇ *Effective communication.* The student demonstrates the ability to use campus technology resources.

◇ *Realistic self-appraisal.* The student evaluates personal and academic skills, abilities, and interests and uses this appraisal to establish appropriate educational plans.

◇ *Enhanced self-esteem.* The student shows self-respect and respect for others.

◇ *Clarified values.* The student articulates personal values and acts in congruence with them.

◇ *Career choices.* The student describes career choice and choice of academic major based on interests, values, skills, and abilities.

◇ *Meaningful interpersonal relations.* The student develops relationships with faculty and others to be engaged with the institution in meaningful ways.

◇ *Independence.* The student operates autonomously by seeking input from advisors in a timely fashion.

◇ *Satisfying and productive lifestyles.* The student achieves balance among academic course load requirements, work, and leisure.

◇ *Achievement of personal and educational goals.* The student can articulate his or her personal and educational goals (Dean, 2006).

## Understanding the Role of Academic Advisors

Ultimately, the responsibility for making decisions about educational plans and life goals should rest with the student. However, the academic advisor plays a key role in helping with that process by challenging students when appropriate, referring them to the many resources on campus that can help with making these decisions, and offering support throughout the process. Advisors need to help students make the best academic decisions possible by encouraging them to identify and assess alternatives and to consider the consequences of their decisions. While the advisor may take the lead in early interactions with the student, he or she should gradually step back, allowing the student to have greater control over the process.

Fox (2008) identified five critical skills or attributes needed by academic advisors to be successful in this role:

1. Starting with a base of *competence*, an advisor must have core knowledge of the institution's policies; its guidelines; and the prerequisite scores, courses, and criteria required to function within the particular academic setting. While students need higher order support from advisors, they frequently seek out their advisors for basic information initially. Thus, it is essential that the academic advisor start from a strong, competent base.

2. Next, the academic advisor must be a skilled *confidence builder*, encourager, and champion for students' best efforts. This requires more than positive affirmation; it requires the advisor to review and relearn the principles of reflection, modeling, and open-ended questioning. The bolstering of confidence must come with an increased understanding of self within the context of the institution and of individual strengths and weaknesses for the interaction to be truly useful.

3. *Cordiality* is the third skill or attribute critical for effective advising. Simple, genuine, intentional courtesy and cordiality are far-reaching and often have a greater impact than one would expect. Most students are unsure, confused, scared, or simply searching. An earnest, kind welcome and response from a skilled professional set a tone for the professional relationship to come.

4. *Credibility* is a core characteristic that the advisor should seek to establish and work to enhance. An academic advisor who is a good facilitator and recognized as a willing and productive collaborator and advocate will be sought after by faculty and leaders of the

institution. Moreover, advisors are excellent partners for first-year students searching for and establishing their academic and career goals.

5. *Creativity*, coupled with the wiliness to collaborate, is the fuel that powers the development process for students and their advisors. Exploring beyond the obvious and seeking the question behind the question are components of creativity. Advisors can help students develop their own creativity by helping them brainstorm what else and what next with regard to academic planning and career decision making. Such activities can also help students see the wisdom in developing multiple pathways or options for accomplishing their goals.

A sixth characteristic of *culture* could be added to complete the ideal toolbox of a new-student academic advisor. Brown and Rivas (1992) describe how the context of one's culture, the history, beliefs, fears, priorities, and the understanding one brings to one-on-one advising sessions shape interactions between advisor and student. Understanding the cultural viewpoints of both student and advisor are essential to accurately understanding student needs and concerns and to effectively guiding them in their development of a plan for success.

## Organizing the Delivery of Advising

*Key Considerations in Designing Academic Advising Programs*

When reviewing the organization of advising services, a number of factors must be considered. The first is the institutional mission. This includes the control of the institution (i.e., public, private, proprietary), the level of educational offerings (i.e., associate, bachelor's, or graduate degrees), the nature of the program offerings (i.e., liberal arts, professional, or vocational) and the selectivity of the institution (i.e., open door vs. highly selective). A second factor is the student population. When the college enrolls a large number of underprepared, undecided, racially and ethnically diverse, first-generation, and/or commuter students, having a highly organized system for advising is critically important, as these are often the students who are less likely to be engaged with the campus and, therefore, more at risk of leaving. The role of faculty in the advising program and their interest in and willingness to advise students must also be considered. Programs and policies, such as the complexity of degree and/or general education requirements, the sequencing of courses, and the extent to which advisor approval is required for a variety of transactions must also be considered. As the complexity increases, the need for highly skilled advisors working in a well-defined advising organization increases.

Three additional factors must also be considered—organizational structure, budget, and facilities. Organizational structure will drive a number of key decisions about the advising center. Components of organizational structure include where advising is located on an institution's organizational chart (i.e., who has ultimate responsibility for advising), who delivers advising to students, and the degree to which advising is centralized or dispersed on a campus. According to a national study of advising practices (Habley, 2004), 32% of advising programs report to the vice president or dean of academic affairs while 39% report to someone at the assistant or associate vice president level. Yet, in two-year public colleges 33% of academic advising programs report through student affairs.

Adequate funding is essential to accomplish the mission and goals of the advising program. Typically, program budgets will include staffing, training and development (including print and online resource materials), equipment and technology, and recognition and rewards. Computerized degree audits and student tracking systems may also make up substantial portions of the advising program budget. Organizational structure will in some measure determine the cost of advising programs and the resources available for funding those programs. Some organizational models and delivery systems are more expensive than others. For example, requiring academic advising responsibilities as part of the full-time teaching faculty load is less expensive than hiring full-time academic advisors. Similarly, using part-time peer or paraprofessional advisors is less costly than hiring full-time professional advisors. Whatever the structure, advising programs must demonstrate fiscal responsibility and cost-effectiveness consistent with institutional protocols.

Facilities need to be considered as well; however, such decisions are determined in part by the structure and delivery of advising services. In decentralized models (described below), very little dedicated space may be needed for the advising program. However, in shared and centralized models, administrators will need to determine how much space is needed, how such space should be configured (e.g., private offices, waiting areas, common rooms for group advising, resource areas), where on campus the program should be housed, and the technological infrastructure needed to support the program. On campuses moving toward more centralized models, discussions might center on whether existing facilities can be upfitted to house a new center or whether there are resources available to build one.

Effective and ethical leadership is an essential component of advising programs (Dean, 2006). Advising program leaders must be empowered and positioned within the administrative structure to be able to accomplish the mission of the advising program. They must articulate a vision for advising, set goals and objectives, prescribe and practice ethical behavior, select and supervise staff, manage both the fiscal and human resources, promote student learning and development, and initiate collaborative interactions with other offices and individuals on campus. Effective advising cannot be done in isolation; rather, program leaders must work in concert with key campus stakeholders. In short, effective program management includes using "comprehensive and accurate information for decisions, clear sources and channels of authority, effective communication practices, decision-making and conflict resolution practices, responsiveness to changing conditions, accountability and evaluation systems, and recognition and reward processes" (Dean, 2006, p. 18).

While title does not translate into leadership effectiveness, it may communicate something about the importance attached to advising by the campus leadership. A national ACT survey of advising practices (Habley, 2004) found that the dominant title for the person responsible for administration of the advising program is Coordinator or Director of Advising. Use of this title has increased from 12% to 28% in two-year public colleges from previous survey administrations.

Finally, effective programs need to have a strong advisor development or training component that focuses on the informational (what advisors need to know, e.g., how to use the computerized student records system), conceptual (what advisors need to understand, e.g., what is academic advising), and relational aspects (what must an advisor demonstrate, e.g., good listening, communication, and referral skills). Assessment and evaluation of both the individual advisor and the overall advising program is also critical as is recognition of and rewards for exemplary services as an advisor. The NACADA Clearinghouse of Academic Advising Resources (NACADA, n.d.) is a good source for examples of assessment instruments and processes, as well as examples of recognition and reward programs.

### Delivery of Advising Services

***Staffing.*** The CAS Standards (Dean, 2006) state that there must be sufficient personnel available to accomplish the program's mission and goals and address students' advising needs without unreasonable delay. Advisor caseload is determined by institutional context and "predicated on understanding the differential needs of your students" (Habley, 2004, p. 2). Whatever staffing is used, academic advisors must have an understanding of relevant cognitive and psychosocial theories of student learning, development, and career decision making. As noted earlier, they should have a comprehensive knowledge of the institution's academic programs, academic requirements, policies and procedures, majors, and support services. They must also have a demonstrated interest and effectiveness in working with and assisting students and participating in professional activities.

Six groups of individuals can be involved in the effective delivery of academic advising: (a) faculty, (b) professional advisors, (c) counselors, (d) graduate students, (e) paraprofessionals (i.e., associate degree or higher), and (f) peers (i.e., fellow students). The relative strengths and weaknesses of each group are briefly discussed here. The strengths of faculty include their knowledge of program and course content, their potential connection with the workforce, and their frequent interaction with students in their classes. As noted earlier, advising models that use faculty may be less expensive to operate if advising responsibilities are part of the faculty's regular load. Research also suggests that student/faculty interaction has a positive impact on student retention (Pascarella & Terenzini, 1977, 1979). Having faculty serve as advisors is one strategy for engineering those interactions outside the classroom. Potential drawbacks of using faculty as advisors may include their lack of enthusiasm for advising and their unwillingness to participate in training to support their academic advising role.

While faculty possess an in-depth knowledge of specific courses and programs, professional advisors are generalists with the ability to advise across all programs. Their education, background, and training may better prepare them to work with special populations, such as undecided students and developmental students. Professional advisors may also have more knowledge of the various services available to help students be successful and are frequently housed in a central location that is easily accessible for students. Counselors have many of the same strengths as professional advisors, yet they may prefer personal and career counseling to academic advising. They may also find that academic advising is less challenging professionally than personal counseling and, thus, may approach it with less enthusiasm (Pascarella & Terenzini, 1977, 1979).

Graduate students, paraprofessionals, and peers can be invaluable in supporting academic advising services. Because they are accessible to students in times and places where faculty and professional advisors are not, they can effectively supplement the services provided by professional advisors and faculty. For example, student advisors might provide basic advising services (e.g., reviewing courses required, helping build a course schedule), thus freeing faculty and professional advisors to focus on the more complicated aspects of advising. Using undergraduate and graduate students in these roles may also reduce the cost of advising programs. While student advisors are likely to bring great enthusiasm to their work, they must be carefully selected, trained, and supervised. Because they do not have the benefit of the background and experience of faculty and professional advisors, their responsibilities must be carefully structured.

*Individual and group advising.* Advising services can be provided individually or in groups. While an individual advising session can specifically focus on that particular student's needs, interests, or concerns, there is value in small group advising as well. As King (2008) notes, group advising is more aligned with teaching. Topics that can be covered well in groups would include general education requirements, the registration process, course selection, policies and procedures, general career planning advice, and providing a framework for selecting a major. Strengths of group advising are that it allows an advisor to potentially serve more students in less time, provides an efficient way to share common content, frees advisors for more one-to-one contact, and establishes peer interaction and contacts.

*Incorporating technology into program delivery.* Technology is another tool in the delivery of advising. Synchronous technology (e.g., videoconferencing, Internet chats, audio conferences, telephone) facilitates same time, same pace, different place, person-to-person advising. Asynchronous technology (e.g., Web pages, e-mail, listservs, social networking sites, blogs, pod casts) facilitates different time, different pace, different place person-to-person advising. The use of technology brings many strengths to an advising system, including reduced costs, increased accuracy and accessibility, and the ability to deliver advising at a distance. Unequal access to technology, increased opportunity for anonymity, and changes in the dynamics of the advisor/student relationship may represent challenges to the effective delivery of advising in exclusively or predominantly online environments.

Having multiple delivery systems is a benefit, as students access advising services from different points and have different needs. Multiple delivery options can also capitalize on advisor strengths while offsetting potential weaknesses.

### Organizational Models of Advising

A chapter on academic advising would be incomplete without a brief review of the seven organizational models of academic advising (Habley, 1983, 2004; Habley & McCauley, 1987). Pardee (2000) classified the models as decentralized, centralized, and shared. In the decentralized models, advising services are provided by faculty and/or staff within academic departments. While overall coordination may be centralized, advisors are accountable to their respective departments. In the centralized model, all advising takes place in an administrative unit such as an advising or counseling center, with a director and staff generally housed in one location. In the shared models, advising services are located within both a central administrative unit and individual academic departments. With the exception of the Faculty-Only model, the organizational models do not presume a specific delivery system (i.e., faculty, professional advisors, counselors, paraprofessionals, or peers).

**Decentralized models.** There are two decentralized models, the Faculty-Only model and the Satellite model. In the Faculty-Only model, each student is assigned a faculty advisor. There may be a campus coordinator of advising, but advisors are accountable to their respective departments. Exploratory students are typically assigned to liberal arts or specially selected faculty. The Faculty-Only model was used by 25% of the institutions responding to ACT's Sixth National Survey of Academic Advising, a decline from 33% in an earlier survey. It is particularly common in private two- and four-year institutions (Habley, 2004). As noted early, strengths of faculty-delivered advising include in-depth knowledge of program and course content, their potential workforce connections for those in career programs, increased student/faculty interaction, and reduced cost.

While many of the shared models (discussed below) have shown slight increases in prevalence according to the ACT advising survey, use of the Faculty-Only model has declined. Given the growing complexity of academic advising, it is unrealistic to expect any one group of people to be able to know and do it all. It is also important that there be sufficient personnel available to address the students advising needs without unreasonable delay and to accomplish the mission and goals of the advising program. Sharing the advising responsibilities makes that much more feasible.

The Satellite model, which is sometimes referred to as the multiversity model, finds advising offices maintained and controlled within academic subunits (i.e., schools, colleges). A satellite office specifically for exploratory students generally provides campus-wide coordination. Within this model, advising responsibilities may also shift from an advising office to specific faculty within the subunits. This model was found in 7% of the institutions surveyed by ACT, a slight increase from the prior survey, and is more common in public universities and large community colleges (Habley, 2004). One strength of this model includes tying advising services to the individual school or college, which can help personalize the experience for the student. However, inconsistent application of policies that apply to all students across departments may present a problem. Similarly, special care may need to be given to students who declare or change majors as well as to those with special needs. Students often make a connection with the first advisor they meet so transition to a new advisor following a major change can be difficult. Because the way advising services are organized in each of the departments or schools may differ, preparing transitioning students for potential changes is helpful.

*Centralized model.* There is one centralized model—the Self-Contained model, in which all advising from orientation to departure takes place in a centralized unit, such as an advising center or counseling center. The unit could be staffed with full- or part-time advisors, counselors, faculty, paraprofessionals, or peers. Typically, a dean or director supervises all advising functions. Found in 14% of the institutions surveyed by ACT (up slightly from a previous survey), the Self-Contained model is the second most popular model in community colleges (Habley, 2004). Strengths of this model include dedicated professional advisors who are housed in a central location that is easily accessible to students. Training, evaluation, and recognition or reward processes may also be more easily accomplished within a self-contained unit that shares common priorities and goals. If only professional advisors are used, opportunities for student/faculty contact may decrease. However, it is possible to build faculty into the model.

*Shared models.* The first of the shared models is the Supplementary model. In this model, faculty are assigned as advisors for all students. A centralized office provides support to faculty, which may include being a referral resource, providing training, creating an advising handbook, or being an information clearinghouse. As such, the office provides only indirect assistance to students and has no original jurisdiction for approving academic transactions (e.g., registration clearance, drop/add, program change), which rests exclusively with faculty. In this model, the advising office is generally small, sometimes headed by part-time or volunteer faculty with trained peer advisors. This model was found in 17% of the institutions surveyed by ACT and is the second most popular model in two- and four-year institutions (Habley, 2004). The central coordination provided by the advising office in this model is a benefit, yet if faculty do not value the services provided by the office or do not find them credible, its success would be questionable.

In the Split model, the initial advising of students is divided between an advising office and academic subunits. The office advises specific groups of students, such as those who are exploratory or developmental. Once specified conditions are met (e.g., choosing a major or completing developmental coursework), students are assigned to an academic subunit, where faculty, full-time advisors, paraprofessionals, or peers may advise them. In this model, a director or coordinator may have campus-wide coordinating responsibilities and provide training and resources for advisors. Found in 27% of the institutions surveyed by ACT, the Split model is the most popular model in public four-year institutions and has been the most prominent organizational model across all campuses since the 1998 survey (Habley, 2004).

Strengths of this model include having trained advisors with the skills to advise the higher risk students. However, as with the Satellite model, there is a need to pay close attention to transitioning students from one advisor or advising system to another and to have close coordination between the advising office and the academic units. It is important that students receive consistent and accurate information and if coordination does not exist, it could lead to confusion and mistakes, which ultimately hurt the students.

Students have two advisors in the Dual model. Faculty advise regarding the students' program of study (i.e., core program requirements, electives), and a centralized office advises regarding general education requirements, registration procedures, academic policies, and the like. In this model the advising office has overall coordinating responsibility and advises exploratory students. This model was found in 5% of the institutions surveyed by ACT, a slight increase from an earlier survey (Habley, 2004). Strengths include the advantages of two delivery systems. However, it is essential that the responsibilities of each advisor and/or advising system be clearly articulated so students know who to see for what.

In the Total Intake model, all of the initial advising occurs through one office, which may be staffed by professional advisors, counselors, faculty, paraprofessionals, or peers. Students are assigned to faculty or academic subunits once specified conditions are met (e.g., after their initial registration, after completion of the first semester, after completion of 45 credits). The director of the office has campus-wide coordinating responsibility and may also have responsibility for the development and enforcement of policies and procedures as well as the development and administration of curriculum and instruction. This model was found in 6% of the institutions surveyed by ACT, a slight increase from a previous survey (Habley, 2004). The key strength of this model is the ability to front load the system and provide a strong start for students. However, attention must be paid to transitioning the students from that initial contact to the assigned advisor.

Perhaps the most useful purpose of assessing an advising organizational model is to better understand an institution's system as it relates to serving students. Insight into one's own model as well as how other models work can be an excellent guide for augmenting services, redesigning processes, and engaging colleagues from across the campus in the common focus on academic advising and student success.

## Identifying the Ideal Model for Community Colleges

Given the demographics of first-year community college students, there are special challenges for academic advisors in terms of preparing students for the collegiate experience and giving them a roadmap for their time in college. An ideal model for community college advising would be the Total Intake model where there is a centralized advising office with a full-time director who reports to the chief academic or student affairs officer. The advising office would provide all advising for first-time students with continued advisement for students who are underprepared, exploratory, in academic difficulty, or changing majors. Once students have made some of the initial adjustments to college and declared a major, they would be assigned to teaching faculty in their program of study.

Full-time advisors and/or counselors, faculty, and paraprofessionals or peers would staff the advising office. All advisors would be carefully selected, receive systematic training, be evaluated annually, and be recognized and rewarded for exemplary advising. They would also interact regularly with key offices, such as admissions, financial aid, the registrar, the testing center, counseling, academic support services, and the academic departments. The office would have campus-wide responsibility for academic advising services.

This model allows the campus to front load the advising system, as entering students are meeting with dedicated advisors who know the system, programs, and support services available for students. They are able to advise across programs so that when students are undecided about or want to change a major, advisors can help without referring the student elsewhere. They can also help first-year students develop an academic plan for their two or more years and are able to respond to the wide variety of questions from entering students. Reassigning students to faculty once they are more settled in their program allows students to then take advantage of faculty expertise related to career connections, transfer, and research. For institutions that do not require advising beyond the first contact, students should have the information they need to self-advise or know where to go for assistance if they feel they still need it.

In 2005, Tacoma Community College (WA) launched a Total Intake academic advising model, which employed intrusive advising, a first-year seminar, group advising, and an array of related services. These programs have combined to create an effective, multi-intervention strategy to increase first-year persistence and move TCC students from admission to declaration of major and preparation for ongoing study. TCC reported a 14% increase in the fall-to-fall retention rate of first-time, degree-seeking students from 2007 to 2009 (Tacoma Community College Office of Institutional Effectiveness, 2010).

## Conclusion

Given the diversity of community college students, it is important to get them started where they are, assist them in creation of an academic plan, make them aware of and help them connect to the different support programs and services available, help them feel connected to the institution, and monitor their progress. In working with first-year students, academic advising can be the framework through which all student services are coordinated to assist new students in assessing, designing, and implementing a plan toward success. An academic advising program that is purposefully structured, well-coordinated, adequately funded, and that provides sound advisor development, recognition, and reward can put first-year students on the right track, helping them engage in their education, feel a connection to the institution, and ultimately achieve their educational and career goals.

## References

Brown, T., & Rivas, M. (1992). Multicultural populations for achievement and success. *New Directions for Community Colleges, 21*(2), 83-96.

Center for Community College Student Engagement. (2009). *Making connections: Dimensions of student engagement.* Austin, TX: The University of Texas at Austin, Community College Leadership Program.

Crockett, D. S. (1984). *Advising skills, techniques and resources.* Iowa City, IA: American College Testing.

Dean, L. A. (Ed.). (2006). *CAS professional standards for higher education* (6th ed.). Washington, DC: Council for the Advancement of Standards in Higher Education.

Fox, R. N. (2008). Delivering one-to-one advising: Skills and competencies. In V. N. Gordon, W. R. Habley, & T. J. Grites (Eds.), *Academic advising: A comprehensive handbook* (2nd ed., pp. 342-355). San Francisco, CA: Jossey-Bass.

Habley, W. R. (1983). Organizational structures for academic advising: Models and implications. *Journal of College Student Personnel, 24*(6), 535-540.

Habley, W. R. (1995). *Foundations of advising.* Presentation delivered at the Summer Institute on Academic Advising. Iowa City, Iowa.

Habley, W. R. (Ed.). (2004). *The status of academic advising: Findings from the ACT Sixth National Survey* (NACADA Monograph, 10). Manhattan, KS: National Academic Advising Association.

Habley, W. R., & McCauley, M. E. (1987). The relationship between institutional characteristics and the organization of advising services. *NACADA Journal, 7*(1), 27-39.

King, N. (2008). Advising delivery: Group strategies. In V. N. Gordon, W. R. Habley, & Associates, *Academic advising: A comprehensive handbook* (2nd ed., pp. 279-291). San Francisco, CA: Jossey Bass

National Academic Advising Association (NACADA). (n.d.). *Clearinghouse of academic advising resources.* Retrieved from http://www.nacada.ksu.edu/Clearinghouse/AdvisingIssues/index.htm

National Academic Advising Association (NACADA). (2005). *NACADA statement of core values of academic advising*. Retrieved from the *NACADA Clearinghouse of Academic Advising Resources* website: http://www.nacada.ksu.edu/Clearinghouse/AdvisingIssues/Core-Values.htm

Noel Levitz. (2005). *Five-year trend study: National student satisfaction report*. Iowa City, IA: Author.

Noel Levitz. (2009). *National student satisfaction and priorities report*. Iowa City, IA: Author.

Pardee, C. F. (2000). Organizational models for academic advising. In V. N. Gordon, W. R. Habley, & Associates, *Academic advising: A comprehensive handbook* (pp. 192-210). San Francisco, CA: Jossey-Bass.

Pascarella, E., & Terenzini, P. (1977). Patterns of student-faculty informal interaction beyond the classroom and voluntary freshman attrition. *Journal of Higher Education, 48*(5), 540-552.

Pascarella, E., & Terenzini, P. (1979). Student-faculty informal contact and college persistence: A further investigation. *Journal of Educational Research, 72*, 214-218.

Schenectady County Community College. (n.d.). *College mission, vision and goal areas*. Retrieved from http://www.sunysccc.edu/about/mission.htm

Tacoma Community College Office of Institutional Effectiveness. (2010, November). *Declared and prepared: Increasing student retention at Tacoma Community College* (An unpublished report). Tacoma, WA: Author.

# Chapter 9
## Career Development: An Essential Component of First-Year Experiences and Student Transitions

Patricia Stanley

Much is written about the multiple missions of community colleges, but three primary elements are career preparation, transfer, and lifelong learning. Career development is central to all three. The National Career Development Association (2008) defines career development as the total constellation of psychological, sociological, educational, physical, economic, and change factors that combine to influence the nature and significance of work in the total lifespan of any given individual. Herr and Cramer (1996) define it as "the lifelong psychological and behavioral procedures as well as contextual influences shaping one's career over the life span" (p. 7). As such, it involves the integration of an individual's decision-making style, life roles, values and beliefs, and self-concept.

Organized career development efforts, like community colleges, have been a part of the higher education landscape in the United States for more than a century. The career development process helps students understand the essential connection between education and career, as well as the life they wish to live. Career development represents the entire sequence of activities and events related to one's career, and it encompasses organized educational qualifications, certifications, and the career path options available at community colleges.

Indeed, most students come to community colleges to advance their career goals, including those that require transitions to other institutions. While community college students are aware of their need for postsecondary education, they are often not aware of the career options that may match their goals, interest, values, and aptitudes or how their limitations may impact available options. Given the vocational mission of many community colleges, career centers or career services often emphasize job placement late in the educational experience, rather than developing comprehensive services related to the entire spectrum of the career development process. Yet, first-year community college students need career development assistance as they declare majors, select career programs, or plan a career pathway. Getting involved in the career decision-making process early in the college experience can have positive results related to program completion and student success. Moreover, appropriate career choices translate not only to future job satisfaction but also to enhanced quality of life for community college students.

Because self-concept and quality of life are intertwined with career choice, career development is an essential component of comprehensive first-year experience programs, especially in the community college. This chapter will provide an overview of the career development process, describe the essential role this process plays in community college career pathways initiatives, and explore the connection between career development and student retention in the first-year of college and beyond. It will also describe several community college career development programs that might be adapted for other contexts. The chapter concludes with recommendations for program enhancement and development.

## The Community College as the Nexus of Career Pathways

A review of the National Career Development Guidelines (NCDG) Framework (National Training Support Center, 2004) helps align career development and community college goals. The Guidelines framework include three domains: (a) Personal and Social Development, (b) Educational Achievement and Lifelong Learning, and (c) Career Management. Under each domain are goals, which define broad areas of career development competency.

### Personal and Social Development Domain
◇ Develop understanding of self to build and maintain a positive self-concept
◇ Develop positive interpersonal skills including respect for diversity
◇ Integrate growth and change into your career development
◇ Balance personal, leisure, community, learner, family, and work roles

### Educational Achievement and Lifelong Learning Domain
◇ Attain educational achievement and performance levels needed to reach your personal and career goals
◇ Participate in ongoing, lifelong learning experiences to enhance your ability to function effectively in a diverse and changing economy

### Career Management Domain
◇ Create and manage a career plan that meets your career goals
◇ Use a process of decision making as one component of career development
◇ Use accurate, current, and unbiased career information during career planning and management
◇ Master academic, occupational and general employability skills in order to obtain, create, maintain and/or advance your employment
◇ Integrate changing employment trends, societal needs, and economic conditions into your career plans (para. 1)

Community college missions often include statements reflecting the NCDG Framework concepts, such as enhancing personal and social development, providing education for lifelong learning, and assisting students in acquiring skills to manage their education and career plans. As open-access institutions, community colleges serve students at various points in the lifespan and with a range of career development needs (e.g., launching a first career, changing career fields, enhancing skills for career advancement), making career development an essential component of community college education.

Education career plans are central to the career development process; likewise, community colleges are often central to providing career planning and pathways for students. Currently, career pathways are used in all states based on the U.S. Department of Education's (U.S. DOE) 16 career clusters, which include, for example, Health Sciences, Finance, and Human Services. Each cluster has numerous career pathways within it, ranging from entry-level to management, including technical and professional career specialties. There are 78 career pathways in the U.S. DOE model, such as Business Financial Management and Accounting, and Health Informatics. Career specialties in the U.S. DOE model are numerous with examples that include bookkeeper, marketing manager, geoscientist, and epidemiologist. The goal of the career pathways process is to prepare students to transition successfully from high school to postsecondary education where career decision making leads to more specific career pathways and career specialties followed by employment in the chosen career field. Career clusters, pathways, and specialties are often all encompassed when educators use the term career pathways.

Hull and Parnell (1991) recognized the importance of programs that required education beyond the secondary level while also creating a smoother transition from secondary to postsecondary education. Tech Prep 2+2 programs span high school and community college career occupational areas, blend the liberal and practical arts, and have support through federal funding from the Perkins Act (i.e., Carl D. Perkins Vocational and Technical Education Act and Carl D. Perkins Career and Technical Education Improvement Act of 2006). Tech Prep is a national educational initiative that involves restructuring traditional curricula and introducing new teaching approaches at the secondary and postsecondary levels. It also integrates career decision making appropriate to each level and links high school career and technical programs to postsecondary certificate or degree programs to become a streamlined 2+2 program.

The Tech Prep concept has been expanded to Programs of Study (POS), which may begin before the junior year of high school and continue beyond community college enrollment to baccalaureate and graduate level education. This extension is critical as the Department of Labor projects that by 2014 the value of postsecondary credentials and skills will rise in high-demand fields with close to 4 million job openings in areas such as health care, education, and computer and mathematical sciences (Hecker, 2005). As a result, the Perkins Act calls for programs of study, or comprehensive, structured approaches for delivering academic and career education to prepare students for postsecondary and career success. An example is the Teacher Academy of Maryland (TAM), which seeks to increase the number of students entering college-level teacher preparation programs. Developed collaboratively among local school systems; community colleges; four-year institutions; and representatives from the university system of Maryland, the Maryland Higher Education Commission, and Maryland State Department of Education, TAM is aligned with the Education and Training Career Cluster and is also part of College and Career Transitions Initiative (CCTI) Education and Training Institute at Anne Arundel Community College in Arnold, Maryland (U.S. Department of Education, 2010).

### Experiential Education and Career Pathways

Career pathways often include work experiences for students as they engage in early career decision making. These experiences may take the form of service-learning, a teaching and learning strategy that integrates meaningful community service with instruction and reflection to enrich the learning experience, teach civic responsibility, and strengthen communities (National Service-Learning Clearinghouse, 2010). With objectives closely aligned to the mission and goals of community colleges, it is no surprise that 60% of the nation's community colleges currently offer service-learning opportunities and another 30% are interested in doing so (AACC, 2009). The American Association of Community Colleges (AACC) has a national project, Broadening Horizons through Service-Learning, funded by Learn and Serve America wherein colleges participate in compiling long-term community impact, retention, and persistence rates.

Richardson (2006) suggests service-learning is particularly useful for secondary and post-secondary career and technical education (CTE) instructors: "Like CTE, service-learning puts coursework into context, mixes rigor with relevance and builds concrete skills" (p. 38). Richardson also notes that students who participate in service-learning report gains in career skills, communication skills, and career exploration knowledge. Teachers also believe that participation in service-learning increases career awareness. Reese (2010) describes a service-learning opportunity that connects career exploration to the criminal justice program at Monroe Community College in Rochester, New York. Here, students work to increase safety in their neighborhoods through the Safe Passages Program, which ensures that elementary students make it safely to and from school.

Other workplace experiences that may be included along the career pathway in community colleges to assist student with career decision making are cooperative education, internships, and apprenticeships. Cooperative education is a structured strategy integrating classroom studies with learning through productive work experiences in a field related to a student's academic or career goals. Co-op is a partnership among students, educational institutions, and employers, with specified responsibilities for each partner (National Commission for Co-operative Education, 2010). The structure of cooperative education leads to degree completion of an academic program and may include Tech Prep 2+2, Programs of Studies, and School-to-Work. Like Tech Prep and Programs of Study described above, School-to-Work has roots in federal legislation. The School-to-Work Opportunities Act of 1994 called for programs to include school-based learning, work-based learning (cooperative education), and connecting activities. Work-based learning is very often a component of community college postsecondary career preparation programs and is helpful as students make career decisions that will affect their current and future lives.

Internships have many of the same components as cooperative education. Students participate in planned, supervised work; internships may be paid or unpaid and are often a capstone experience for a career program. Apprenticeships may also be a part of the student's pathway in a program of study. Registered apprenticeships "connect job seekers looking to learn new skills with employers looking for qualified workers, resulting in a workforce with industry-driven training and employers with a competitive edge" (Office for Apprenticeship, 2010, para. 8). Members of the Apprenticeship Advisory Committee for Registered Apprenticeships have commented that within a career pathway program, the student benefits from dual enrollment in an apprenticeship and an educational institution. Registered apprenticeship programs have the potential to increase student retention by concurrent enrollment in a secondary school and a community college, as well as the apprenticeship experience.

### Adult Education and Career Pathways

Pathways from adult education programs are also important to community colleges, as many adult students require additional skills for advancement in their current careers or to support a career change. Two Office of Vocational and Adult Education (OVAE) projects, Ready for College and Career Connections, funded through grants from the U.S. DOE, provide insights into facilitating career pathways for adult learners. In successful pathways, curricula must be aligned for seamless transition, and the League for Innovation in Community Colleges' College and Career Transition Initiative (2006) has completed this type work in 16 career clusters. Also, cooperation and trust must be built and maintained between education segments as secondary teachers, adult education instructors, and postsecondary faculty work together with career development advisors. The goal is to create curricular frameworks in the broad career clusters that can prepare students to move seamlessly from high school or adult education to postsecondary education and employment. The selection of a career area that is later refined to a specific career choice requires progressing through the steps in the career development process in order for the ultimate career goal to be achieved.

The role community colleges play in career pathway reform cannot be overemphasized as these colleges work with many partners—business and industry, secondary and adult basic education, as well as private and public baccalaureate institutions. Wise and Rothman (2010) note the importance of designing specific programs to support career pathways for adult learners:

> Increasing the supply of postsecondary certificate earners to meet the demands of a skilled workforce requires...recognizing that many adults are balancing families, work obligations, and finances. The more flexible and accessible the education experience, the more likely that adults will be able to participate. (p. 3)

Community colleges are well positioned to provide these educational experiences for first-year adult learners.

## Baccalaureate Programs in the Two-Year College

A number of community colleges are adopting a baccalaureate option to assist students in completing a career pathway that requires the baccalaureate degree. These opportunities are often called higher education centers or Communiversities. Community colleges offer some baccalaureate degrees independently, as is currently the case with 54 public community colleges nationwide (Russell, 2010). Yet, the Community College Baccalaureate Association (2009) acknowledges that collaborative programs are more common than independent community college baccalaureate degrees. For some adult learners, these options are often the only means they have to access baccalaureate education and complete their identified career goals. While data show that community colleges students who transfer to four-year colleges and universities perform well compared to their peers who start college at four-year institutions, the number who successfully transfer falls far below what is needed in the nation's workforce (Center for Innovative Thought, 2008). As lifelong education providers, community colleges can assist students in reaching their ultimate career goals through multiple options, including access to baccalaureate degrees, which may take a number of years as well as a number of career educational plans or career pathway revisions.

## Career Development Services Online

Historically the growth of computer technology aligns with the growth of community colleges, and many examples of excellent web-based student services (e.g., course, registration, library access, academic support) can be found in the nation's community colleges, which frequently have missions to offer education (and services) any time, any place, anywhere (O'Banion, 1997). Therefore, it should be no surprise that some colleges are also providing effective career services to students online. Colleges without walls, such as Coastline Community College in Southern California and Rio Salado in the Maricopa Community College District in Arizona, have provided online student support services for many years. The state of California has adopted the international program, The Real Game, to align with California Academic Content Standards, Career Technical Education Model Curriculum Standards, and the Future Content Standards for Adult Literacy and Lifelong Learning. This new digital program is also aligned with the 2004 National Career Development Guidelines; the American School Counselor Association National Standards for Student Academic, Career and Personal/Social Development; and the U.S. Secretary of Labor's Commission on Achieving Necessary Skill (SCANS) Employability Skills. Partners in this endeavor include the Chancellor's Office for California Community Colleges, the K-20 Education Technology Collaborative, and the California Career Resource Network. Real Game is a creative method of teaching career skills through a set of six career development programs targeted to various ages, including adults. The programs encourage participants to learn more about themselves, to focus on the process in addition to the end goal, to identify and reach out to important allies, to develop resilience in the face of change, and to cultivate an appreciation for lifelong learning.

### The Impact of Career Pathways Initiatives on Student Retention

At the Community College Symposium held in 2008 by the Office of Vocational and Adult Education in collaboration with the Community College Research Center at Columbia University, a number of researchers expressed concern that data were not available to support pathways, a well-received education reform (Karp, 2008). While career pathways and programs of study with their career development components certainly appear to be the right thing to do for community college students, comprehensive national data on increased completion and retention rates remain to be collected. Valentine et al. (2009) underscore the need for such research, noting "many interventions supporting transition that are of interest to policymakers lack even one experimental evaluation and most existing non-experimental evaluations are of undetermined inferential strength" (p. 52). At the same time, they highlight the potential contribution of career development to the first-year experience, suggesting "that there is reason to be optimistic about the potential for relatively comprehensive interventions to help students earn better grades and stay in school, at least in the short term" (p. 5). In fact, the initial retention data from the College and Career Transition Initiative project, which aligned the curriculum and career development within pathways, are encouraging. Additional support for the efficacy of career pathways programs comes from campus-based studies.

Cunningham, Cardenas, Martinez, and Mason (2006) report on a study done on the Lucero Program at Lansing Community College (Lansing, MI), which provided the growing population of Latino students with computers, helped them make connections to the community, and offered them academic assistance (e.g., tutoring; reading, writing, and assessment exams; a summer institute) and mentoring. The Lucero Program also offered a workforce development component, which assisted students in defining a career path, preparing for job interviews, and connecting with local employers by assigning mentors or professionals from their chosen fields. Students in the program (2003-2004) had an 80% retention rate compared to 56% for the college overall. They took an average of 11 credits and earned a mean GPA of 2.63. As an outcome of program participation, students identified themselves as degree seeking (90%), with half of those planning to transfer to a four-year institution.

Another study (Baron,1997) indicated that career development contributed to increased retention in the first year of college when it was an integral component of first-year experience initiatives. The FOCUS (Freshman Outreach, Caring, Understanding and Support) Center at Bronx Community College (Bronx, NY) offers holistic counseling, including vocational counseling, psychological assessment, relevant educational and occupational information, peer counseling and tutoring, an Occupational Preference Survey, and a revised orientation and career development course. The FOCUS Center also provides immediate contact with absent and at-risk students. The retention rate for first-year students participating in the program was 76.5% compared to 59.3% for students who did not participate.

While not specific to community college students, Lepre's (2007) work highlights the critical importance of encouraging undecided first-year students to take advantage of career counseling. She concluded that by targeting first-year students and possibly first-semester sophomores, career counseling professionals could optimize the chances of helping these students persist. Lepre noted that if the principles of student involvement theories are applied to the career decision-making process, then the students who are more involved in thinking about their future careers have a better chance of pursuing the academic programs that can help them achieve their goals.

Research (Calcago, Crosta, Bailey, & Jenkins, 2006) has shown that students who reach certain milestones, or momentum points, such as obtaining 20 credits or completing 50% of a program have a higher probability of graduating. To the extent that career pathways help students achieve these milestones, they should become an integral part of the first-year experience for community college students. The next section offers examples of programs designed to help students achieve a variety of milestones related to retention and academic success.

## Programs That Work

No two community colleges are exactly alike, as each college serves a community with distinctive educational needs. Accordingly there is no one-size-fits-all career development approach that meets the needs of diverse situations. Yet, the principles identified in first-year programs that successfully incorporate career development can serve as a road map for other colleges to use in developing initiatives for their unique contexts.

In order to highlight a variety of institutional types and locations—small, midsized, and large; rural, urban, and suburban—a number of sources were consulted. Several national associations, such as the National Council on Student Development (NCSD), an affiliate of the American Association of Community Colleges, and the National Academic Advising Association (NACADA), acknowledge program excellence in academic advising and career development. Their lists of recognized programs were mined for possible examples. Colleagues who are principals in the National Career Development Association, the Rural Community College Alliance, and the Guidance and Career Development Division of the Association for Career and Technical Education (ACTE) were also contacted for recommendations of exemplary programs. Principals from the California Institute for Career Development, the Office of Vocational and Adult Education, and career development professionals who were former members of the National Cadres of Trainers for the National Career Development Guidelines also supplied suggestions and contacts. Interviews with program directors focused on the following questions: (a) What is the mission (or goals) of the program? (b) How is the program structured? (c) How is program effectiveness measured? and (d) Could aspects of the program be used in other contexts?

### Northwest Vista College

Northwest Vista College (NVC) is part of the Alamo Community College District in San Antonio, Texas. The program "creates exemplary models for learning to be, learning to work, learning to serve and learning to lead ...together" (Northwest Vista College, 2010, p. 1.). Previous results from the Community College Survey of Student Engagement (CCSSE) on the importance, satisfaction, and use of career services were a red flag for NVC administrators. Students reported that career services and advising were very important to them, but their frequency of use was low. The large number of students who were undeclared majors, along with low transfer and graduation rates, indicated that NVC needed a strategy that could engage and increase awareness of programs and majors to students on a larger scale while also increasing their awareness of educational goal planning. The Career and Transfer Services (CaTS) Center Team concentrates on decreasing the number of students who have not declared an area of concentration.

A career assessment instrument called CaTS in the Classroom helps students validate their choice of major or explore different possibilities through various career decision-making services available at the college. NVC also has a self-paced, modular, virtual advising experience for students. Faculty, staff, and advisors collaborate twice a year in Major Mania, an opportunity to explore majors and visit with program faculty. Good participation and a 96% positive experience are reported for this awareness event. Colorful, easy to use materials have been developed for Northwest Vista's Academic, Career, Transfer Services: One is related to career planning and the second to milestones (momentum points) in the path to completion, with reminders to students as they gain credit hours. By combining CaTS with a student development seminar and other strategies, the number of undeclared students at NVC dropped from 23% in 2005 to 6.6% in 2009. NVC institutional research suggests that "students who have an education goal and plan are likely to be more successful than those who remain undeclared" (Northwest Vista College, 2010 p .1).

## Bucks County Community College

Bucks County Community College (Newton, PA) is a three-campus college with two one-stop centers: one for enrollment development (i.e., admissions, financial aid, and registration) and one for Student Planning Services. Both offer virtual as well as physical services to support students. Student Planning Services consists of academic advising support and faculty advising coordination, career and job services, counseling services, disability services, prior learning assessment, success grant programs, transfer planning resources and services, and the dean of Student Affairs office. The goal of the one-stop model is to reduce the need for of students to seek information and services from multiple campus locations and websites. Rich Fulton at Frederick Community College (personal communication, May 22, 2002) likens separated services to the Bermuda Triangle. Before student services at the college were moved to one location, students needed to visit three different buildings to complete necessary transactions. Just like ships in the mythic Bermuda Triangle, students would often disappear en route and not be seen again.

At Bucks, the motto "Student First Student Fast" reflects the desire to provide students with what they need in a timely way and is actualized in the center's physical organization, cross training of staff, enhanced efficiency, and more. Evaluations include college-based questionnaires completed by students after all sessions (via e-mail, phone, or face to face), the Noel Levitz Student Satisfaction Inventory, and the CCSSE. The Institutional Research Office administers CCSSE; both academic and student service areas use the results. At Bucks, the student is viewed holistically, and the college mission mandates no more silos (C. Hagedorn, personal communication, October 19, 2008). Thus, career development is an integral part of a larger program to assist students during their first year in a number of ways.

## Montgomery Community College

At Montgomery Community College (Blue Bell, PA), the Career Services Office is managed by the director of Career Services who reports to the vice president of student services. The Career Services goal is to offer programs, activities, and services that will provide individuals with lifetime tools for successful career and personal development in a rapidly changing world. Ongoing support is available to students (and alumni) at all times and the personalized and in-depth attention they receive has been reported as a major factor in making these services exemplary.

Master's degree-level counselors are available by appointment or on a walk-in basis to guide students through the career exploration and decision-making processes as part of an effort to promote self-awareness and support students in selecting appropriate career options and college majors.

Counselors are also available to teach students how to prepare résumés and portfolios, write cover letters, develop effective job search strategies, and overcome job search obstacles. Opportunities are provided to enable students to practice responding to questions to maximize confidence in job interviews. Further, a designated counselor is available to assist students interested in exploring internship opportunities.

In addition to diverse print, video, and web resources, students have access to DISCOVER, a self-directed, interactive career assessment and exploration program. For those interested in jobs or internships, College Central, an online job listing and information service, is available. A counselor provides each student with extensive and detailed feedback, encourages follow-up individual appointments for assistance, and reviews résumés uploaded on College Central.

Workshops and classroom presentations on a variety of topics are conducted to help students maximize success in career planning. For students enrolled in a two-credit first-year seminar, a specially developed classroom presentation, Preparing Now for a Successful Future Job Search, teaches current strategies for enhancing the success of future job searches. A two-credit career development course is also available to students. Finally, career fairs are scheduled regularly throughout the school year to provide students with networking and job or internship search opportunities as well as to obtain first-hand career information from employers. Attendance at career fair preparation workshops is encouraged prior to these events.

Vice president for student affairs Steady Moono (personal communication, November 12, 2009) suggests that other colleges can replicate their multiple assessment strategies at minimal costs to the institution. These include the Noel Levitz Student Satisfaction Inventory, point-of-service surveys, employee surveys, graduate surveys, placement data, alumni feedback, and retention data for students using the services. The common theme and lesson learned in all these surveys is the emphasis on career service staff getting connected with students very early in their first semester and performing multiple checkups throughout the subsequent semesters.

## Quinsigamond Community College

At Quinsigamond Community College (Worcester, MA), the Career and Academic Services (CAPS) program is intended to further student success by employing a developmental career and advising model that provides assistance during all stages of a student's college experience. The model used at Quinsigamond is organized in four stages, defined by number of credits earned toward a degree, and prepares students to assume larger responsibility for decision making as they progress through a program of study. A staff of full- and part-time advisors offers courses in career planning, academic advising and strategies for student success, web-based support, and other services on a year-round basis. All advisors, including faculty advisors, have ongoing, innovative professional development opportunities that focus on current trends in advising (e.g., working with millennial students, using technology, and identifying hot jobs in the state).

The Early Alert system at Quinsigamond also addresses both career and academic planning through a formal, proactive, feedback system, which alerts nonperforming students and student-support agents to early signs of academic failure or withdrawal from the college. Timely, appropriate intervention services can prevent potential first-year student dropouts. The structure at Quinsigamond has the CAPS director reporting to an assistant dean in the Division of Academic Affairs, thus reinforcing the connection to instruction and faculty in academic areas. Data collected over six years for a Title III grant show that the college orientation course, Strategies for College and Career, one third of which is career development content, has increased student persistence to the second semester 15-25% above the baseline, indicating that career development strategies are making a difference.

## Manchester Community College

Career Services at Manchester Community College (MCC, Manchester, CT) offers job skills workshops, job and career fairs and expos, special programs/events, professional development, and a job-listing service. Career Services also promote a number of resources including a web page, an annual employee newsletter, a tool kit for success, ex-offenders resources, and summer brochures. The web page (Manchester Community College, 2010) contains promotion and connection to cooperative education and internship programs so that students can gain academic credit while refining their career choice and gaining experience in a chosen field.

The job fairs include résumé critiquing by nationally certified résumé writers and opportunities to learn about and apply for internships and cooperative education. MCC graduates who are now professionals offer insights to various industries as well as continuing education opportunities. The Connecticut Career Counseling and Development Association, a division of the Connecticut Counseling Association, cosponsored John D. Krumboltz, author of *Luck is No Accident,* on the Manchester College campus as a professional development event for academic and career counselors from a number of colleges in the state. College-sponsored speakers have included Brian Jud, an expert in foreign-born workforce development and author of *Job Search 101*, and Richard Nelson Bolles, author of *What Color is My Parachute*. College partners help to cosponsor career and job fairs.

At MCC, Career Services offers the opportunity to use an online career information delivery system called Choices Planner that helps students compare, connect, and choose from a vast network of education options. This interest-based assessment tool enhances self-awareness and helps career explorers make more informed decisions about where they fit into the world of work. Results are saved in a personal portfolio.

Coordination with other services that fall under the first-year experience is accomplished by recommendations and referrals. The Career Services staff presents a career choice-focused workshop to first-year seminars at the request of the teaching faculty.

Recognizing the importance of assessment, Manchester Career Services is moving from gathering data on client satisfaction to focusing on what learning has occurred as a result of the program. Currently, all workshops are evaluated at their conclusion via an online survey with questions focused on why students came, whether their goals were achieved, and related queries. A year-end report compiles these data and shows that 85-95 % of the participants indicate satisfaction levels of *very good* or *excellent*. Employers evaluate job fairs and the Vocational Day programs in much the same manner, with similarly positive results.

## Orangeburg-Calhoun Technical College

As a rural community college, Orangeburg-Calhoun Technical College (O-C Tech) in Orangeburg, South Carolina is part of the majority of American community colleges that serve the needs of unique rural communities. Career development initiatives at O-C Tech facilitate the pursuit of careers in STEM fields. Using funding from the National Science Foundation Advanced Technology Education division, O-C Tech has developed Diverse Engineering Pathways, a project that incorporates a focus on green technology.

The South Carolina Education and Economic Development Act (2005) established Personal Pathways to Success, a system for students to transition seamlessly from the state high schools to postsecondary education. With secondary school contacts and basic understanding of the secondary education curriculum in place, O-C Tech built a formal alliance (i.e., consortium) with 10 school districts, industry, Claflin University, and South Carolina State University. Grant funds supported summer workshops and other initiatives, such as credit recovery to assist secondary students in getting ready for college. O-C Tech, in conjunction with the University of South Carolina and the South Carolina Department of Education, adapted the nationally recognized pre-engineering Project Lead the Way curriculum to increase dual credit and articulation opportunities, while adding rigor to the traditional technical courses and relevance to traditional academics. OC-Tech provides instructors for three alliance school districts in order to attract larger numbers of students to the STEM career and advanced manufacturing career cluster. Student interest in these areas has increased from 10% to 33% over a three-year period, and the college has added calculus and physics course offerings to meet program demand.

College counselors have all completed career development facilitation certification, and one full-time college counselor is assigned to the high schools. All eighth and ninth grade students in the consortium were given interest inventories (i.e., Kuder and Explore), and no match was found between students' stated career interest and the area's industry job needs. Thus, career development workshops for parents and teachers now include information on where jobs are in the college service area. The college and their secondary partners pool Perkins Career and Technical Education Act funds (restricted to career pathways or programs of study) to jointly fund career guidance initiatives.

O-C Tech collects completion, retention, and enrollment data to assess outcomes of the pathway projects. Enrollment data in targeted career areas needed in the community industries are especially critical to the consortium alliance. Achieving the Dream guidelines and grant assessment requirements assist the college in acquiring data for future decisions. New opportunities reflect the success of the pathway collaboration. For example, a five community college consortium has received grant funds to provide training in the STEM related area of megatronics, a program that includes both technology and electrical skills. O-C Tech is also working with other colleges to provide professional development for teachers in high schools. Such collaborations have resulted in consistent course numbers at the various colleges and shared course offerings so all the colleges need not offer each course required in often expensive, special programs. Next in the pathways programs at O-C Tech will likely be health careers as the alliance members look at the need for additional skills to be learned in high school biology, anatomy, and other science disciplines.

Key to the success of the O-C Tech pathways project is collaboration with secondary schools—starting at eighth grade—and four-year baccalaureate institutions. Such collaboration builds trust for articulation and transfer of credits. The pathways grants and the collaborative work has also led, in part, to revamping and updating the first-year program course at O-C Tech. Another change in the first-year program is the result of three years of data collection on Supplemental Instruction (SI). The data show that the program is working, as students who participate in SI have a pass rate 10 points higher than those who do not participate. To help students succeed with their career plans, the college is now mandating tutoring in some sections based on the information and analysis.

## Recommendations and Implications

The trend in community colleges to focus on success for all first-year students appears to be a force in merging and integrating career planning and advising with other student support services. The one-stop approach to a number of student services is prevalent as is offering such services online or via the college website. Faculty, staff, and advisors working together may be an outgrowth of the learning college movement, described by Boggs in chapter 1, as that concept suggests that all college personnel are responsible for student learning and success. It also makes students responsible for their own learning as seen in the Quinsigamond program example.

The community college professionals who work with and direct the programs described in this chapter suggest aspects of their successful initiatives that might be adapted at other colleges. Specific recommendations follow.

◇ *Make career development a core component of first-year experiences and student services programs.* The college could require a career development component in the first-year seminar and/or merge or integrate the management of such courses with career planning and advising.

◇ *Front load services via a Welcome Center, orientation program, or other initiative so that career development concepts are introduced to students early in their college experience.* Noel, Levitz, and Saluri (1985) argue that

> One of the first objectives of an institution ought to be to help students think through, in a very rational and informed way, the kinds of careers or majors that are most appropriate for them...It should be a process that begins in and continues throughout the first year, perhaps even throughout the second. (p. 11)

◇ *Build a strong relationship between student and academic affairs (i.e., between learning support, instruction, and student success services) in which faculty are equal partners with counselors.* Good programs can successfully report to the dean, provost or vice president of academic affairs, or student services administrators. However, program excellence and collaborative relationships take a tremendous investment of time, patience, and political skill to develop.

◇ *Provide excellent professional development for faculty, staff advisors, and counselors to emphasize the importance of career development as an integral part of every student's college experience.* To ensure that students receive the information and services they need when and where they need them, cross-train college faculty, staff, advisors, counselors, and others to deliver career education on a continuous basis

◇ *Work cooperatively with secondary schools and baccalaureate-level institutions so that career development is a continuous pathway of ever more refined student decision making.* Academic experiences should also be supplemented by appropriate work experiences throughout the career pathway (i.e., at the secondary and postsecondary level). Such opportunities might take the form of service-learning, cooperative education, practica, or internships. However, all have the potential to assist in career exploration and planning.

◇ *Use accountability measures that provide insight into student goal achievement to improve services and to make other program decisions.* As noted earlier, there is limited research demonstrating the effectiveness of career pathways initiatives. In order for such initiatives to flourish, institutions must be able to demonstrate their value to students, to employers, and to the larger community served by the college.

◇ *Provide program reports to college faculty, staff, decision and policy makers to gain a strong commitment to this career aspect of student success from the top down as well as from across the college program areas.* Regular communication with the career program advisory committees that are recommended (often required) for all career-focused programs at community colleges and with local business and industry leaders will ensure that career pathways initiatives are relevant and serving the needs of the community. Moreover, presenting program assessment results will help them understand how the college is attempting to address their concerns—and how successful the college has been in doing so. Providing opportunities for internal and external constituents to respond to assessment results may also open up new avenues for program development and improvement.

◇ ***Support national data collection efforts on career pathways programs.*** While institutional-level assessment and research are critical for program improvement and expansion at the local level, they may have limited usefulness in informing practice and policy decisions on a state, regional, or national level. Comprehensive national studies on the impact of career pathways programs on achievement of critical milestones in the first college year and long-term persistence are needed to institutionalize such efforts on more campuses.

Students come to community colleges to gain knowledge and skills for careers that provide a quality life for themselves and their families. First-year experience programs in community colleges that are carefully developed to increase retention and foster transitions cannot short change career development components in their design and implementation. A student's success in life is dependent on lifelong career development and learning, just as lifelong education is central to the community college mission.

## References

American Association of Community Colleges (AACC). (2009). *Service learning*. Retrieved from http://aacc.nche.edu/Resources/aaccprograms/horizons/Pages/default.aspx

Baron, W. (1997). *The problem of student retention: The Bronx Community College Solution – The Freshman Year Initiative Program*. (ERIC Document Reproduction Services No. ED 751 698).

Calcago, J. C., Crosta, P., Bailey, T., & Jenkins, D. (2006). *Stepping stones to a degree: The impact of enrollment pathways and milestones on community college student outcomes*. New York, NY: Columbia University, Teachers College, Community College Research Center.

Center for Innovative Thought. (2008). *Winning the skills race and strengthening America's middle class: An action agenda for community colleges*. New York, NY: The College Board.

Community College Baccalaureate Association (2009). *Philosophy, mission and purpose*. Retrieved from http://.www.acccbd.org/

Cunningham, P. D., Cardenas, J., Martinez, R., & Mason, M. L. (2006). Lucero: Shining light on Latino retention. *Community College Journal of Research and Practice, 30*,139-140.

Hecker, D. E. (2005, November). Occupational employment projections to 2014. *Monthly Labor Review, 128*(11), 70-101.

Herr, E. L., & Cramer, S. H. (1996). *Career guidance and counseling through the life span: Systematic approaches* (5th ed). New York, NY: Longman.

Hull, D., & Parnell, D.(1991). *Tech-prep associate degree: A win/win experience*. Waco, TX: Center for Occupational Research and Development.

Karp, M. M. (2008, July 19). *Towards a community college research agenda: Summary of the National Community College Symposium*. New York, NY: Columbia University, Teachers College, Community College Research Center.

League for Innovation in Community Colleges. (2006). *College and Career Transition Initiative*. Retrieved from http://www.league.org.league/projects/ccti/index.html

Lepre, C. R. (2007). Getting through to them: Reaching students who need career counseling. *Career Development Quarterly, 56*(1), 74- 84.

Manchester Community College. (2010). *Career services*. Retrieved from http://www.mcc.commnet.edu/students/career/

National Career Development Association. (2008). *Career development: A policy statement of the National Career Development Association Board of Directors*. Retrieve from http:// www.ncda.org

National Commission for Co-operative Education. (2010). *The cooperative education model*. Retrieved Nov. 15, 2010 from http://www.coop.edu/aboutcoop2.html

National Service-Learning Clearinghouse. (2010). *What is service-learning?* Retrieved Nov 15, 2010 from http://www.servicelearning.org/what_is_service-learning/servicelearningis

National Training Support Center. (2004). *National career development guidelines (NCDG) framework*. Retrieved from Alliance of Career Resource Professionals (ACRP) website: http:// www.acrna.net/

Noel, L., Levitz, R., Saluri, D., & Associates. (1985). *Increasing student retention*. San Francisco, CA: Jossey-Bass.

Northwest Vista College (2010). *Northwest Vista career development*. Unpublished paper. San Antonio, TX: Author.

O'Banion, T. (1997). *A learning college for the 21st century*, Phoenix, AZ: Oryx Press.

Office of Apprenticeship. (2010.) *Registered apprenticeship: Top questions about RA*. Retrieved July 16, 2010 from http://www.doleta.gov/OA/eta_default.cfm

Reese, S. (2010, April). Learning and serving through CRE. *Techniques: Connecting Education & Careers*, 17-20.

Richardson, S. (2006, January). The power of service-learning. *Techniques: Connecting Education & Careers*, 38-40.

Russell, A. (2010, October). Update on the community college baccalaureate: Evolving trends and issues. *Policy Matters*. Retrieved from the AASCU website http://www.congressweb.com/aascu/startpage.htm

South Carolina Education and Economic Development Act (EEDA). (2005). Section 59-59-30 of the South Carolina Code of Laws.

U.S. Department of Education, Office of Vocational and Adult Education (OVAE). (2010, July 29). *OVAE Connections*, p. 1. Retrieved from http://www2.ed.gov/news/newsletters/ovae-connection/2010/07292010.html

U.S. Department of Labor. (2010). *Registered apprenticeship*. Retrieved from http:// www.doleta.gov/OA

Valentine, J. C., Hirschy, A. S., Bremer, C., Novillo, W., Castellano, M., & Banister, A. (2009). *Systematic reviews of research: Postsecondary transitions – identifying effective models and practices*. Louisville, KY: University of Louisville, National Research Center for Career and Technical Education.

Wise, B., & Rothman, R. (2010, February). *The online learning imperative: A solution to three looming crises in education* (Issue Brief). Washington, DC: Alliance for Excellent Education.

# Chapter 10

## Learning Communities and Community Colleges: The Challenges and Benefits

Randy Jedele with Vincent Tinto

Originally, learning communities were created to provide more powerful learning experiences and improve student success in college. Beyond coregistration and the social affiliations they spur, learning communities are designed, in their fullest implementation, to build educational settings that require students to collaborate and use the knowledge and skills they acquire from the different courses in the community to build more powerful learning experiences. For underprepared students, for instance, such a setting enables them to acquire basic academic skills in the context of a content course. The result is not only increased academic and social engagement, via the educational activities of the community, but also increased learning and enhanced retention. In fact, Shapiro and Levine (1999) concluded:

> Regardless of how we choose to define success in college—whether it is a statistical measure of persistence and retention, or gains in critical thinking and writing abilities that show up as positive outcomes on student learning assessments—we now have compelling evidence to suggest that creating learning communities on campuses leads to greater student success in college. (pp. 14-15)

Even though learning communities have received much acclaim and many accolades, Minkler (2002) notes, "there continues to be a lively debate among community college educators as they examine this innovation and assess how it might help them serve a changing and diverse population of learners" (p. 46). Yet, it is the very diversity of learners in community colleges that should, more than any other factor, encourage faculty, staff, and administrators to seriously consider launching a learning community initiative, redesigning an existing program, or increasing activity in the learning community program. This chapter seeks to lay out some of the possibilities related to learning community initiatives for community college educators.

It is beyond the scope of this chapter to provide a detailed history of learning communities or the theoretical perspectives that support them. Similarly, we have chosen not to review the literature describing student, faculty, or institutional outcomes related to learning communities. Rather, readers are referred to the numerous journal articles and books describing, research, theory, and practice in learning community programs (see for example, Gabelnick, MacGregor, Matthews, & Smith, 1990; Lenning & Ebbers, 1999; Levine Laufgraben, Shapiro, & Associates, 2004; Shapiro

& Levine, 1999; Smith, MacGregor, Matthews, & Gabelnick, 2004). Instead, the primary focus for this chapter is on the following three research questions:

1. Do learning communities look different at community colleges than at four-year institutions?
2. What special challenges do learning communities present for community colleges?
3. What are the unique benefits of having learning community initiatives on community college campuses?

Before taking up these questions, the chapter will offer a rationale for adopting learning communities and a brief description of some common learning community models. The chapter closes with descriptions of learning community programs at 10 community colleges.

## A Rationale for Learning Communities

In the mid- to late-1980s, several publications, such as Bloom's (1987) *The Closing of the American Mind* and Ravitch's (1988) *What Our Seventeen-Year-Olds Don't Know*, raised questions about the curriculum of higher education, the role of faculty, student involvement, and high attrition rates. In addition to these calls for reform in higher education, changing student demographics, new methods of curriculum delivery, and new understandings about how people learn led colleges and universities to implement learning community initiatives (Levine Laufgraben et al., 2004). As Gabelnick et al. (1990) note, "learning communities are a vehicle for responding to all of the issues at once" (p. 6). Similarly, Smith et al. (2004) suggest that learning communities

embody an analysis of what is needed to reform higher education (curricular restructuring), a theory of learning (based on current research), a commitment to certain educational goals (putting student learning at the center of our work), and a commitment to the importance of community (a necessary condition for learning). (p. 22)

Finally, Schoem (2002) states that

The name "learning community" affirms two important principles: that of learning and that of a community of learners. It suggests that course content, pedagogy and learning are inherently intertwined, and it explicitly puts forward the long-standing, though sometimes overlooked, notion of a community of scholars—both faculty and students—coming together for deeper learning. (p. 53)

As such, Shapiro and Levine (1999) note that the structure of learning communities allow colleges and universities to

◇ Organize students and faculty into smaller groups
◇ Encourage integration of the curriculum
◇ Help students establish academic and social support networks
◇ Provide a setting for students to be socialized to the expectations of college
◇ Bring faculty together in more meaningful ways
◇ Focus faculty and students on learning outcomes
◇ Provide a setting for community-based delivery of academic support programs
◇ Offer a critical lens for examining the first-year experience (p. 3)

In this way, learning communities are "an effective way to address some of the most pressing concerns of the academy—disengaged, passive, and unevenly prepared students, a fragmented curriculum with little connections between and among courses, and a high freshman to sophomore year attrition rate" (Strommer, 1999, p. 41).

Research on learning communities seems to bear this out. Retention and persistence are natural byproducts of students' making connections with other students and faculty members who participate in learning communities. The combination of student bonding and active learning facilitates what Tinto (1987) saw as a critical factor in student retention: "membership in at least one supportive community, whatever its relationship to the center of campus life" (p. 68). Further, a qualitative study by Gabelnick et al. (1990) revealed that students expressed a sense of belonging, an appreciation for collaboration and working with other students who did not always have the same insights or ideas about classroom subjects and materials, an ability to establish connections between courses, and a deeper understanding and appreciation of self as a result of learning community participation. For the most part, students commented on "their sense of involvement more than anything else—with their peers, their faculty, with college in general, and with themselves as maturing learners" (p. 57).

As higher education moves into the 21st century, it is becoming increasingly obvious that learning communities are not a fad. More and more college campuses are implementing learning community programs. A 2002 study by the Policy Center of the First Year of College (now the John N. Gardner Institute for Excellence in Undergraduate Education) found that 62% of all institutions enrolled at least some of their entering students in a learning community (Barefoot, 2002). When asked about the continued interest in learning communities, Cross (1998) suggested that learning communities continue to be relevant because "they are compatible with changing epistemologies about the nature of knowledge, because research generally supports their educational benefits, and because they help institutions of higher education meet their missions of educating students for lives of work and service" (p. 11). Further, when fully implemented, learning communities enhance student social and academic engagement, improve student learning, and increase first-to-second-year persistence (Engstrom & Tinto, 2008; Tinto, 1996; 1997; Tinto, & Russo, 1994).

## Learning Community Models

According to Levine Laufgraben et al. (2004), "there is a sense that no 'one size fits all,' and classifications, as well as models of learning communities, vary as needed to adapt to distinct campus cultures" (p. 20). Yet, most learning communities can be categorized as one of four types: "(1) paired or clustered courses, (2) cohorts in large courses or FIGS . . ., (3) team-taught programs, and (4) residence-based learning communities, models that intentionally link the classroom-based learning community with a residential life component" (Levine Laufgraben et al., p. 5).

Paired or clustered (sometimes referred to as linked courses) learning communities are designed for integrating curriculum and helping students make connections with other students. These are usually the first type of learning community formed on campuses. Gabelnick et al. (1990) note these communities are the simplest to create because while some degree of syllabi or assignment coordination takes place, faculty teach their courses independently.

Cohort models—sometimes referred to as freshman interest groups or FIGs—are a type of community formed within larger classes. FIGs are more commonly found in large university settings, and they are designed as a support group for students in the FIG. Each member of a FIG attends two or three larger classes together, and they meet at least once a week, usually with a peer advisor, to discuss issues related to the larger classes or to share frustrations and concerns about the first-year experience (Levine Laufgraben et al., 2004; Smith et al., 2004; Gabelnick et al., 1990).

Team-taught communities, also known as coordinated programs, can involve two to five faculty members who work together in one coordinated effort (Levine Laufgraben et al., 2004). These types of communities demand the "most radical restructuring of typical course offerings . . . as both faculty and students are engaged . . . in interdisciplinary, active learning around themes" (Gabelnick et al., 1990, p. 28).

Residence-based learning communities, also referred to as living/learning communities, add another dimension to the curricular models. In addition to registering in a cohort of classes, the students live together. One of the benefits of living/learning communities is that academic discussions often spill from the classroom to the residence halls more so than in regular residential or learning community situations.

## Research Method

As noted above, a considerable amount of research conducted on a wide range of learning community topics exists; however, very little of this work focuses specifically on community colleges. Lenning and Ebbers (1999) and Smith et al. (2004) have a brief list for community colleges in their indexes, but neither work addresses this setting specifically. Several journal articles or book chapters (Bystrom, 1999; Engstrom & Tinto, 2008; Hodge, Lewis, Kramer, & Hughes, 2001; Killacky, Thomas, & Accomando, 2002; Matthews, 1986; Tinto & Russo, 1994) and doctoral dissertations (Emmerson, 2009; Faga, 2006; Gerkin, 2009; Jedele, 2007; Reynolds-Sundet, 2007; Rye, 1997) have examined learning communities in the community college. However, none has specifically addressed the three research questions asked here (i.e., the differing structures, challenges, and benefits of the learning community in a two-year setting as compared to a four-year setting).

For the current study, learning community coordinators at select community colleges across the country were invited to respond to the research questions. A convenience sampling of learning communities was selected from the Washington Center for Improving the Quality of Undergraduate Education's registry of community colleges. In addition to these institutions, community colleges that have well-established learning community programs (i.e., Kingsborough Community College, LaGuardia College, and Seattle Central Community College) and those involved in the promotion of learning community work (i.e., Delta College, Harper College, and Metropolitan Community College in Kansas) were also included in the sample. The learning community coordinators at 27 institutions were invited via e-mail to participate in the research. They were asked to provide a brief history of their learning community initiatives and respond to the three research questions. In some cases, the coordinators supplied the information about their learning community programs and answered the questions, while in other instances, the coordinators asked their learning community team or advisory board to participate with them to answer the questions.

Of the 27 coordinators contacted, 10 agreed to participate. Their responses shaped the discussion of the findings below. Additional details about their initiatives are included in the Practices section of this chapter.

## Findings

*Institutional Differences*

Although both community colleges and four-year institutions use the same models—linked, coordinated, clustered, FIGs—there are some differences between the makeup and types of learning communities offered. According to Julie Simanski (e-mail communication, November 19, 2009) at Des Moines Area Community College (DMACC), "heterogeneous populations of students with varying abilities and motivation, unlike the four-year institutions with entrance standards that somewhat equalize the playing field" impact the composition of learning communities at community colleges. For example, developmental learning communities, which link two or more remedial classes (e.g., reading, writing, math) or link a remedial class to a credit-bearing class (e.g., a developmental reading class connected with a sociology or psychology class), are more common at community colleges than at four-year institutions.

Study strategies classes, while not necessarily developmental, are designed to help underprepared students acquire the academic skills for college success. These classes may also be frequently linked to other courses. DMACC has had success with several study strategies classes linked with such classes as Composition I, Introduction to Psychology, and Western Civilization. The sole purpose of these types of learning communities, besides having integrated learning opportunities, is to create cohort situations where students will hopefully make connections with other students, their faculty in the cohorts, or the institution in some way. The emphasis on academic skills development may make such linkages more common at open enrollment institutions.

The vast majority of community college students commute to campus as very few two-year institutions have residence halls. As a result, living/learning communities are, for the most part, only found at four-year institutions. These residence hall communities, often based on majors, create a completely different cohort of students. Students make connections in their classes and within the social space of the residence hall, where entire floors may be devoted to students in the same major. Thus, "four-year community experiences may be more long-lasting as [students] pursue their career interests in major-oriented communities, rather than the [classroom-only] communities more frequently found on community college campuses" (J. Simanski, e-mail communication, November 19, 2009).

Differences in institutional mission may also shape learning community offerings. Similar to the major-oriented learning communities found at four-year institutions, community colleges frequently form learning communities in career program areas such as automotive, culinary, or criminal justice. Students involved in career programs usually form cohorts because they take so many classes together. As such, career program learning communities are not designed for cohort building as much as to improve academic skills and increase the rate of program completion. For example, at DMACC, the writing component was completely integrated into the automotive arena, and the required speech component was introduced in a learning community in the culinary department. The students in these programs found it easier and more comfortable to write or speak about automotive and culinary topics with their peers in those programs than to explore topics outside their areas of expertise. As a result, more students successfully completed their program requirements and received their certificates.

A similar learning community initiative was added in the criminal justice department in the fall of 2009, where a group of first-year criminal justice majors at DMACC were encouraged to join a learning community linking Introduction to Criminal Justice and Composition I. Similar to the two programs described above, the writing instructor in these learning communities based the majority of the writing assignments on criminal justice topics. The instructor also used the criminal justice textbook to design assignments based on the readings and the major topic of each chapter. A second learning community is planned for Juvenile Law and Composition II. At the time of this writing, data reporting on program effectiveness were not available; however, anecdotal evidence suggests that both instructors and students were pleased with the integrated learning experiences and the improvement in writing skills for the students who participated.

## Special Challenges

Though not a unique challenge to community colleges, the simple act of encouraging student participation in learning communities seems to be an ongoing problem. Until the learning community culture is well established, it is very difficult to get students to participate. This may be especially true for underprepared and first-generation college students who may have limited understanding of the nature and benefit of integrated learning models. Also, the large number of students who register online without any assistance from the academic advising staff may limit participation. At J. Sargeant Reynolds Community College, establishing a level of awareness has always been the "greatest challenge" since "approximately 75 percent of students self advise and use online registration" (M. McCrimmon, e-mail communication, December 3, 2009). For commuter students, the benefits of learning community participation may pale in comparison to personal obligations. Simanski notes,

> Community college students not only go to school, but also they have families, financial, work, and social obligations that often weigh more heavily in their day-to-day lives. Adding one more component, such as the obligations of a learning community could possibly burden an already overwhelmed student. (e-mail communication, November 19, 2009)

To help raise student awareness about the value of such initiatives, several institutions promote individual scheduling sessions with advisors and counselors who are well-informed about learning community opportunities. Tracey McKenzie at Collin County Community College maintains that "academic advisors have played a key role in promoting learning communities and informing students of these unique course options." (e-mail communication, December 3, 2009). Because Des Moines Area Community College has summer orientation for program areas, the two instructors involved with the criminal justice learning communities visited the orientation sessions to promote the value of taking the criminal justice learning communities. This targeted promotion was successful because both of the fall classes filled to capacity. At Collin County Community College, the faculty have participated in a variety of marketing techniques including, "Banner ads on the college homepage, streaming videos of professors promoting their courses, e-mail blasts, and movie theater ads. In addition, faculty continue to play a significant grassroots role in recruiting students for their LCs" (T. McKenzie, e-mail communication, December 3, 2009).

As at many institutions, one of the primary challenges for launching and sustaining educational initiatives is funding. Susan Jensen (e-mail communication, November 24, 2009) at Grossmont College notes, "In my experience over 25 years, money, or the lack of it, has always come into play in respect to the growth of" learning communities on this campus. Jensen recommends that colleges building a learning community initiative from monies received "from grants or other sources run the risk of losing participation from instructors when the grants run out." However, even once the grant money was spent, Grossmont College managed to build a culture of collaboration where faculty are willing to participate in the learning community program without receiving stipends for development or reassigned time for teaching together.

*Unique Benefits*

As noted above, commuter students may present a special challenge to learning community organizers. Yet, they also stand to gain unique benefits from their participation in such programs. Simanski suggests,

> given the lack of activities often available at a community college, learning communities offer students an opportunity to connect socially, as well as academically. Sometimes the learning community is the only opportunity for some students to connect with the institution or other students because they spend more time with these students than the students in their 'stand alone' classes. (e-mail communication, November 19, 2009)

Learning communities may also offer benefits to students who are at greater risk for dropping out—those attending part-time, late enrollees, and those required to take remedial classes. Gonzalez (2009) notes that "students who enroll part time are less engaged than their full-time peers, and more likely to drop out of college. Such likelihood is high at community colleges, where close to two thirds of students attend part time" (p. A19). Part-time students, especially those who work full-time, are often more concerned about filling a schedule, than signing up for specific classes. In an attempt to schedule classes around their jobs, part-time students often take whatever is available, which may mean enrolling in a learning community because a block schedule makes managing work obligations easier. While they benefit from the scheduling convenience, the opportunity to become more engaged with their studies, their peers, and their faculty members may also increase their likelihood of persisting.

Another group with high dropout rates are students who enroll late, many as late as the first week of classes during a new semester. Usually, these students lack direction and motivation. However, many community colleges have designed learning community environments in an attempt to help students make connections to faculty and other students and decrease the likelihood of their dropping out (Emmerson, 2009). For example, at Des Moines Area Community College, first-time, full-time students who enroll seven days prior to the first day of classes are required to see a counselor or advisor to register, and based on their COMPASS/ACT scores, they must take at least one learning community or a supported course, such as a college preparatory course or SDV 108, The College Experience, which is the college's orientation to college seminar.

Jensen believes that the sense of community gained through learning community participation is also extremely beneficial for those students who are placed into developmental classes. Because these students "often lack self-confidence, academic and/or personal goals, and motivation, the learning community gives them much more than academic preparation" (S. Jensen, e-mail communication, November 24, 2009). The fact that community college missions stress the teaching and learning environment allows them, as Jensen maintains, to be in "a unique position because [community college faculty] can 'nurture' while they teach." Similarly, Benjamin Sloan from Piedmont Virginia Community College also discusses the benefits for developmental or other at-risk students, noting that "learning communities can provide a sturdier safety zone for those who are on the knife's edge, academically and otherwise. . . . The learning community provides a strong framework for collaboration, and all of the benefits are on the side of the at-risk student" (e-mail communication, November 30, 2009). Engstrom and Tinto (2008) concur, suggesting that at-risk students who participate in learning communities "are significantly more likely than their peers to persist from freshman to sophomore year—a crucial point at which many students leave higher education" (p. 19).

Although faculty at community colleges are not the only learning community instructors who benefit from collaboration, it only stands to reason that this group will benefit more because of their devotion to teaching. Indeed, from their inception, community colleges were designed as teaching institutions where "a large majority of the faculty are oriented more toward teaching than toward research" (Huber, 1998, p. 2). In fact, Cain (1999) stated that "the teaching faculty is the key to community college's work" (p. 47). In his study of community college learning community faculty, Jedele (2007) discovered passionate teachers who were tremendously impacted by collaboration that was connected to learning community preparation, which carried over to their teaching experiences in future stand-alone classes. In some cases, such as at Grossmont, the collaboration goes beyond the learning communities and has "helped build a culture of community on the campus . . . that gives us opportunities to promote student growth [and learning] that are not comparable to a four-year college" (S. Jensen, e-mail communication, November 24, 2009).

## Practices: Learning Communities in the Community College

Learning communities have been used in a variety of ways for a range of students. Most frequently, they have been employed in the first semester as an academic and social gateway that helps students make a successful transition to college. That is the case because their very structure, namely having students co-enroll in two or more courses, helps students develop early social and academic affiliations that underlie successful transitions. In addition, when directed to students who begin college academically underprepared, as they are at DeAnza College and El Paso Community College, among many others, they help students make the transition to college-credit work by connecting one or more developmental courses to a content course. In this way, students are getting academic assistance while also earning college credit.

In other instances, community colleges have employed learning communities more directly to help students transition by including a first-year seminar among the courses that comprise the learning community. In these instances, such as at Des Moines Area Community College and Inver Hills Community College, the first-year seminar can take on a variety of forms from the more traditional orientation course. For example, some courses stress study and time management skills, others have attended to issues of advising and counseling, and others combine elements of all three areas. These have been highly successful at many community colleges. For example, in an attempt to improve student success, Inver Hills Community College (2010), collected data regarding their learning community initiative; their first-year seminar, OnCourse; and students who participated in both a learning community and OnCourse from 2006-2008. Learning community participation appears to support student retention, with persistence from fall to spring ranging from low- to mid-80% for students in a learning community, OnCourse, or a combination of the two, as compared to a low 70% in their control group. Des Moines Area Community College also collected data from 2005 to 2009. The students were enrolled in learning communities with at least one college prep course, such as orientation to college, study strategies, or a developmental course (i.e., reading or writing), linked to a content-based course, such as psychology or history. Their persistence rate from fall to spring with learning community students ranged 94.6 % learning community students persisting, as compared to 60.7% in the control group in 2005 to 74.6% learning community students persisting, as compared to 63.6% in the control group in 2009 (J. Dehart, e-mail communication, March 15, 2010). Regardless of the emphasis, the benefit of including a first-year seminar in the learning community is that it enables the instructor to align the seminar activities with the needs of students in the linked course, and therefore, more directly attend to the many issues that shape students' transitions to college. The program descriptions that follow highlight additional strategies for structuring learning communities to support student academic success and persistence.

## Collin County Community College

Learning communities at Collin County Community College (Dallas, TX) follow a model of fully integrated paired classes in which faculty members from two different disciplines collaborate to blend and coordinate the course curriculum around a common theme or central question. Faculty design and propose courses and the variety of course offerings changes each semester. The courses are truly interdisciplinary in that faculty members are present for the duration of the combined sessions. All course work is blended (i.e., class discussions, experiential projects, exams, field trips, and grades). Each faculty member is fully engaged in every aspect of each course. Bringing together faculty members from different disciplines in this fashion changes the essential nature of the educational experience making it substantially more collaborative and participative than typically found in stand-alone courses. Students are exposed to aspects of issues they would rarely have the opportunity to consider in a stand-alone class where only one discipline and faculty perspective is presented. The faculty members serve as role models for questioning, challenging, and integrating perspectives from the other discipline. Students engage with the faculty members and each other, and the nature of the learning community experience invites them to discuss, collaborate, integrate, and explore (T. McKenzie, e-mail communication, December 3, 2009).

## Delta College

The learning community program at Delta College (University Center, MI) is a faculty-led initiative that averages 30 learning communities during an academic year, enrolling between 750-800 students in a variety of offerings (e.g., developmental, transfer and general education, special topics, career track). The faculty at Delta College have created both linked and fully coordinated models, with learning communities ranging from two to five courses. Delta College provides its faculty and staff development through a special course on pedagogy in learning communities. The National Learning Communities Conference was founded by Delta College, and the college continues as one of the six rotating host institutions for the conference (A. Colenbrander, e-mail communication, December 22, 2009).

## Des Moines Area Community College

Learning communities have been a part of the academic culture at Des Moines Area Community College (Des Moines, IA) since 2001. The program is marketed with the tag phrase "Turn your commuting experience into a community experience." The college has had success with a range of types of learning communities, such as linking the first-year seminar and Composition I, developmental reading and writing, and study strategies and content-based classes. In addition, they offer several boutique options, specially designed learning communities faculty create because they want an interdisciplinary team-teaching experience. Some examples are Sex and Syntax (linking Composition II and Marriage and Family), which integrates writing and sociology; Art, Music, and Ideas (Composition I and Introduction to Humanities), combining writing and humanities; and Three Peas in a Pod, merging public speaking with children's literature. Usually, these learning communities are coordinated and taught in a block schedule of time. To facilitate the transfer of engineering students to Iowa State University and to ensure their persistence to a degree, the College has launched another type of learning community initiative. An initial focus group of the community college students suggested that once they arrived at the four-year campus, they felt left out and somewhat lost. With this in mind, the community college will seek to establish a cohort of students who would transfer to the engineering program as a group. The program is one of several initiatives funded by a joint National Science Foundation grant to the College and Iowa State. Data on the impact of the program are not yet available; however, partnerships like these seem well positioned to foster greater opportunities for student success in the community college and beyond.

### Grossmont College

Project Success at Grossmont College (El Cajon, CA) is a 25-year-old learning community program that regularly offers about 40 sets of two or more course links. Because linked instructors teach the same students in back-to-back classes, they are able to integrate curriculum and share course goals, content, texts, and activities. A sense of community develops among students who work together productively and support each other in a safe learning environment. Such environments are especially important for the approximately 1,000 students enrolled in linked basic skills courses each semester. Both institutional and independent research conducted over the life of the program has shown that basic skills students in Project Success far exceed the achievement and retention levels of basic skills students enrolled in stand-alone courses. In 2008, Project Success developed a linked basic skills reading, writing, and math learning community contextualized to prepare students for the nursing program. Research on this community is expected to show superior student achievement in math, as well as in writing, and thus promote the development of additional contextualized course links (S. Jensen, e-mail communication, November 24, 2009).

### Harper College

As of 2010, learning communities approach their 20th year as an important feature of the educational landscape at Harper College (Palatine, IL). Learning communities currently run in three main models: (a) a fully coordinated course, which means faculty design and coteach a multi-disciplinary program of study around a theme involving two courses; (b) linked courses consisting of two or more discrete courses with faculty working together to coordinate the syllabi and/or assignments, but teaching their own course individually; and (c) business simulation, where students sign up for a business course and gain exposure to six different business disciplines by working to create a comprehensive business plan for a local entrepreneur. In recent years, Harper College has typically run 10 to 12 learning community courses per semester with total enrollments running at approximately 225 students. Learning community offerings have included more than 40 courses from a wide range of disciplines. (R. Middleton-Kaplan, e-mail communication, March 14, 2010).

### Inver Hills Community College

Learning communities were first offered at Inver Hills (Inver Grove Heights, MN) in the mid-1990s for students who were English language learners. At that time, the programming was not sustainable, but in 2006, when learning communities were suggested as a strategy for improving student success and retention, the English for Academic Purposes (EAP) faculty were eager to re-establish learning communities for English-language learners. EAP faculty found that combining developmental EAP reading and writing courses with carefully selected college-level content courses not only motivated students but also gave them opportunities to immediately apply the skills and principles taught in the EAP courses (J. Costello, e-mail communication, June 26, 2010).

## J. Sargeant Reynolds Community College

In the fall of 2009, the third year since the inception of learning communities at J. Sargeant Reynolds (Richmond, VA), 15 learning communities were offered, serving approximately 700 students. This enrollment was a 25% increase in learning community participation from the previous year. These learning communities are primarily targeted to serve 18- and 19-year-old first-year students, and the retention rate was 9% higher than nonlearning community students. The majority of these learning communities were linked with either the first-year experience class or Composition I. Although the initiative is young, it has already affected the culture of teaching and learning at the college. Training has been added to assist faculty in developing techniques and resources for improving student engagement. (C. Peterson, e-mail communication, December 1, 2009).

## Kingsborough Community College

Learning communities at Kingsborough Community College (Brooklyn, NY) have increased in number over the past 14 years. Beginning in 1995, with the institution of the Intensive ESL Program and the emergence of the Opening Doors Program in 2003, Kingsborough's learning communities have grown from serving approximately 120 first-time, first-year students each semester to more than 1,000. The majority of these students are underprepared for college-level courses, and approximately 75% test into developmental English. Although research suggests that the underprepared students are more likely to stop out of college, Kingsborough's learning community program has been able to demonstrate a significant and consistent rise in academic success and persistence in college.

Kingsborough offers three learning community programs: (a) Open Doors, a program for first-time, first-year college students; (b) ESL Intensive, a program for students with English language acquisition needs; and (c) Career Focused, a program for second-semester and other advanced students pursuing their major areas of study. Kingsborough's evaluation results have shown that students in the program groups felt more integrated and engaged than students in control groups. Program students attempted and passed more courses and earned more credits during their first semester, and they were more likely to take and pass English skills assessment tests that are required for graduation or transfer.

The impact of learning communities at Kingsborough has reached beyond the documented academic success of the students. The development and growth of the learning community program has had a direct impact on the College's process, policy, and practice. For example, more intrusive advising is being used, so that students are more appropriately registered in classes, especially in the developmental education area. The program has also transformed the way faculty teach and work within the college community through student-centered pedagogy, cross-curricular connections, and ongoing collaboration among faculty, advisors, tutors, librarians, and students. (R. Singer, e-mail communication, December 4, 2009).

## Metropolitan Community College

AIM for Success is a learning community designed to give some of Metropolitan Community College's (Omaha, NE) most at-risk students a stronger start. In 1994, a Developmental Education Task Force was created to study the success rates of developmental students. What the task force found was that students who tested into all developmental courses—math, writing, and reading—had a very low success rate. Based on Tinto's (1996; Tinto & Russo, 1994) research on learning communities, Metro decided to create a learning community for developmental students. The extra support these students find in a learning community seemed likely to help them be more successful in their classes and their overall college experience. The AIM for Success learning community, which focuses on three developmental courses—math, writing, and reading–was piloted in 1997. The success of the pilot led to its expansion to all three campuses. Feedback from counselors suggested that more of the AIM students continued to attend Metro and that they tended to register for classes together to continue the learning community experience on their own. Because of word of mouth, more students began to ask about AIM (T. Quick, e-mail communication, December 1, 2009).

### Piedmont Virginia Community College

Piedmont Virginia Community College (Charlottesville, VA) began its learning community initiative in 2004 as a result of a report completed by the Learning Communities Task Force, which recommended it as a worthwhile investment of campus resources. Funding for the program has come through the College's foundation-sponsored Teaching and Learning grants and Title III money aimed at strengthening student support services and developmental education-related areas. The project is directed by a coordinator for learning communities and a Learning Communities Advisory Board, comprised of faculty who have taught in learning communities, two deans, and a librarian. Developmental English and math classes have always been a part of the learning community program. Other communities have been consciously designed and structured to improve retention and success by linking such classes as English and American history or math and chemistry. Data collected in 2007 suggest that persistence rates for students participating in learning communities are significantly higher than the general student population (88% vs. 76%, B. Sloan, e-mail communication, November 30, 2009).

## Conclusion

There is little question that, within reason, learning communities can do much to enhance the success of community college students. But achieving success requires the understanding that coregistering students for two or more courses does not, in itself, make for a learning community. Coregistration is only the foundation upon which a learning community is built. Robust learning communities require that the content of the linked courses be coherently integrated and structured to allow application across the learning community.

Such integration does not arise by chance; rather, it is the result of an intentional policy that facilitates collaborative work among faculty and professional staff. In community colleges where faculty and staff are more than fully occupied with teaching courses and working with students, the time for successful integration of course content is sorely lacking. Without an institutional policy that invests in the development and sustainability of learning communities, it is too often the case that learning communities never really move beyond coregistration models.

But even when supported by the institution, the development of effective learning communities does not occur over night. Typically, such communities take three to four years to reach full effectiveness. This gestation period is a reflection of a number of issues, not the least of which is that it takes time to learn how to implement learning communities well in a particular context with a particular population of students. As students learn in a learning community, so too must faculty and staff. Ongoing quantitative and qualitative assessment must be part and parcel of the work of faculty and staff, not only to monitor their progress in implementing the communities, but also to learn how to manage learning communities more effectively.

Though the challenges of collaboration and assessment may seem daunting, it is clear that many institutions, such as those described above, have faced those challenges successfully. We need to learn from their experience and use that knowledge to the benefit of our students. They deserve no less.

## References

Barefoot, B. O. (2002). *Second national survey of first-year academic practices.* Brevard, NC: Policy Center on the First Year of College. Retrieved from http://www.jngi.org/2002nationalsurvey

Bloom, A. (1987). *The closing of the American mind.* New York, NY: Simon & Schuster.

Bystrom, V. A. (1999). Learning communities in the community college. In J. H. Levine (Ed.), *Learning communities: New structures, new partnerships for learning.* (Monograph No. 26, pp. 87-96). Columbia, SC: University of South Carolina, National Resource Center for The First-Year Experience and Students in Transition.

Cain, M. S. (1999). *The community college in the twenty-first century: A systems approach.* New York, NY: University Press of America.

Cross, P. (1998, July-August). Why learning communities? Why now? *About Campus,* 4-11.

Emmerson, J. E. (2009). *Leading them to water: A study of the efficacy of a mandatory placement project in first-year academic courses at a community college* (Unpublished doctoral dissertation). Ames, IA: Iowa State University.

Engstrom, C. M., & Tinto, V. (2008). Learning better together: The impact of learning communities on the persistence of low-income students. *Opportunity Matters: A Journal of Research Informing Educational Opportunity Practice and Programs, 1,* 5-21.

Faga, K. (2006). *Paired, developmental learning community: A case study of one institution* (Unpublished doctoral dissertation). Ames, IA: Iowa State University.

Gabelnick, F., MacGregor, J., Matthews, R. S., & Smith, B. L. (1990). *Learning communities: Creating connections among students, faculty and disciplines* (New Directions for Community Colleges No. 41). San Francisco, CA: Jossey-Bass.

Gerkin, D. (2009). *The impact of a first-year learning community on student persistence: Perceptions of a community college students* (Unpublished doctoral dissertation). Minneapolis, MN: Walden University.

Gonzales, J. (2009, November 20). Connecting with part-times is key challenge for community colleges, survey finds. *The Chronicle of Higher Education,* A19.

Hodge, G., Lewis, T., Kramer, K., & Hughes, R. (2001). Collaboration for excellence: Engaged scholarship at Collin County Community College. *Community College Journal of Research and Practice, 25,* 675-690.

Huber, M. T. (1998). *Community college faculty attitudes and trends.* Stanford, CA: National Center for Postsecondary Improvement.

Inver Hills Community College. (2010). *2010 systems portfolio.* Retrieved from www.inverportfolio.project.mnscu.edu

Jedele, R. E. (2007). *Teaching and learning in community: A phenomenological study of community college faculty pedagogy and learning communities* (Unpublished doctoral dissertation). Ames, IA: Iowa State University.

Killacky, J., Thomas, C., & Accomando, A. (2002). Learning communities and community colleges: A case study. *Community College Journal of Research and Practice, 26,* 763-775.

Lenning, O. T., & Ebbers, L. H. (1999). *The powerful potential of learning communities: Improving education for the future.* Washington, DC: The George Washington University.

Levine Laufgraben, J., Shapiro, N. S., & Associates. (2004). *Sustaining and improving learning communities.* San Francisco, CA: Jossey-Bass.

Matthews, R. (1986). Learning communities in the community college. *Community, Technical, and Junior College Journal, 57*(2), 6-8.

Minkler, J. E. (2002). ERIC review: Learning communities at the community college. *Community College Review, 30*(3), 46-63.

Ravitch, D. (1988). *What our seventeen-year-olds don't know.* New York, NY: Harper & Row.

Reynolds-Sundet, R. (2007). *Toward a greater understanding of student persistence through learning communities* (Unpublished doctoral dissertation). Austin, TX: The University of Texas.

Rye, A. M. (1997). *The impact of teaching in coordinated studies programs on personal, social, and professional development of community college faculty* (Unpublished doctoral dissertation). Corvallis, OR: Oregon State University.

Schoem, D. (2002, November/December). Transforming undergraduate education: Moving beyond distinct undergraduate initiatives. *Change,* 50-55.

Shapiro, N., & Levine, J. H. (1999). *Creating learning communities: A practical guide to winning support, organizing for change, and implementing programs.* San Francisco, CA: Jossey-Bass.

Smith, B. L., MacGregor, J., Matthews, R. S., & Gabelnick, F. (2004). *Learning communities: Reforming undergraduate education.* San Francisco, CA: Jossey-Bass.

Strommer, D. W. (1999). Teaching and learning in a learning community. In J. H. Levine (Ed.), *Learning communities: New structures, new partnerships for learning* (Monograph No. 26, pp. 39-50). Columbia, SC: University of South Carolina, National Resource Center for The First-Year Experience and Students in Transition.

Tinto, V. (1987). *Leaving college: Rethinking the causes and cures of student attrition.* Chicago, IL: University of Chicago Press.

Tinto, V. (1996). Persistence and the first year in the community college. In J. N. Hankin (Eds.), *The community college: Opportunity and access for America's first-year students* (pp. 97-104). Columbia, SC: University of South Carolina, National Resource Center for The Freshman Year Experience and Students in Transition.

Tinto, V. (1997). Classrooms as communities: Exploring the educational character of student persistence. *Journal of Higher Education, 28*(6), 599-623.

Tinto, V., & Russo, P. (1994). Coordinated studies programs: Their effect on student involvement at a community college. *Community College Review 22*(2), 16-25.

# Chapter 11

## Increasing Access and Success for First-Year Students in Science, Technology, Engineering, and Math

Kim Armstrong

A national crisis is emerging for the United States in global technological competitiveness (Committee on Science, Engineering, & Public Policy, 2007). In the coming decade, the retirement of scientists and engineers will significantly drain the labor pool in science, technology, engineering, and math (STEM) fields. The nation is also experiencing a brain drain as Chinese and Indian scientists and mathematicians who have worked in the United States return to their home countries (Nelson, 2009). At the same time, data on the state of education in the United States indicate a decreasing number of students choose to major in and successfully compete in an emerging global economy fueled by rapid innovation and technological breakthroughs. However, a major question is whether the science and high technology sectors in the United States will have sufficient numbers of STEM graduates to compete in the changing global marketplace (Froschauer, 2006).

In fall 2009, the Obama Administration presented a plan to bolster the nation's economic competitiveness by improving education in and attracting more students to STEM fields. The passage of the America COMPETES Reauthorization Act (2010) supports this goal by investing in modernized manufacturing, spurring American innovation through basic research and development of high-risk and/or high-reward clean energy initiatives, and strengthening math and science education to prepare students for the 21st century workforce (Pelosi, 2010) Yet, this goal cannot be achieved by government intervention alone. Institutions of higher learning must play a crucial role in preparing all students to be competitive in the global economy.

However, all along the educational pipeline, students are being lost in the fields of science, technology, engineering, and mathematics. This is particularly true for historically underrepresented groups and women whose participation and persistence rates in these fields are dramatically lower than in the general student population (Johnson & Woodin, 2002). By 2050, minorities are projected to account for 47% of the U.S. population. Currently, minorities comprise approximately 30% of students enrolled at American community colleges. As a result of their accessibility, open door admission policies, and reduced costs, community colleges are likely to continue serving this increasingly diverse student population (Szelenyi, 2001).

This chapter examines the important role that community colleges play in preparing students for STEM careers. It opens with a discussion of current levels of participation in STEM fields and highlights some barriers to participation and success, particularly for historically underrepresented students and women. Strategies for increasing the pool of potential STEM students and supporting their progress to degree completion, with highlights from exemplary programs, are also explored.

## Participation in STEM Fields

There are nearly 1,200 two-year colleges in the United States enrolling 11.5 million students. Community colleges are an important segment of the STEM pipeline, offering associate degrees, which prepare students for entry-level employment in various STEM careers. Some school districts and community colleges have designated programs for high school students that often include transfer courses leading to a certificate or associate degree, including those in STEM fields (Blomberg, 2007). In 2002-2003, some 92,640 associate degrees (14.6% of all associate degrees) were awarded in STEM fields (National Center for Education Statistics [NCES], 2007). Computer science is a popular choice for students, with the number of earned degrees in computer science increasing at an average annual rate of 5.6% between 1990 and 2000. In 1998, computer science degrees represented 45% of all science and engineering degrees awarded, while degrees in engineering technology declined 36% between 1991 and 1997 (Johnson & Woodin, 2002). Health care workers, veterinary assistants, pharmacy technicians, forensic-science technicians, dental hygienists, and nurses are among the fastest growing occupations in this decade requiring a minimum of an associate degree (Blomberg).

Community colleges also support students whose ultimate goal is the completion of a bachelor's degree or higher. According to a report from the National Center for Education Statistics (NCES, 2007), 44% of recipients of bachelor's and master's degrees in science and engineering had taken at least one course in a two-year college. Other students may opt to complete the first two years of study at a community college before transferring to baccalaureate programs since math and science courses are an integral part of the general educational requirements for nearly all college students. This may be particularly true for historically underrepresented populations: More than 35% of ethnic minorities graduating with a bachelor's degree in science and engineering began their career at community college (National Science Foundation, 1996). Increasing numbers of community colleges are also providing opportunities for students to earn bachelor's degrees in STEM-related fields, such as nursing, through concurrent enrollment partnerships with colleges and universities.

Two-year colleges, because of the diversity of students they enroll, have the potential to contribute significantly to increasing the racial, ethnic, and gender diversity of those pursuing education and careers in STEM fields (Moore, 2009). Yet, participation of historically underrepresented populations, especially Hispanics and women, continues to lag behind other groups.

### Historically Underrepresented Populations

Until recently, minorities and women have held few jobs in STEM fields. Despite comprising more than two thirds of the population, women and minorities fill fewer than 25% of STEM positions in the United States. These low levels of job placement can in large part be explained by patterns of participation in STEM education. Although the number of degrees awarded to minority student groups continues to increase slightly, the largest proportion of degrees earned is at the associate level. Among minority student groups, nearly 30% of associate degrees are in the social sciences; however, the proportion of computer science degrees earned by minority students has almost doubled since 1985 from 2,052 to 3,615 (Johnson & Woodin, 2002). In 1998, minority students were awarded approximately 23% of the mathematics and computer science degrees at the associate level, a far higher percentage than degrees awarded to minority students at the bachelor's, master's, or doctoral level (Johnson & Woodin). Since nearly half of all undergraduates in the United States enroll in community colleges, the associate degree is an important milestone in attaining a STEM-related job, especially among underrepresented populations and women.

*Hispanic students.* A large number of students who are eligible to enroll in college have not done so, thereby creating a pool of undeveloped talent (Harrell, Forney, & Scott, 2003), especially among Hispanics/Latinos. The U.S. Hispanic population will triple by the year 2050 and grow from 15% to 30% of the total population (Government Accounting Office [GAO], 2006). The number of Latino students participating in higher education has more than doubled in the past 20 years, and those participation rates will continue to increase as the Hispanic population grows. Yet, Latino participation in STEM has not experienced the same growth (Dowd, Malcom, & Bensimon, 2009). Moreover, increased participation has not necessarily translated to degrees in any field. Latinos comprised 19% of the college-aged population in 2006 (18 to 24 year olds), but only earned 8% of the bachelor's degrees awarded. Such low completion rates have critical implications for the ability of the United States to meet its STEM labor force needs.

While the proportion of Hispanics employed in STEM fields almost doubled from 1994 to 2003 (5.7% to 10%, respectively, GAO, 2006), Hispanic representation in STEM-related fields (10%) was still lower than their representation in the labor force as a whole (13%, GAO). Participation in STEM-related programs of study mirrors Hispanic labor force participation. The majority of Hispanics who enter higher education will initially enroll in two-year colleges (Johnson & Woodin, 2002), and most will pursue fields of study in social science or business. In 2006, only 0.03% of all first-year Hispanic female students planned to major in computer science (Johnson & Woodin). Yet, Hispanic students are not necessarily uninterested in STEM fields: 36% of Latino students expressed an interest in majoring in a STEM field, and Latinos enter STEM majors at rates similar to White and African Americans (Johnson & Woodin). Trends among Hispanic students showed an increase in the number of associate degrees earned in engineering technology until 1995 when participation in this field began to decline. Since the mid-1990s however, there has been an increase in degrees awarded in computer science (Johnson & Woodin). Still, only 6.7% of computer science bachelors' degrees are earned by Hispanic/Latinos.

*Women.* In 2003, women accounted for approximately 26% of all STEM workers (Thorius, 2009). When looking at women's participation by race or ethnicity, Hispanic women comprised 24% of the STEM workforce in 2003 compared to 27% of Asian American women and 35% of African American women (Johnson & Woodin, 2002).

Among minority groups, a growing number of girls are completing high school well prepared in math and science and capable of pursuing STEM majors in college. Female students are equally as likely to have taken and earned high grades in the prerequisite math and science classes in high school and have confidence in their math and science abilities (Johnson & Woodin, 2002). Although large numbers of women are capable of succeeding in STEM courses, fewer women than men pursue STEM majors (Thorius, 2009). Native American women earn less than 1% of computer science degrees, and African American women represent only 4.8% of the graduate enrollment in computer science (Simard, 2010). Among first-year college students, women are much less likely to say that they intend to major in STEM fields than their male counterparts, and those women who do pursue STEM majors leave them early in their college careers (Simard).

For both Hispanic students and women, as with other historically underrepresented populations, increasing STEM participation requires a two-prong solution, involving both recruitment and retention of eligible students.

## Barriers to Participation and Success

A large body of research enumerates the barriers that limit participation and success of women and minority students in STEM courses and careers. For example, students from historically under-represented groups, such as African American and Hispanic students, both female and male, are less likely to have access to advanced courses in math and science in high school, which has a negative impact upon their ability to perform successfully on standardized tests or complete STEM majors in college. In 2005, 31% of Asian American and 16% of White high school graduates completed calculus, compared to 6% of African American and 7% of Hispanic high school students. Also, 25% of Asian American and 10% of White students took either an advanced placement or International Baccalaureate exam in calculus, compared to 3.2% of African American and 5.6% of Hispanic students (Johnson & Woodin, 2002).

Lack of exposure to math and science course work may also lead to lower feelings of self-confidence among these students. Such feelings may be compounded by the fact that STEM industries do not communicate to girls and minorities that they are needed in these areas. Similarly, high school teachers and, later, college faculty and staff may have negative attitudes regarding the ability of women and minorities to achieve high levels in math and science. Such stereotyping may result in students' receiving subtle messages about their ability (or lack of it) to pursue STEM careers or experiencing overt discrimination and harassment in the classroom. The result is an academic system, which is still not blind to gender or color and which throws numerous roadblocks in students' paths to success (Robinson, 2010).

A related barrier for student entry into and success in STEM fields is a lack of mentors or role models for women and students of color. Faculty of color are rare in the STEM fields. For example, American Indians account for less than 1% of engineering faculty (Johnson & Woodin, 2002). Without role models and mentors, students may lack information about STEM careers and, as a result, are less likely to develop an interest in those fields. Students who decide to study STEM disciplines may feel isolated from their peers and instructors because of cultural and gender differences.

The presence and guidance of peer and/or faculty mentors have been shown to positively affect retention (Powell, 2006). Seventy percent of women and minorities stated that teachers had the most influence in their developing interest in STEM areas, and 88% reported that their high school teachers played the most influential role in sustaining their interest in STEM. Yet as noted above, negative attitudes of faculty and staff can be powerful disincentives. Despite an early interest in science and high regard for their science teachers, 40% of students surveyed stated that they were discouraged from pursuing a STEM career at some point in their lives. While 41% indicated that high school was where the initial discouragement occurred, more than 60% reported that the most devastating experiences occurred in college, with 44% specifically citing college professors as the individuals responsible (Nagel, 2010).

Aside from the challenges of recruiting women and minority students as STEM majors, institutions may have difficulty retaining these students. Science, mathematics, and engineering report the lowest retention rates among all academic disciplines. Approximately 50% of students entering college with an intention to major in one of these areas change majors within the first two years of study (Johnson & Woodin, 2002). As noted above, these retention rates may be worse for women and minorities.

Students may leave STEM majors for a number of reasons. Again, lack of adequate precollege preparation may make it difficult for students to succeed in college-level science and math courses. Teaching and learning environments can also fail to support the different learning styles of women and minority students. Competitive versus cooperative learning environments, large lecture classes, and limited exposure to experiential activities in STEM course work may undermine the performance of even well-prepared students. Such learning environments can lead to students' negative perceptions of the subject matter and career options. In a survey of college students who left STEM majors, the most frequently cited reasons contributing to the change in major included (a) the belief that non-STEM majors would be more interesting, (b) a loss of interest in the STEM major itself, and (c) a rejection of the STEM career-associated lifestyle (Seymore, 1992).

## The Role of Community Colleges in Preparing Students for STEM Careers

The pool of students available for recruitment will depend on the success of precollege efforts to create interest in and provide motivation to learn science and math. At the same time, building a broader base of STEM talent requires intentional interventions within the first year of college and beyond. Precollege and postsecondary programs designed to increase diversity in STEM courses and careers should include the following educational components:

- ◇ Challenging content in science and math
- ◇ Contextual learning that enhances personal meaning and motivation to learn
- ◇ Experiential math education that offers connections and applications to everyday life and emphasizes the use of math in the workplace (Institute for Women in Trades, Technology & Science, 2010)
- ◇ Development of college readiness through on-campus experiences or other college connections
- ◇ Substantive, ongoing professional development for math and science instructors at all levels
- ◇ Broad-based, collaborative partnerships that promote high expectations and a college-going culture (Davis-Butts, 2006)
- ◇ Mentoring programs that help to socialize students, especially women and minorities to STEM fields
- ◇ Opportunities for collaboration learning through small work groups, cohorts, and/or learning communities

This section highlights some specific initiatives designed to support the recruitment and retention of first-year community college students into STEM fields.

### Developmental Education

Many minority, first-generation, and low-SES students are not prepared to pursue majors in science and engineering fields. In 2002, 690,000 minority students graduated from high school, but only 28,000 had taken the necessary math and science courses to be fully prepared for an engineering curriculum. The *Science and Engineering Indicators - 2002* (National Science Board, 2002) found that 1 in 8 eighth-graders attended schools that did not offer an algebra class. The report also indicated that high-minority, low-SES high schools had a lower proportion of experienced math and science teachers than those with lower minority and higher SES rates. These disparities contribute to a reality wherein only 1.3% of the available pool of minority high school graduates are awarded engineering degrees (Nealy, 2008).

Community colleges offer a wide array of courses that can enable students to develop the academic backgrounds needed to succeed in STEM fields. Students and faculty must understand that many students are underprepared due to socioeconomic and educational issues that were beyond their control. Supporting students to be task-oriented with regard to developmental courses is essential. These courses should be presented as the bridge between where students are and where they plan to be in terms of program, major, or career. Faculty and staff play a critical role in helping students recognize that progress towards a goal is a process. They must also be willing to stand by and with students as they encounter the doubts and fears, which might lead students to abandon their aspirations.

Understanding where the barriers to student success exist is also critical. In 1994, Montgomery College (Takoma Park/Silver Spring, MD) enrolled approximately 25% of the graduating class from the public high schools in the county. During the assessment for course placement of these students, the college found that surprisingly high numbers of graduating students were not prepared for college-level work. After further research it was determined that students in the county used three pathways through high school to college. The first pathway—completion of precalculus and honors English—led to college readiness for most students who followed it. No students who took this path needed developmental courses at the college level. In the second pathway, students took intermediate algebra or trigonometry and nonhonors English. This pathway resulted in one third of the students needing remedial work while in college. In the third pathway, students completed geometry and an English course that was below grade level. All who followed this path were required to enroll in remedial courses.

In chapter 4, Brown and Rivas offer an in-depth treatment of strategies for helping underrepresented students succeed in the first college year. Such strategies have broad applicability to students wanting to enter STEM fields.

## Bridge Programs

Summer and precollege bridge programs are another strategy for preparing students to enter and succeed in STEM fields. While these programs typically involve formal preterm learning experiences, they may also extend throughout the first academic term or year. Such programs may serve academically underprepared students and/or historically underrepresented student populations. Bridge programs include exposure to and skill building in fundamental courses and more advanced introductory level STEM courses. Classroom instruction is frequently combined with experiential learning opportunities, allowing students to apply their new knowledge immediately while exposing them to STEM career opportunities. Partnerships with business and industry STEM professionals lead to rich learning opportunities for students, including guest speakers, job shadowing, internships, plant and/or company tours, and involvement in research projects. These kinds of opportunities are usually reserved for upper-level students, but they can have a profound impact on students during their first year. Comprehensive bridge programs typically include some of the following components:

◇ Study skills preparation classes (e.g., note taking, test taking, reading strategies, time management)
◇ First-year seminars
◇ Tutoring and/or Supplemental Instruction
◇ Mentoring by second-year students, professionals in the community, or faculty
◇ Learning communities and study groups comprised of bridge students
◇ Early-alert systems to identify students in need of academic and social resources and assistance
◇ Student engagement opportunities, such as clubs and organizations, to strengthen the learning environment and to foster community development

The STEM Summer Bridge Program at Passaic County Community College (PCCC, Paterson, NJ) was designed to bridge the transition from high school to college for the first-year students entering college for the first time. The summer program allows students to attend an eight-day session where they experience a stimulating environment that includes high-tech and hands-on group learning. The discovery program provides students with a broad exposure to different areas of science and technology (PCCC, 2010).

The goals of the program are to help students better understand the relationships among STEM disciplines by the use of interactive experiences and to develop the scientific skills of observation, data analyses and documentation, and interpretation of results. Since it is recognized that math and mathematical concepts may be a barrier for many students, this summer bridge program emphasizes the application of math in such topics as computer technology, environmental science, and forensics, among others (PCCC, 2010).

### Careers and Technical Education Models

As stated earlier, some students leave STEM fields because they do not find the academic work engaging, or they may perceive the coursework to be irrelevant. Other students may experience academic difficulty because they fail to grasp mathematical concepts and scientific theories without a relevant application. The National Science Board (2002) recommends restructuring the undergraduate STEM curriculum to include more investigative learning, technology, laboratory experiences, and collaborative work. Programs that provide students with hands-on engagement (e.g., experiential learning, real life projects) have been successful in increasing recruitment and retention of women and minorities (Powell, 2006). Further, changing the curriculum to promote more collaborative group work also helps students develop peer networks. Such social support systems, including learning communities, are of particular benefit to underrepresented students in fields that have been perceived as difficult and unwelcoming (Powell).

Career and technical education (CTE) programs provide excellent models of hands-on, cohort-based instruction. CTE programs typically include job shadowing, mentoring experiences, school-based enterprises, apprenticeships, internships, and major-based student organizations—all of which expose students to career fields. Research (Harrell et al., 2003) suggests that rigorous CTE engages and motivates students, lowers dropout rates, and increases student achievement and graduation rates. Expanding and strengthening CTE programs is one solution to increase the pool of students in the STEM pipeline (Harrell et al.). CTE might also be adapted to associate degree programs to make STEM instruction more relevant and accessible for students. In chapter 9, Stanley explores one type of CTE—Tech Prep—as a strategy for ensuring that students make progress along a chosen career pathway.

### Transfer Pipelines

Along with changing demographics and increasing college costs and workforce expectations, there has been significant growth in demand for access to community colleges. While all sectors of the higher education community must play a role in helping the country meet its educational workforce needs, the community college with its open door policy, proximity, and affordable tuition will be a leader in this effort. Transfer is particularly important since 31% of college-qualified, low-income students enroll in community colleges (Powell, 2006). Yet, students often need encouragement to complete bachelor's degrees. Programs like the Community College Summer Research Program at Occidental College (Los Angeles, CA) have successfully transferred groups of students who continue in the pursuit of the higher degree (Powell). However, to significantly increase minority and female participation, educators need to strengthen the educational pipeline at the precollege level where interest in math and science develops. To this end community colleges have partnered with elementary and secondary schools (Powell).

Eastfield Community College (Mesquite, TX), the National Science Foundation, local high schools, and business and industry partnered to offer underrepresented students a 2+2+2 transition in their course of study in science, technology, engineering, and mathematics through three levels of academia—high school, community college, and four-year college. The Science Talent Expansion Program (STEP) is a model that was developed with the assistance of a National Science Foundation grant to provide a seamless transition from the community college and to completion of a four-year college in the STEM curriculum in Texas. The STEP project demonstrated how the two-year and community college systems could nurture students to engage "in the very business of science through the generation of new knowledge" (Eastfield College & National Science Foundation, 2002, para 3).

## Faculty Development Initiatives

As noted above, faculty at the precollege and college levels play a critical role in encouraging (or discouraging) student pursuit of STEM careers. The pool of minorities and women in STEM faculty positions is frequently low, so students may lack adequate career role models. Further, White and male faculty may be less likely to step up as mentors for historically underrepresented students. STEM faculty typically focus on the cream of the crop, the top-tier student or the like-me student (Tobias, 1996). Their teaching style may reward students who are like them, dissuading women and students from diverse backgrounds from continuing in STEM fields.

As Brown and McPhail noted in chapter 5, faculty need to develop cultural competence so they can more effectively engage increasingly diverse student bodies. Cultural competency training should provide faculty with tools to examine and eliminate stereotypical views regarding the abilities of women and minorities to succeed in STEM. The training should also provide faculty members with tools to effectively engage diverse populations in and outside the classroom. In addition, faculty must be supported to develop curricula using a range of pedagogical strategies to respond to various learning styles associated with diverse student populations.

While many institutions offer excellent faculty development initiatives, programs need to be developed that focus exclusively on STEM issues. Stem-focused professional development opportunities will ideally (a) engage STEM researchers and professionals in the development and delivery of workshop experiences, (b) model inquiry-based and cooperative learning strategies, and (c) engage science education professors who can speak to standards-based activities. Faculty should also experience substantive, ongoing opportunities for learning and development (Loucks-Horsley, 1995, as cited in Lee, 2001). Faculty development must include strategies for creating a culture of success and meeting the needs of minority, low-income, and women students (Allen-Sommerville, 1996; American Institutes for Research, 1998; Culotta & Gibbons, 1992).

Through the Iowa Mathematics and Science Partnership (IMSEP), an advisory board of state education experts has defined how the community college faculty prepares students for STEM education. The advisory board recognizes that more students are attending two-year and community colleges prior to four-year colleges. The project states that when community college faculty who are certified in STEM recognize the potential in students and can create learning communities within the classroom, the schools are on the right path to increasing STEM students in the pipeline. Instructors will be able to earn community college teaching certificates with emphases on STEM fields and participate in a summer institute developed to establish a community of STEM instructors and experts. Additionally, the advisory team is working with Iowa Central Community

College, Fort Dodge Animal Health, and Iowa State University to develop science curriculum units for high school students earning dual credit. The summer seminars were designed to prepare new and current community college faculty in STEM areas. The Iowa Legislature continues to support IMSEP despite budget cuts (Dillavou, 2009).

## Conclusion

Patton (2008) made several recommendations for increasing access to and success in STEM fields, which are offered as concluding thoughts to this chapter. First, partnerships involving all sectors of education—K-12, community colleges, and four-year institutions—are needed to improve student progression through math, science, and technical curricula. Such partnerships allow for the alignment of curricula and assessment plans, enabling institutions to maximize limited technical, human, and fiscal resources. Moreover, such alignment increases the possibility of students' making a smooth transition from one educational experience to the next and for institutions being able to demonstrate those successful transitions. As a critical partner, Patton suggests that the community college build on existing standards for curriculum and pedagogy for each particular STEM field.

As an institution with a teaching mission, the community college has the infrastructure to support excellence in student learning. Patton (2008) argues that this expertise be used to foster the development of student-centered STEM instructors. Faculty development initiatives should encourage instructors to engage in fieldwork, observations, and internships in STEM areas. In addition to helping faculty develop content-area knowledge, professional development experiences can expose them to divergent teaching philosophies and methodologies. Finally, because role models and mentorship are critical to the success of underrepresented populations in STEM fields, Patton also argues for community colleges taking the lead in hiring a diverse pool of well-qualified STEM instructors and providing all STEM faculty with opportunities to develop cultural competency and strategies for adapting instruction to diverse learning styles.

In order to expand the pool of STEM talent, institutions must move beyond top-tier students and identify those who can be nurtured to succeed. They must also seek to involve more women and minorities in these fields. Yet, students from historically underrepresented groups will need substantial guarantees of being welcomed and assurances that they can and will succeed (Tobias, 1996). It is imperative that these future STEM professionals know that they are not expected to become carbon copies of their professors, and are encouraged to embrace their individuality and bring their unique experiences to the table.

Community colleges are well positioned to help the United States achieve its economic and technical needs for the new century by widening the pipeline for students to enter STEM fields and by encouraging them to do so.

## References

Allen-Sommerville, L. (1996). Capitalizing on diversity. *The Science Teacher 2*, 20-23.

America COMPETES Reauthorization Act, H.R. 5116, P.L. 111-358 (2010).

American Institutes for Research. (1998). *Gender gaps: Where schools still fail our children* (Executive Summary). Washington, DC: American Association of University Women Foundation. Retrieved from http://www.aauw.org/learn/research/all.cfm

Blomberg. J. (2007, September). *STEM initiatives in community colleges: A program review.* Tallahassee, FL: Florida Department of Education. Retrieved from www.fldoe.org/cc/Vision/PDFs/PR2007-01_STEM.pdf

Committee on Science, Engineering, & Public Policy (COSEPUP). (2007). *Rising above the gathering storm: Energizing and employing America for a brighter future.* Washington, DC: The National Academies Press. Retrieved from http://books.nap.edu/catalog.php?record_id=11463

Culotta, E., & Gibbons, E. (1992). Minorities in science: The pipeline problem. *Science, 258,* 1157-1276.

Davis-Butts, E. (2006). *Fostering STEM diversity.* Retrieved from http://opas.ous.edu/Committees/Resources/Staff_papers/DIVR_WhitePaper_2006.pdf

Dillavou, L. (2009, March 16). Ebbers, ELPS team work with instructors for better STEM preparation. *Inside Human Sciences.* Retrieved from http://www.hs.iastate.edu/news/inside/view/202

Dowd, A. C., Malcom, L. E., & Bensimon, E. M. (2009). *Benchmarking the success of Latino and Latina students in STEM to achieve national graduation goals.* Los Angeles, CA: University of Southern California.

Eastfield College & National Science Foundation. (2002). *STEP Science Talent Expansion: Project Overview.* Retrieved from http://www.efc.dcccd.edu/rcd/nsf/overview.htm

Froschauer, L. (2006, November 2). How can we attract students to STEM careers? *NSTA Reports.* Retrieved from http://www.nsta.org/publications/news/story.aspx?id=52862

Government Accounting Office (GAO). (2006). *The changing workforce: Demographics facing the federal government.* Retrieved from http://www.gpoaccess.gov/gaoreports/

Lee, H. (2001). *Enriching the professional development of mathematics teachers.* ERIC Digest. (ERIC Reproduction Services No. ED 465 495)

Harrell, E., Forney, P., & Scott, W. (2003). Ready or not, here we come: Retaining Hispanic and first-generation students in postsecondary education. *Community College Journal of Research and Practice, 27*(2), 147-156.

Institute for Women in Trades, Technology, & Science. (2010). *Gender difference in learning and achievement in mathematics, science and technology and strategies for equity: A literature review.* Retrieved from http://www.iwitts.org/proven-practices?task

Johnson, J. M., & Woodin, T. S. (2002). Higher education in science and engineering: Increasing global capacity in S&E. In National Science Board, *Science and engineering indicators – 2002* (NSB-02-1). Arlington, VA: National Science Foundation. Retrieved from the National Science Foundation website: http://www.nsf.gov/statistics/seind02/c2/c2h.htm

Moore, J. (2009). Two-year colleges: Guidelines and exemplary teaching. *Journal of Chemical Education, 86*(7), 779.

Nagel, D. (2010, March 23). Colleges, professors discourage women from pursuing STEM careers. *Campus Technology.* Retrieved from http://campustechnology.com/articles/2010/03/23/colleges-professors-discourage-women-from-pursuing-stem-careers.aspx?sc_lang=en

National Center for Education Statistics (NCES). (2007). *Persistence and attainment of 2003-04 beginning postsecondary students: After three years.* Washington DC: U.S. Department of Education.

National Science Board. (2002). *Science and engineering indicators – 2002* (NSB-02-1). Arlington, VA: National Science Foundation. Retrieved from the National Science Foundation website: http://www.nsf.gov/statistics/seind02/c0/c0s1.htm

National Science Foundation. (1996). *Women, minorities, and persons with disabilities in science and engineering* (Report No. NSF 96-311). Arlington, VA: Author. (ERIC Document Reproduction Services No. ED 402 192)

Nealy, M. J. (2008, September 15). Scholars blame low minority retention in STEM on affirmative action. *Diverse Issues in Education*. Retrieved from http://diverseeducation.com/article/11684/

Nelson, L. (2009, September 2009). Minority students needed in math and science to combat "brain drain," professors say. *The Chronicle of Higher Education*. Retrieved from http://chronicle.com/article/Minority-Students-Needed-in/48568/

Passaic County Community College (PCCC). (2010). *STEM project details*. Retrieved from http://www.pccc.cc.nj.us/headlines_feed2/headlines-stories/pccc-gets-1/stem-project-details

Patton, M. (2008). *Teaching choice: Community colleges extend K-12 pathways and practices*. Washington. DC: American Association of Community Colleges.

Pelosi, N. (2010). *America competes reauthorization act*. Retrieved from http://www.speaker.gov/newsroom/legislation?id=0373

Powell, R. M. (2006). Improving the persistence of first-year undergraduate women in computer science. *Proceedings of the 39th SIGCSE Technical Symposium on Computer Science Education*, 518-522. doi:10.1145/1352135.1352308

Robinson, L. (2010, May 21). Discouraging lessons: Study reveals barriers to pursuing STEM careers erected at an early age for women, minorities. *Materials Education*. Retrieved from http://materialstechnology.tms.org/edu/article.aspx?articleID=3468

Seymore, E. (1992, February). "The problem iceberg" in science, mathematics, and engineering education: Students explanations for high attrition rates. *Journal of College Science Teaching*, 230-238.

Simard, C. ( 2010). *Obstacles and solutions for underrepresented minorities in technology*. Palo Alto, CA: Anita Borg Institute for Women and Technology.

Szelenyi, K. (2001). Minority student retention and academic achievement in community colleges. *ERIC Digest*. (ERIC Document Reproduction Services No. ED 451 859)

Thorius, K. K. (2009). *Gender equity matters*. Tempe, AZ: Arizona State University, The Equity Alliance.

Tobias, S. (1996). *They're not dumb, they're different: Stalking the second tier*. Tucson, AZ: Research Corporation.

# Chapter 12
## Fulfilling the Promise: Summary and Recommendations

Thomas Brown, Margaret C. King, and Patricia Stanley

Community colleges continue to play a pivotal role in U.S. higher education. They provide access to high-quality educational opportunities for millions of Americans aspiring to acquire the skills needed to advance in their current careers, compete in the new economy, and/or to transfer to four-year colleges and universities. Increasing persistence and success is a continuing concern in community colleges, especially as they enroll high percentages of students who are from low socioeconomic backgrounds, first generation in college, or from historically underrepresented ethnic and racial minority groups. If more students are to achieve their personal, academic, and career goals, community colleges must engage all members of the campus community in enhancing students' first-year experiences.

Nearly all community colleges emphasize their commitment to provide all students with opportunities to achieve their visions and dreams—regardless of background or skills levels at entry. Yet, as noted elsewhere in this monograph, nearly half of students who enter America's community colleges withdraw before beginning a second year of studies. While some students leave having achieved their goals (e.g., successful transfer to a four-year institution, completion of course work for new skill acquisition or professional development), the evidence suggests that too many students leave because they have not become fully engaged in their campus communities. Recognizing the significance of this challenge, an increasing number of community college leaders have focused their attention on programs, services, and interventions that can help their students move into college successfully and persist until they have achieved their goals.

This monograph has offered readers a compendium of demographic data, research, theories, and practical information that can be used to increase persistence and success for first-year community college students. Underprepared students are given particular attention, as the community college must address issues surrounding the gap between students' academic backgrounds and the skills and knowledge they need to achieve their goals. While community college students are frequently underprepared, so too are many community college faculty and staff, who lack specific training or skills to respond to the needs of the diverse students enrolling on their campuses. The monograph emphasizes the importance of effective professional development for community college faculty, staff, and administrators to enhance the understanding, skills, and behaviors that can increase first-year student engagement, learning, and persistence.

While the chapter authors have focused on different aspects of the community college, as a whole, the monograph provides a framework for the essential elements of comprehensive first-year experience programs in community colleges.  First-year seminars, learning communities, academic advising, and career development are described as interventions that can benefit newly entering community college students and the institution in important ways. Increasing access and success for students in science, technology, engineering, and math (STEM) programs is critical to meet current and future educational, career, and employment needs at the local and national level. The community college plays a vital role in helping first-year students enter and succeed in STEM fields. Strategies for planning and implementing first-year initiatives have been described throughout the monograph.

## Recommendations

Comprehensive first-year programs in a community college can be effective in fostering student success. Yet, the models and concepts presented throughout the monograph must be adapted to specific campus settings. With this caveat in mind, we present the following recommendations gleaned from chapter authors and community college leaders (i.e., presidents, vice presidents, deans, and trustees).[1] The recommendations encompass strategies for designing, implementing, and gaining support for comprehensive first-year experience initiatives.

### Creating Intentionally Designed Comprehensive Programs

While the specific components will vary from one institution to the next, community colleges should seek to develop comprehensive first-year experiences that are intentionally organized to help students make a successful transition into higher education, achieve their individual goals, and move on to additional educational opportunities or a career. Programs and services that help students make the initial adjustment to campus include welcome centers, preterm orientation programs, and first-year seminars or college success courses. Such initiatives should be a priority for all campuses. Learning communities provide opportunities for academic and social integration, while helping students achieve academic success and persist in the critical first year of college. Other aspects of a comprehensive first-year experience should focus on learning support, academic skills assessment, academic advising, and career development. Community college leaders must also look to interventions that have been found to be very effective but have not yet been widely adopted, such as organized study groups and mentoring programs. A review of the literature will also offer insight into the kinds of initiatives that hold promise for supporting a college's unique student population and mission.

An effective academic advising program is a key component of a comprehensive first-year program. As recognized by the Council for Advancement of Standards (CAS, Dean, 2006), there is a need for someone to be in charge, empowered, and positioned to accomplish the mission of the advising program. The program should be supported by strong advisor development and training, recognition or reward, and have adequate funding to accomplish the program mission and goals. To ensure that all first-year students receive the guidance, information, and support needed to move into college successfully, community colleges should consider adopting the Total Intake Academic Advising Model described in chapter 8 where feasible.

Equally important and closely related to academic advising is career development. Community colleges must work cooperatively with secondary schools, adult education programs, and baccalaureate-level institutions so that career development is a continuous pathway of ever more refined student decision making. Offering a variety of opportunities along career pathways for students to have experiences in the workplace will assist them in career exploration and planning. Both academic advisors and career counselors should be trained to deliver culturally relevant support programs and services.

Stand-alone services on community college campuses are being replaced by one-stop centers that house a number of services in one centrally located area. Isolated islands of special services for students are being grouped together and often provide cross-training of professional staff and faculty. A single first-year experience program component may be a good start, but experienced program leaders know that no one strategy or service works for all students, many of whom require a compendium of services.

## Bringing Programs to Scale

Building comprehensive and effective first-year programs takes time and, most importantly, institutional dedication and commitment. Many excellent first-year initiatives start as boutique programs, serving a particular population. Often such programs may be grant funded; and without the institutional commitment for ongoing support, the program disappears when the grant ends. Community colleges should seek to serve at least 75% of new students through first-year initiatives. While initiatives may reasonably begin as pilot programs with much smaller groups of students, one way to bring them to scale is to link them to regular accreditation processes (e.g., Academic Quality Improvement Programs or Quality Enhancement Plans).

Another way to bring programs to scale is to overcome the reluctance to require student participation. Assessment for placement should be mandatory, allowing institutions to identify and reach out early to students who are underprepared for college-level work. These students should be required to participate in programs and services known to increase learning, persistence, and graduation, such as tutoring. Active outreach through early-warning programs and intrusive academic advising are other strategies for ensuring that students are connected to the programs they need.

## Cultivating Support From Campus Leadership

Leaders at all levels are reluctant to support what they do not understand. Therefore, those charged with developing and implementing first-year initiatives must take the time and make the effort to educate the campus leadership, who can become the biggest advocates for (or roadblocks to) program institutionalization. Formal reports or informal discussions with academic deans, the president's council or staff, the board of trustees, the foundation board, academic or college senate, dean's council, and other campus leadership groups should highlight relevant research and national studies on the need for and effectiveness of specific kinds of initiatives. Campus leaders are very likely to be committed to the mission or multiple missions of the college. Therefore, it is important to connect first-year experience program development to these college-guiding mission, vision, and values statements as a means to secure leader support. Campus leaders should also be involved in and/or kept abreast of first-year experience planning meetings, task forces, teams, visits to exemplary programs, and similar activities to help them gain a sense of understanding and ownership for the program.

Initial support from campus leaders to develop a first-year program must be maintained during subsequent critical developments, such as budget cuts, new leadership, data-driven program adjustments, enrollment shifts, and more. Hiring or selecting the right people to manage or coordinate the first-year experience program is vital to maintaining momentum and continued leader support. Presidents, vice-presidents, deans, and board of trustees members described the professionals they desire as individuals who are totally committed and engaged in the program, work well with others, and collaborate effectively. An overarching ability to put student needs first and make student success their mission is essential.

Interviews with colleges leaders suggest that their engagement and support for first-year programs is often based on three major components: (a) a strong program connection to the college mission or vision, (b) data supporting the need to assist students in meeting theirs goals and/or data showing the program is or will make a positive difference for students, and (c) broad-based college support from both academic and student affairs. The bottom line is that effective campus leaders support first-year experience programs because they know it is the right thing to do for students, for the college, and for the community.

### Building Coalitions on Campus

Campus leaders are also more likely to support bottom-up approaches that reflect collaboration between academic and student affairs. Faculty and student affairs staff should be equal partners in planning and implementing first-year initiatives. Further, the kind of comprehensive, integrated first-year experience advocated here cannot succeed without strong partnerships that span divisions, departments, and campus roles. By working with all areas of the college community, the program is never finished but is constantly improving and evolving as support from various constituencies is added.

### Developing Community Partnerships

While those working in community colleges have an understanding of the special mission and challenges in this sector of higher education, continuing efforts must be made to enlist the support and advocacy from political, business, and community leaders.  For example, specific efforts should be made to emphasize the fact that community colleges are increasingly the first choice of students because of their quality, access, and diversity of program offerings.  Additionally, these colleges should share their remarkable record of success in placing career and technical education graduates in jobs shortly after program completion.

Career-focused programs at community colleges are often required to have an advisory committee drawn from local business and industry leaders. Regular communication with these advisory committees helps keep the community college apprised of the needs and concerns of local industry, while offering community college leaders the opportunity to educate external community members about educational programs and innovations. These committees provide a model for other programs at the community college and for the college as a whole, as they may offer a way to build support for first-year initiatives among policy makers.

### Providing Campus-wide Professional Development Opportunities

Ongoing professional development should be an institutional priority and included in all part- and full-time faculty and staff job descriptions. Professional development opportunities need to be tailored to the unique institutional context so that faculty, staff, and administrators are prepared to address the learning needs of the students on their campuses. Successful programs will (a) create institutional structures that provide opportunities for faculty and staff to reflect together on the most effective ways to support student learning and success; (b) cross-train college faculty, staff, advisors, counselors, and others to deliver resources on a continuous basis; and (c) provide reward and recognition incentives for all employees to participate. Ideally, preservice and in-service professional development should be required for all professional staff, as well as for instructional faculty engaged in first-year initiatives.

## Supporting Transfer

While community colleges have multiple missions, an increasingly important one is to serve as a pipeline for students hoping to achieve a four-year degree. As such, community colleges need to promote a culture of transfer that recognizes that successful transfer begins when students enter the community college. In order to facilitate student transfer, community colleges should examine their existing programs and policies and work collaboratively with four-year baccalaureate institutions to ensure that students can make a smooth transition from one institution to another. Effective transfer programs will incorporate academic advising, career development, and academic support services to assist students in becoming well-prepared to enter the four-year institution and to increase the likelihood of their success after transfer. Specific transfer initiatives designed to support students in STEM fields are highly desirable. Colleges must make information about successful transfer initiatives a central part of their internal and external marketing efforts.

## Establishing Relevant Benchmarks for Success

Community colleges are uniquely defined by access, inclusion, community responsiveness, innovation, small class sizes, and a focus on instruction. They are also defined by a distinctive learning-centered model. While community colleges have adopted a success and completion agenda, the diverse nature of community college students challenges the traditional standards for measuring postsecondary completion (i.e., two years for the associate degree plus two additional years for the baccalaureate degree). The majority of community colleges students attend part time, work while attending college, and have limited economic resources, making standard measures of progress almost meaningless. New and appropriate measures for assessing and reporting community college student success and completion that reflect the complex and comprehensive missions of community colleges are long overdue.

Because persistence data continue to be important for all institutions, community colleges should examine the extent to which first-year initiatives impact student retention. While institutions will establish an overall goal for retention, they also need to establish a set of goals that acknowledges multiple definitions of student success. Connected to these goals must be a realistic timeframe for achieving them. Finally, to ensure that the institution is making satisfactory progress toward those goals, an individual should be designated to oversee the coordination of retention initiatives.

## Building a Culture of Evidence

While it is difficult to ignore heart-felt stories from students who have overcome enormous odds to gain success, for which they credit college programs and personnel, testimonials are not adequate measures of program effectiveness. Many, if not most, campus leaders and external constituents react only to solid quantitative data. These data need to be based on a consistent definition of success, program completion (including transfer), and attrition as described above. Building a culture of evidence on the campus ensures that faculty, staff, and administrators have the data they need to advocate for program adoption, expansion, or improvement. Strategies for building a culture of evidence encompass (a) establishing comprehensive information and tracking systems, including student cohort tracking; (b) employing accountability measures that provide meaningful data about student goal achievement; (c) using data for program decision making; and (d) supporting national data collection and research studies in areas that are specific to community colleges, such as effectiveness of career development, learning communities, and professional development programs as a means of enhancing student retention.

## Conclusion

First-year experience programs take time to develop fully and are often part of other transformations that have occurred, at times simultaneously, on community college campuses. The Learning College movement transformed community college education, and the more recent theme of matching student access with student success is currently affecting college transformations. Community college missions, visions, values, and goal statements reflect these transformations and have set the stage for comprehensive first-year programs to be an integral part of the community college educational delivery system.

Community colleges that support a comprehensive and effective first-year experience are likely to possess the following characteristics: (a) a history of working collaboratively across programs, academic disciplines, and services; (b) well-designed learning communities; and (c) the ability to make data-driven decisions and plan strategically. These colleges also appear to be mission driven and focused on student learning. Likewise, colleges that are clear about their vision and understand that student needs, goals, and ultimate success are the collective job of everyone at the college also provide an inviting climate for first-year experience programs.

As community colleges are being asked to play an ever increasing role in U.S. efforts to regain global leadership through improved college completion rates, the information presented here is significant. This monograph offers insights from highly credible researchers and practitioners, community college leaders, as well as principals from the first-year experience and students in transition movement. We thank all who contributed to the monograph, as it represents a collective effort to bring together current research, exemplary programs, and professional educators to focus on the first year in community colleges—where nearly half of our nation's students begin their postsecondary educational journeys. Student success is more important than ever before in the lives of new high school graduates, returning and adult students, underprepared students, and all the others who look to community colleges to help them achieve their dreams. Local communities, states, and the nation will continue to depend on community colleges to enhance the quality of life for all citizens and to keep the United States competitive in the world. Therefore, first-year programs in these colleges must be well supported and highly effective for the many who come through the community college's open doors.

## Notes

[1]The authors would like to acknowledge and thank the community college leaders who helped shape these recommendations by offering their perspectives as to why and how they support first-year programs at their colleges. They include presidents, administrators, and trustees from Aims Community College in Greeley, Colorado; Parkland College in Campaign, Illinois; Delta College in University Center, Michigan; Century College in White Bear Lake, Minnesota; Pasadena City College in Pasadena, California; and Frank Phillips College in Borger, Texas.

# References

Dean, L. A. (Ed.). (2006). *CAS professional standards for higher education* (6th ed.). Washington, DC: Council for the Advancement of Standards in Higher Education.

# About the Contributors

**Paul Arcario** is dean for Academic Affairs and professor of English as a Second Language (ESL) at LaGuardia Community College. He has overall responsibility for curriculum and pedagogy and, in that capacity, provides guidance for the College's electronic portfolio, outcomes assessment, and first-year experience programs. Arcario has a long-standing interest in technology-based pedagogy, having conducted ESL teaching workshops using video and other media at Teachers College, Columbia University, as well as having produced educational videos for teaching ESL, including the first American English-language teaching video broadcast in The People's Republic of China. In 2007, Arcario was named an Outstanding First-Year Student Advocate by the National Resource Center for The First-Year Experience and Students in Transition.

**Kim Armstrong** is assistant dean of Student Support Services at Black Hawk College, where she provides administrative leadership for student engagement, enhancement, and retention, with an emphasis on minority populations. Armstrong received her BS, MS, and PhD degrees from Howard University in physiological neuropsychology with an emphasis in child development. She completed postdoctoral training at Northwestern Medical School and the Beckman Institute for the Advancement of Science and Technology at the University of Illinois at Champaign-Urbana. Armstrong's background spans the research, clinical, and administrative strata, as she has worked for the National Science Foundation, the Schwab Rehab Center, and the Provena Medical Center, where she was responsible for developing health initiatives for African Americans and Amish populations. She has co-authored reports for the National Science Foundation on diversity in the work place; for the U.S. Congress on mental health services in rural minority populations; as well as others, including the American Psychological Association.

**Betsy O. Barefoot** serves as vice president for the John N. Gardner Institute for Excellence in Undergraduate Education in Brevard, North Carolina. She is directly involved in the development of instruments and strategies to evaluate and improve the first college year. In addition, she conducts seminars on the first-year experience across the United States and in other countries and assists colleges and universities in implementing and evaluating first-year programs. Barefoot has authored and co-authored a number of publications, including *Achieving and Sustaining Institutional Excellence for the First Year of College* and *Challenging and Supporting the First-Year Student: A Handbook for the First Year of College*. She has also edited *The First Year and Beyond: Rethinking the Challenge of Collegiate Transition*, a 2008 volume of New Directions for Higher Education.

**George R. Boggs** is president and chief executive officer emeritus of the American Association of Community Colleges (AACC), which represents more than 1,100 associate degree-granting institutions and some 13 million students. Prior to AACC, Boggs served as faculty member, division chair, and associate dean of instruction at Butte College, and he was the superintendent/president of Palomar College for 15 years. He was as a member of the Committee on Undergraduate Science Education of the U.S. National Research Council and has participated on several U.S. National Science Foundation panels and committees. Boggs holds a bachelor's degree in chemistry from The Ohio State University, a master's degree in chemistry from the University of California at Santa Barbara, and received his doctorate in educational administration from The University of Texas at Austin.

**Thomas Brown** has served as an academic and student affairs educator for nearly 40 years, most recently as dean of Advising Services/Special Programs at Saint Mary's College of California. He is currently managing principal of Thomas Brown & Associates, a consulting group that has served more than 350 two- and four-year colleges in the United States and abroad. As a campus dean, Brown developed and implemented a nationally recognized academic advising program and was responsible for new student and family transition programs; academic support and achievement (e.g., tutoring, services for students with disabilities); and units serving Asian Pacific American, Black, Latino, and international students. He also created the Saint Mary's High Potential Program, which provides access and support to first-generation students from historically underrepresented backgrounds. He has held numerous positions in the National Academic Advising Association (NACADA), including vice president and chair of the Multicultural Concerns Commission. Brown has published and presented extensively on student retention, staff development, academic advising, and promoting the achievement and success of multicultural and at-risk students.

**Rusty N. Fox** serves as vice president for Student Development Services at Tarrant County College Southeast Campus. He was previously the dean of Student Development and director of Counseling/Advising at Oklahoma City Community College and coordinator of Academic Advising at Brookhaven College. Active in his profession, he presents at national and regional conferences and is a member of the National Academic Advising Association (NACADA) Consultant's Bureau. As a past board member, Fox served twice as the Association's national Commission Chair for Two-Year Colleges. He holds a BA in speech communication from Texas A&M University, an MS in counseling from Texas A&M University-Commerce, and he is a doctoral candidate in higher education at Capella University.

**Thomas J. Grites** has been directly involved in the academic advising process in higher education for almost 40 years. He has served as a consultant, program evaluator, and faculty development workshop leader to more than 100 different campuses. He was instrumental in forming the National Academic Advising Association (NACADA) and held the position of president for two terms. He has authored more than 60 journal articles, position statements, book chapters, program evaluations, and consultant reports, and has delivered over 80 conference presentations. Grites co-edited the second edition of *Academic Advising: A Comprehensive Handbook* and recently co-authored an orientation textbook for transfer students entitled the *Transfer Student Companion*. He earned his bachelor's and master's degrees from Illinois State University and completed his doctoral work at the University of Maryland. Both institutions honored Grites with Distinguished Alumni awards, and he was inducted into the College of Education Hall of Fame at Illinois State.

**Ana Margarita (Cha) Guzman** is the first female president of Palo Alto College. A native of Cuba, Guzman has been in educational administration for more than 30 years and is a leading voice for Hispanic Americans in education. She served as senior advisor to Education Secretary Richard Riley during the Clinton administration, as well as chair of President Clinton's White House Commission on Educational Excellence for Hispanic Americans from 1993 to 2000. Guzman's breadth of experience in education spans from service as a public school teacher to her position as vice chancellor of the Texas A&M System. In addition, she has been president of the Texas Association of Chicanos in Higher Education and is currently on the Board of Trustees for The College Board.

**Wesley R. Habley** is the coordinator of State Organizations and principal associate in Educational Services at ACT, Inc. One of the nation's foremost experts in the field of academic advising, Habley has more than 50 published works on academic advising and student retention. His most recent publications include *Academic Advising: A Comprehensive Handbook, Status of Academic Advising,* and *What Works in Student Retention.* Habley is a founding board member of the National Academic Advising Association (NACADA) and has held positions such as president and treasurer. He is the founding director of the NACADA Summer Institute on Academic Advising and the recipient of NACADA's awards for service and for outstanding contributions to the field of advising. Habley has delivered more than 200 presentations at professional meetings and has consulted or led workshops at more than 125 colleges in the United States, Canada, and the Middle East.

**Randy Jedele** is the chair of the Humanities Department, coordinator of Learning Communities, and a member of the writing faculty at Des Moines Area Community College. He is a former Commission Chair for the National Academic Advising Association (NACADA) and a recipient of the Outstanding Advisor Publication award for his faculty advising handbook, *Small Things Make Big Connections.* Jedele teaches in a variety of learning communities each semester and has several years of experience of working with first-year students, either as an advisor or a writing coach. He received his doctorate in educational leadership and policy studies from Iowa State University, where the majority of his doctoral research, including his dissertation, focused on learning communities.

**Margaret C. (Peggy) King**, recently retired, served as associate dean for Student Development at Schenectady County Community College (SCCC), where she provided leadership for the Division of Student Affairs and reported directly to the president. She directed the Academic Advisement Center and supervised Counseling and Career and Employment Services. Prior to her work at SCCC, King was assistant director of Counseling at Ocean County College. She was a founding member of the National Academic Advising Association (NACADA) and the first Association president who represented a community college. King has published, presented, and consulted widely in the field of academic advising and increasing student success. A leading expert on academic advising models and systems, she also served as an editor and author for a NACADA monograph focused on academic advising in community colleges. She received her BA degree in history from Ursinus College and her MS and EdD degrees from the University at Albany. King was a recipient of the State University of New York Chancellor's Award for Excellence in Professional Service, the NACADA Award for Service to the organization, and the NACADA Virginia N. Gordon Award for Excellence in the Field of Advising.

**Kay McClenney** is director of the Center for Community College Student Engagement and the Sid W. Richardson Endowed Fellow in the Community College Leadership Program (CCLP) at The University of Texas at Austin (UT). Within the CCLP, she is also senior consultant to the UT work on the national Achieving the Dream initiative, codirector of the California Leadership Alliance for Student Success (CLASS), and director of the MetLife Foundation's National Student

Success Project. Prior to her move to UT, McClenney served for 10 years as vice president and chief operating officer of the Education Commission of the States (ECS). She received the 2002 PBS O'Banion Prize for contributions to teaching and learning in America.

**Christine Johnson McPhail** is managing principal for the McPhail Group LLC, a higher education consulting firm and is emerita professor of higher education and founder of the Community College Leadership doctoral program at Morgan State University. Prior to this, she was president and chief instructional officer at Cypress College. McPhail serves on the Advisory Council for the Community College Survey of Student Engagement, the National Center for Postsecondary Research at the Community College Research Center, and is also an Achieving the Dream coach. McPhail is a past recipient of the AACC National Leadership and the League for Innovation's Terry O'Banion Leadership awards. She has served on the Board of Directors for the American Association of Community Colleges, the Council for the Study of Community Colleges, the American Education Research Association (AERA), and the editorial board for the *Community College Journal of Research and Practice*. In addition to many articles and book chapters, McPhail is the editor of *Establishing and Sustaining Learning-Centered Community Colleges*. Her research interests lie in the intersection of three fields of higher education: leadership, governance, and teaching and learning.

**Mario Rivas** is a counselor and psychology and counseling professor at Berkeley City College, where he has also served as vice president of Student Services. He has been the associate dean of Undergraduate Studies at San Francisco State University and assistant director of the Martin Luther King Advising Center at the University of Minnesota. Rivas has worked with the Mathematics, Science, and Engineering Achievement (MESA) Program for California Community Colleges, the Puente Program, and Educational Opportunity Programs Services at numerous community colleges. He has completed extensive training in Gestalt personal development counseling at the Gestalt Institute in San Francisco, published in the field, and has used the Gestalt Educational Counseling method to assist individuals and groups, particularly ethnic minority groups, to grow beyond self-limiting personal boundaries. He has published and presented extensively on increasing student success and serves as an organizational consultant for faculty, staff, and students on college campuses across the nation. Rivas was a first-generation Latino who began his postsecondary education at Laney Community College in Oakland, California, and went on to earn a PhD in counseling psychology the University of Minnesota.

**Susan Rondeau** currently counsels transfer students at Pima Community College, writes about transfer issues, is a member of the Transfer Student Commission of the National Academic Advising Association, and is semiretired in Tucson, Arizona. She is one of the authors of *Advising Transfer Students: Issues and Strategies* and co-authored *Transfer Student Companion*. For many years, Rondeau taught a popular course on how to transfer from a community college to a university and served as a statewide transfer student ombudsperson.

**Patricia Stanley** is the former president of Frederick Community College and served as the first Deputy Assistant Secretary for Community Colleges in the U.S. Department of Education from 2006 to 2009. Prior to working in the Maryland-DC area, Stanley held a number of positions in California, including administrator for workforce development in the California Community College Chancellor's office, administrative dean at Orange Coast College, executive vice president at Cypress College, and executive director of the California Institute for Career Development. Stanley holds a bachelor's degree from Wittenberg University, a master's degree from the University of Southern Mississippi, and a doctorate from the University of the Pacific. Active in numerous community and educational organizations at both the state and national levels, Stanley has also participated in international education programs in Kuwait, Thailand, the former Soviet Union, China, and a number of countries in Europe and Scandinavia.

**Vincent Tinto** is Distinguished University Professor at Syracuse University and senior scholar at the Pell Institute for the Study of Opportunity in Higher Education in Washington, DC. Tinto is a widely respected scholar in the field of increasing student persistence, and he has published extensively on student retention and the impact of learning communities on student success in both two- and four-year institutions. He has consulted with federal and state agencies, independent research firms, foundations, and two- and four-year institutions on a broad range of higher educational issues. Tinto received his PhD in education and sociology from the University of Chicago.

# Index

NOTE: Page numbers with italicized *f* or *t* indicate figures or tables respectively.